Following God

LEARNING LIFE PRINCIPLES FROM THE WOMEN OF THE BIBLE

BOOK TWO

Following God

LEARNING LIFE PRINCIPLES FROM THE WOMEN OF THE BIBLE

BOOK TWO

A Bible Study by

Wayne Barber

Eddie Rasnake

Richard Shepherd

AMG Publishers™

Advancing the Ministries of the Gospel
God's Word to you is our highest calling.

Following God

LEARNING LIFE PRINCIPLES FROM THE WOMEN OF THE BIBLE
BOOK TWO

Tenth Printing, 2011

ISBN: 978-0-89957-308-3

Cover and text design by Phillip Rodgers
Editing and layout by Rick Steele
Cover illustration by Florence Anderson

Printed in Canada
13 12 11 —T— 12 11 10

This book is dedicated to

Kay Arthur

a devoted friend and faithful follower of our
Lord Jesus Christ. Kay is a modern example of a
woman God is using greatly in the work of His
Kingdom, a woman who knows and teaches
"the grace of God in truth." Thanks for holding
high the standard of the Word of God.

Acknowledgments

This work goes forth to those who have encouraged us in the publication of the first seven books in this series. This series has been a labor of love, and through our study we have made friends with many saints of days gone by. We look forward to getting to know them even better in heaven. We are especially grateful to the body of believers at Woodland Park Baptist Church in Chattanooga, Tennessee, who have walked through many of these studies with us and have been a continual source of encouragement as the writing of new studies progresses. Thanks to the folks at AMG, especially Dale Anderson, Warren Baker, Trevor Overcash, Dan Penwell, Phillip Rodgers, and Rick Steele. Special thanks also go to Linda Gail Shepherd for her proofreading and suggestions offered from a woman's perspective. Most of all, we remain grateful to the Lord Jesus, who continues to teach us and lead us in what it means to follow Him with a whole heart.

 THE AUTHORS

Wayne Barber

WAYNE BARBER has recently become Senior Pastor of Hoffmantown Church, Albuquerque, NewMexico. A renowned national and international conference ministry speaker, the primary goal of Wayne's ministry is in spreading the message of "the sufficiency of Christ." People around the world connect with Wayne's unique ability to make God's Word come alive through his honest and open "real-life" experiences. Wayne has authored or co-authored several books, and his most recent book, *The Rest of Grace*, was published in 1998. He also authors a regular column in AMG's *Pulpit Helps* monthly magazine. For eighteen years he served as Senior Pastor-Teacher of Woodland Park Baptist Church, in Chattanooga, Tennessee, and for many of those years in Chattanooga, Wayne co-taught with noted author Kay Arthur of Precept Ministries and has studied under Dr. Spiros Zodhiates, one of the world's leading Greek scholars. Wayne and his wife Diana have two grown children and now make their home in Albuquerque.

Rick Shepherd

RICHARD L. SHEPHERD has been engaged in some form of ministry for more than twenty years, focusing on areas of teaching, discipleship, and prayer. He has served in churches in Alabama, Florida, Texas, and Tennessee and now serves as Director of Prayer and Spiritual Awakening with the Florida Baptist Convention. For nearly seventeen years (1983–2000), Rick served as an associate pastor at Woodland Park Baptist Church in Chattanooga, Tennessee. The Lord's ministry has taken him to several countries, including Haiti, Romania, Ukraine, Moldova, Italy, Israel, England, and Greece, where he has been involved in training pastors, church leaders, and congregations. Rick has also lectured on college and seminary campuses. He graduated with honors from the University of Mobile and holds a Master of Divinity and a Ph.D. from Southwestern Baptist Theological Seminary in Fort Worth, Texas. He and his wife Linda Gail have four children and make their home in Jacksonville, Florida.

Eddie Rasnake

EDDIE RASNAKE met Christ in 1976 as a freshman in college. He graduated with honors from East Tennessee State University in 1980. He and his wife, Michele, served for nearly seven years on the staff of Campus Crusade for Christ. Their first assignment was the University of Virginia, and while there they also started a Campus Crusade ministry at James Madison University. Eddie then served four years as campus director of the Campus Crusade ministry at the University of Tennessee. In 1989, Eddie left Campus Crusade to join Wayne Barber at Woodland Park Baptist Church as the Associate Pastor of Discipleship and Training. He has been ministering in Eastern Europe in the role of equipping local believers for more than a decade and has published materials in Albanian, German, Greek, Italian, Romanian, and Russian. Eddie serves on the boards of directors of the Center for Christian Leadership in Tirana, Albania, and the Bible Training Center in Eleuthera, Bahamas. He also serves as chaplain for the Chattanooga Lookouts (Cincinnati Reds AA affiliate) baseball team. Eddie and his wife Michele live in Chattanooga, Tennessee, with their four children.

THE SERIES:

Three authors and fellow ministers, Wayne Barber, Eddie Rasnake, and Rick Shepherd, teamed up in 1998 to write a character-based Bible study for AMG Publishers. Their collaboration developed into the title, *Life Principles from the Old Testament.* Since 1998 these same authors and AMG Publishers have produced five more character-based studies—each consisting of twelve lessons geared around a five-day study of a particular Bible personality. More studies of this type are in the works. Two new titles were added to the series in 2001: *Life Principles for Worship from the Tabernacle* and *Living God's Will.* These newest titles are unique in that they are the first Following God™ studies that are topically-based rather than Bible character-based. However, the interactive study format that readers have come to love remains constant with each new release. As new titles are being planned, our focus remains the same: to provide excellent Bible study materials that point people to God's Word in ways that allow them to apply truths to their own lives. More information on this groundbreaking series can be found on the following web pages:

www.followingGod.com
www.amgpublishers.com

Preface

Women are important to the plan of God. This may seem like an unnecessary statement of the obvious, yet often this important message gets clouded by our culture. There are even those in the body of Christ that so promote an imbalanced view of submission, that they leave little room for women to do anything in the service of God except take care of the nursery. Yet God makes it clear that women are important to Him

In Genesis 1:26–28, when the Trinity initiated the creation of mankind, we read, *"Then God said, 'Let Us make man in Our image, according to Our likeness; and let THEM rule over the fish of the sea and over . . . every creeping thing that creeps on the earth.' And God created man in His own image, . . . And God blessed them; and God said to THEM, 'Be fruitful and multiply, and fill the earth, and subdue it; and rule over the fish of the sea and over the birds of the sky, and over every living thing that moves on the earth' "* [emphasis added]. In the plan of God, it takes both male and female to reflect His image.

It was Hagar, the Egyptian slave girl who named God as *El Roi,* "The God Who Sees." It was Bathsheba whom God chose as the mother of Solomon and the kingly line of descendants leading to Jesus. Rachel and Leah bore the sons of Jacob who became the twelve tribes of Israel. It is amazing as one begins to study the Scriptures seriously how many women God has included in His book!

Jesus affirmed women in His public ministry. He reached out to the Samaritan woman at the well, and then used her to take the gospel to a whole village. He rescued the woman caught in adultery from unjust justice. He gave women a prominence in His life and ministry that the culture did not. In fact, His public ministry was financed in large part by a group of women.

What is the message from all of this? Women are important to God. You may be asking, "How can three men write a book of Bible studies about women?" The fact is, what you will learn in the pages of this book is not about what we know of women, but what God's word has to say regarding women. Our goal is to take you to the Word, specifically those passages that introduce us to the prominent female characters of the Bible, and let you see for yourself what God has to say. Through these women of Scripture He has a message for men and women alike about what it means to follow God. It is our prayer that this study will help you to follow Him more closely.

Following Him,

WAYNE A. BARBER   RICHARD L. SHEPHERD

EDDIE RASNAKE

Table of Contents

Hagar 1

Lot's Wife 19

Rebekah 37

Leah 53

Rachel 67

Abigail 85

Bathsheba 101

Jezebel 117

Elizabeth 133

The Woman at
the Well 151

Women of
the Gospels 169

The Submissive Wife 191

How to
Follow God 207

Hagar

TRUSTING THAT GOD SEES

Cast out into the wilderness to die, Hagar had countless hours to reflect on her life, on her choices, and on the hardships she endured because of the choices of others. If any life had cause for despair, it was hers. Yet it was in this lowest of places that she learned her highest truth: *God sees me. Wherever I am, whatever is done to me, whatever I must endure, God sees me.* It was through the providential workings of this God who sees that Hagar's life was forever changed. Through this Gentile slave girl, God revealed a new facet of His character. In fact, it was Hagar who gave God the name, *El Roi*—"the God Who Sees." There is much to learn from this humble visitor from Egypt. She was not sinless—no one but Christ bears that description—but she bears less guilt in this story than her mistress or master. Even though she suffered the consequences of the sinful choices of others, and to a degree, her wrong responses to those choices, she was never out of God's sight. In her low places, the High and Exalted One met with her in a special way. Though she was sent into the wilderness a second time with only a jug of water, it was there she found a well. The God who sees was the One who would meet her needs.

HAGAR

The Egyptian name, Hagar, closely resembles the root of the Arabic word that means "flight." Not only is the word "flight" a prominent characteristic of Hagar's life, but also of her distant descendant Mohammed. As we look at the name, "Hagar," in light of her life, it should be understood to mean **fugitive** or **immigrant**, which is what she became.

WHERE DOES SHE FIT?

2200 B.C.	1950	1700	1450	1200	950	600	100 B.C.	A.D. 1	A.D. 100

HAGAR
2100?–2040?

Daniel
619–534?

ELIZABETH
75 B.C.?–A.D. 10?

REBEKAH
2040?–1915?

Solomon
991–931

WOMEN of the
Gospels
10 B.C.?–A.D. 50?

LEAH
1948?–1885?

Judges Rule
1385–1051

David
1041–971

LOT'S WIFE
2100?–2066

RACHEL
1943?–1899

Joshua
1495–1385

ABIGAIL
1036?–976?

Nehemiah
480?–400?

Jesus Christ
4 B.C.?–A.D. 30?

THE
SUBMISSIVE
WIFE

BATHSHEBA
1016?–961?

Moses
1525–1405

Isaac
2065–1885

Ephesians 5;
1 Peter 2—3

JEZEBEL
889?–841

Abraham
2165–1990

Jacob
2005–1858

Samuel
1105–1022

WOMAN at Well
10 B.C.?–A.D. 50?

THE FAMILY OF ABRAHAM

God delights to reveal Himself to the unlearned. He takes great pleasure to show who He is to the uninitiated. Without God's initiative it would be impossible for us to know Him. He is too high, and we are too limited. But God is knowable because He chooses to make Himself known. It was during an age when He was forgotten that He disclosed Himself to a man named Abram in Ur of the Chaldeans (an area in what is now known as Iraq) and later, to a woman named Hagar. He desires to reveal Himself to us as well. Second Chronicles 16:9 teaches us that *"the eyes of the LORD move to and fro throughout the earth, that He may strongly support those whose heart[s are] completely His."* God saw something in the hearts of Abram and Hagar and intervened in their intertwined lives. Today we want to look at the band of people surrounding Abram and how they came together as we seek to establish a context for what we will study in Scripture of the life of Hagar, the one who recognized God as the One who sees.

God spoke to Abram. He communicated a life-changing message to him, calling him to leave the land of his birth for an unknown destination. In Genesis 12:1 we read, *"Now the Lord said to Abram, 'Go forth from your country, and from your relatives and from your father's house, to the land which I will show you.'"* This invitation from Jehovah came with a promise of blessing, and Abram responded with obedience.

📖 Look at Genesis 12:10.

What did Abram find in the land of Canaan when he arrived there?

_____

_____

_____

What did he do?

_____

_____

_____

When Abram arrived at the land of promise, he found it in a severe famine. He had the reassurance that God was still in the promise (12:7), but it was clear that a detour was first. The verse tells us Abram went down to Egypt to "sojourn" there (to live temporarily among the people).

📖 Read Genesis 12:11–20 and answer the questions that follow.

What is Abram's plan to keep himself safe in Egypt (verses 11–13)?

_____

_____

_____

_____

> "For the eyes of the LORD move to and fro throughout the earth that He may strongly support those whose heart is completely His. . . ."
>
> 2 Chronicles 16:9a

What happens to Sarai when they get to Egypt (verses 14–15)?

_____

_____

_____

_____

What does Pharaoh give to Abram in exchange for Sarai (verse 16)?

_____

_____

What does God do to protect Abram and Sarai, and how does Pharaoh respond (verses 17–20)?

_____

_____

_____

_____

When Abram arrived in Egypt, worry gripped him. He recognized that having a beautiful wife was a liability in a land where the ruler could have any woman he chose. Instead of trusting God to protect them, Abram concocted a lie that protected him but put Sarai in jeopardy. She was taken into Pharaoh's house, presumably to become part of his harem. While there is every reason to judge Abram harshly for his actions in Egypt, we must recognize that though he knew God at this point, he actually understood very little about Him yet. The Law had not been given, and he had no Scriptures to guide him. It is significant that Pharaoh gave Abram livestock and servants. This gift answers the question that will arise later of where Hagar, the Egyptian maid, originated. In spite of Abram's striving to protect himself, God saw their need. God saw, and He manifested His protecting power and took care of Abram and Sarai, sending them on their way.

📖 Back in the land of promise, God visits Abram again. Look at Genesis 15:1–6.

What is God's promise to Abram in verse 1?

_____

_____

_____

What is Abram's worry (verses 2–3)?

_____

_____

How does God answer Abram's concern (verses 4–5)?

_____

_____

While there is every reason to judge Abram harshly for his actions in Egypt, we must recognize that though he knew God at this point, he actually understood very little about Him.

How does Abram respond (verse 6)?

_____

_____

_____

Abram had been following God. It was not a perfect pursuit, stained as it was with his humanity. But Abram had sought to be faithful. In Genesis 15:1, God makes two significant promises: to protect and to provide. God would be his shield, and promised great reward. Abram was old enough to appreciate material blessing, yet also practical enough to recognize its limitations. With a barren wife (Genesis 11:30), even if he had great wealth, he had no one to share it with or leave it to. God reached to the deepest longing of Abram's heart and promised to give him an heir, and descendants as numerous as the stars of the heavens. In Abram's response we see what makes him special. He believed God, and it was credited to him as righteousness (see Galatians 3:6).

Abram is the possessor of a great promise, but now comes the season of waiting. For every expectant father there is much time spent waiting. For Abram, it was a much longer wait than he expected or wanted. It is in this time of waiting that we are introduced to Hagar.

 Hagar DAY TWO

THE FOLLY OF SARAI

A promise given, then waiting . . . a decade of silence. Does God see? Where is the child of promise? One of the greatest temptations a Christian faces is to try and help out God with a shortcut to His promised blessing. One of the most amazing aspects of Jesus' encounter with Satan in the wilderness (Matthew 4) is that every enticement with which Satan tried to tempt Jesus was a shortcut to the perfect plan of God. After Jesus had endured forty days of fasting, Satan bid Him to turn stones into bread. Of course it was God's will that Jesus be fed—but not in that way. Satan had Jesus stand on the pinnacle of the temple and encouraged Him to cast himself on the stones below to see if the angels really would catch Him as the Scriptures promise. It was part of God's plan that Jesus be protected—but not that He test His Father. Satan then revealed all the kingdoms of the world and promised them to Jesus if He would only fall down and worship Satan. Yes, it is God's will that Jesus rule and reign over all—but to do so by way of the Cross, not by worshiping Satan and the evil he represents. Every "gift" that Satan offered was essentially part of the will of God, but not produced in the way of God. As we will see today, the temptation of the shortcut is one of Satan's favorite tricks.

In Genesis 16:1, what are the circumstances that introduce us to Hagar?

_____

_____

_____

_____

God does not want our help, He wants our obedience— Sarai's mistake is in not seeking God's plan.

We find this chapter prefaced with the dismal report that Sarai still has not borne any children to Abram. The promise of God is now hovering over their heads—still unfulfilled—and the couple is asking what should be done. It is understandable that they would feel this way. They may have been asking themselves, "What have we done wrong?" Clearly, they had been trying, albeit unsuccessfully, to have a child, and now the biological clock was ticking. The implication in Genesis 16:1 is that they had drawn a conclusion that Sarai was just too old now to have a child (in spite of God's promise), and that an alternative must be sought. At this juncture we are introduced to Hagar, Sarah's Egyptian maid.

📖 Look at Genesis 16:2–3.

What was Sarai's idea to compensate for her barrenness?

_____

_____

_____

_____

_____

Describe Abram's response.

_____

_____

_____

_____

What choice does Hagar have in the matter?

_____

_____

_____

_____

How long had it been since Abram was promised a child by God?

_____

_____

The bitterness of barrenness must have weighed heavily on Sarai. In her culture to have no children was a shameful thing. We know from 16:15 that Abram was 86 years old when Ishmael was born—meaning Sarai was around 77. The mention of Abram's living in Canaan for ten years gives us the idea it had been this long since the promise of a child was first given. The introduction of a new plan (or shall we say, "shortcut"?) suggests that Abram and Sarai had now given up on having a child together. The plan was the brainchild of Sarai's striving: Abram could have a child via her maid, Hagar. We are told that Abram *"listened to the voice of Sarai."* There is no evidence that he sought God in the matter. The statement that Sarai *"took Hagar . . . and gave her"* to Abram makes it clear that Hagar was given no choice in the matter. As a servant, she was bound to the whims of her mistress.

Put Yourself In Their Shoes
SARAI'S SHORTCUT

While the idea of having a child through a household servant sounds ludicrous to us today, it was a commonly accepted practice in the culture of that day, especially in the Chaldean region that Abram and Sarai had come from. It was not God's plan, but it was a part of the world in which they lived.

📖 Read Genesis 16:4–6.

What is Hagar's response when she becomes pregnant with Abram's child?

_____

_____

Why do you think she responds this way?

_____

_____

_____

_____

How does Sarai view Hagar?

_____

_____

_____

_____

What does Abram do about the situation?

_____

_____

_____

_____

When Hagar became pregnant with Abram's child, we are told *"her mistress* [Sarai] *was despised in her sight."* We are not told exactly why, but the response was probably a combination of Hagar's pride at her new position, as well as pain at having been used in such a way. It did not take Sarai long to regret her ill-fated plan of having Hagar as a bond wife. She now saw Hagar as a rival instead of a tool, and complained to Abram. Abram basically told her, "She's your maid—its your problem." Then Sarai proceeded to treat Hagar so harshly that she fled.

We can see from Hagar's plight that many suffered because of Sarai's folly. However, there is guilt enough to go around for all, and Hagar is not innocent in the matter. She acted in such a way to enrage her mistress. Yet, humanly speaking, we can certainly understand her response. She had been forced into the role of surrogate mother through Sarai's striving and Abram's foolish acquiescence.

Two principles can be quickly gleaned from this lesson so far. The principle we learn from Sarai is that we should not try to help out God with our striving, for it is when we seek shortcuts to God's will that our own choices become our chastisement. The principle we learn from Hagar is that wrong treatment can be compounded by our own wrong responses to the injuries of others.

The Flights of Hagar

 **DAY THREE**

wice Hagar ran away from the conflict she had with Sarai. Once she was sent back, and the other time she was set free. Both occasions are in the context of difficult times. Yet, both times, God saw her situation and met with her in a significant way. There is a powerful lesson for us in this. Our most important meetings with God are often not on the mountaintops but in the valleys. It is in our difficulties that we need to hear from God the most and to be reassured that He sees our situation. Today we want to look at how God met in a special way with Hagar during her lowest points. Although He would meet with Hagar in correction, He would also meet with her in blessing.

📖 Look at Genesis 16:3–7.

Why does Hagar flee from Sarai and Abram?

_____

_____

_____

Why does Sarai treat her harshly?

_____

_____

_____

_____

To where does Hagar flee?

_____

_____

_____

When the pressures of being a wife of Abram grew intense, Hagar couldn't stand the heat and ran away. She fled from Sarai because once she became pregnant, Sarai began treating her harshly. While Sarai is not to be excused for her misdeeds, Hagar is not completely innocent in the matter. The text tells us Sarai was *"despised in her sight."* Hagar fled from her mistress in the direction of Shur, a wilderness area between Egypt and Assyria. It doesn't appear she had any particular destination in mind. It is more that she ran **from** Sarai, than that she ran **to** any particular place.

📖 Read Genesis 16:8–16 and answer the questions that follow.

Where does the Angel of the LORD find Hagar, and what does He ask her?

_____

_____

_____

_____

Word Study
"THE WAY TO SHUR"

Hagar fled to the wilderness on the way to Shur. The word "Shur" means "wall" and referred to a great barrier of some kind across the great northeastern highways out of Egypt, near the eastern boundary line of Egypt mentioned in records from the Twelfth Dynasty, circa 2000–1775 B.C. With this landmark called "Shur," it was logical that the wilderness region surrounding it would take on the same name, serving as a wall of sorts itself. It was this same wilderness that the Israelites entered after they had crossed the Red Sea (Exodus 15:22–23).

How does He respond to Hagar's answer?

_____

_____

_____

What does this suggest about Hagar's problem?

_____

_____

_____

_____

Word Study

HOW DID ABRAM AND SARAI BECOME ABRAHAM AND SARAH?

It was God who changed Abram's name to Abraham. The name "Abram" literally means *"exalted father,"* which must have been painful to a man who was childless until he was eighty-six. "Abraham" means *"father of a multitude."* God also changes "Sarai" *("my princess")* to "Sarah" *("princess").* At a casual glance, the change of Sarah's name seems much less significant, but there is a point to the change. No longer is Sarah to be Abraham's princess only. Now he will share her with a family that will multiply beyond belief.

The Angel of the LORD found Hagar by a spring in the wilderness. There is no indication that she cried out to the Lord, but He met with her anyway. He saw her need. The angel asked two questions—where was she coming from, and where was she going—but Hagar only had an answer for the first question. She was fleeing from her mistress. The angel drives to the heart of Hagar's problem: *"Return to your mistress, and submit yourself to her authority."* Apparently, the root of the problem was in Hagar's attitude. Once she became pregnant with Abram's child, she began to see herself as his wife and as superior to Sarai. As we will see in tomorrow's study, the Angel of the LORD went on to pronounce blessing on Hagar and the infant she carried inside of her. In verse 15, we see that she obeyed the Lord and returned, giving birth to a son, Ishmael.

Now take a look at Genesis 21:9–15.

What does Sarah (Sarai) want to do with Hagar and Ishmael once Isaac is born?

_____

_____

_____

_____

What does God tell Abraham (Abram) to do?

_____

_____

_____

_____

Where do Hagar and Ishmael end up?

_____

_____

Once Isaac arrived, Sarah saw trouble between Ishmael and him and wants to get rid of that problem once and for all. At first, Abraham was worried by Sarah's request to dismiss Hagar and Ishmael, but God put his mind at ease. It is significant to note that the first time Sarah had an idea (having a child by Hagar) Abraham *"listened to the voice of Sarai,"* and ended up lamenting the day he made that decision. Now, he was hardly willing to listen to another idea by Sarah regarding Hagar until he had heard from God. He had learned from his original mistake. God made it clear that He knew what was going on (He sees), and that Abraham could trust Him with the entire situation. So Abraham sent Hagar and Ishmael away with a jug of water. The mother and her son traveled into the wilderness as far as that water would take them and then sat down, expecting to die.

📖 Read Genesis 21:16–21 and answer the questions that follow.

When did God intervene in the situation (verses 16–17)?

_____

_____

_____

_____

_____

What significance do you find in the irony that Hagar was about to give up on life only a few feet away from a well of water (verse 19)?

_____

_____

_____

_____

_____

_____

What do you think it means that *"God was with the lad"* (verse 20)?

_____

_____

_____

_____

_____

_____

_____

ISHMAEL

It is noteworthy that when Hagar fled the second time, Ishmael was probably around sixteen or seventeen years old. He was born when Abraham was eighty-six (16:16), and Isaac (who was born when Abraham was one hundred years old) had just been weaned, making him about two or three. Ishmael was no longer a child. He needed to meet with God too.

What a powerful message there is in these short verses, especially when you look at them in light of the fact that God sees! God saw their need, but He waited for them to cry out to Him. God heard both Hagar's cry and Ishmael's as well. When they cried, God saw their tears and met with them. Don't you find it astounding that they gave up within a short distance of a well. God knew exactly when they would reach the end of themselves, and He allowed them to capitulate at the very place He had provision for them. He didn't let them see this well though, until they looked to Him. Once God met with them, He took the lesson He taught Hagar and taught it to the lad as well. **He sees!** We don't know exactly what it means that *"God was with the lad,"* but it suggests that Ishmael walked with God in some way. He would never forget the despair he felt in the wilderness, dying of thirst; nor would he forget that God saw his despair and met his need.

THE FUTURE OF ISHMAEL

What happened to the son of striving? What future could one hope for a son who was a discarded mistake? Ishmael was unloved and unlovely, yet God had purpose for his life. While Hagar was still pregnant with this son, God began to unveil the plans He had for the boy. It was in the place of despondency as Hagar fled to the wilderness that God revealed their future and hope. God had promised to bless Abraham and his descendants, and Ishmael was Abraham's son. God would fulfill His word, regardless of the circumstances of Ishmael's birth. Today we want to look at the future God planned for the son of Abraham and Hagar.

📖 Read through Genesis 12:1–3 and summarize all that is promised to Abraham there.

_____

_____

_____

_____

_____

_____

Abraham was promised that if he would go at God's bidding, the Lord would make a great nation of him and bless him. God also promised to *"make* [his] *name great"*—in other words, to give him a lasting reputation. Not only would Abraham be blessed, but he would also be a blessing to all the families of the earth. While this ultimately is accomplished through Christ, born through the line of Isaac, part of this blessing applies to Ishmael, for all his descendants call Abraham their father.

📖 Look at the promises in Genesis 15:1–6 and reflect on how they relate to Ishmael.

_____

_____

_____

_____

_____

_____

_____

_____

God promised to be a shield to Abraham, and we see this same protection exercised on his son, Ishmael. God also promised great reward. When the Lord promised descendants more numerous than the stars of the heavens, this is fulfilled not just through Isaac but through Ishmael as well.

Did You Know?

? THE ANGEL OF THE LORD

Throughout the Old Testament, there are many appearances of "the Angel of the LORD." Sometimes when angels appear, they are revealed by name, but when **the** Angel of the LORD appears, it is none other than the Lord Jesus Christ in His pre-incarnate form. The Angel of the LORD appeared to many, including Gideon and Manoah, the father of Samson, both of whom acknowledged Him as God and feared death for having seen Him. But it is significant that He appeared first to Hagar.

📖 When God met with Hagar the first time in the wilderness, He revealed to her some of the plans He had for her son, Ishmael. Read Genesis 16:10–12 and answer the questions that follow.

What is the promise of verse 10, and who are the descendants mentioned?

_____

_____

_____

_____

What does the name "Ishmael" mean (verse 11)?

_____

_____

What does verse 12 reveal of Ishmael's character?

_____

_____

_____

_____

_____

_____

Word Study
ISHMAEL

The name "Ishmael" means, *"God shall hear,"* and was probably not fully understood by Hagar or her son until they both cried out to God in the wilderness (Genesis 21:9–21). Not only does God see, but He hears too.

God makes it clear that the promise of multiplied descendants was not just a plan for Abraham through Isaac. The same promise is made to Hagar for Ishmael. It is significant that God picked out the lad's name. In biblical times, a name was an important thing, communicating something about the history or character of the one bearing it. The name "Ishmael" means "God shall hear" and was probably not fully understood by Hagar or her son until they both cried out to God in the wilderness (Genesis 21:9–21). God reveals that Ishmael will be *a wild donkey of a man,"* painting a picture of one who would be marked by stubbornness and strife.

📖 Look at Genesis 21:18 and write what you learn there of the future God promises to Hagar for Ishmael.

_____

_____

_____

_____

_____

_____

Again, God affirms His promise to do great things for Ishmael. In the same way that He had promised to make a great nation of Abraham (Genesis 12:2), God had planned the same for Ishmael. The nation He would make of Abraham was Israel, and the nation He would make of Ishmael was the Arabs. Even though Ishmael was the son of striving, God would be faithful to him. "The God Who Sees" saw him at every point of his life and met him there.

FOR ME TO FOLLOW GOD

The single most important lesson we learn from Hagar's life is that God sees. Jehovah has many names in the Bible, and in each He reveals something of His character and power. *El Roi,* "The God Who Sees," was a name selected for Him by the Egyptian slave girl, Hagar. What a powerful concept it must have been to one in her position. To be a slave was to be one of no rights and position in life. Slaves were the "unseen" in their culture. Like other slaves, Hagar was cruelly used for the selfish purposes of her master and mistress. Their pleasure was her pain. Although she was not sinless (none of us are), she was certainly victimized. Imagine her despair to be cast out to fend for herself while carrying a child. But hers is not a hopeless situation, for the God of hope **sees**. What a massive change comes over every situation we fall into when we understand that our loving Heavenly Father sees. He knows. He is aware. Today we want to look at how this revelation of Hagar applies to us right now.

 Take some time to think honestly about your life. Think about the difficult things that you have experienced or are currently experiencing. Take some time for honest reflection. Then write down the things in your life that you think God doesn't see.

Painful things inflicted on me by others:

_____

_____

_____

_____

_____

_____

_____

_____

Impossible situations in which I find myself:

_____

_____

_____

_____

_____

_____

_____

_____

_____

_____

Sinful things I have done that I thought I could hide from God:

_____

_____

_____

_____

_____

_____

_____

God sees. Nothing escapes his notice. What others or we thought could be hidden by darkness, He has seen. In Psalm 139:12 we read, *"Even the darkness is not dark to Thee, And the night is as bright as the day. Darkness and light are alike to Thee."* God has seen what others have done to me. God has seen my trails and trials. God has even seen the things I have done that I thought were hidden. Most important, He not only knows what I have done, but He knows why I have done it. First Corinthians 4:5 tells us that when He judges, He will *"both bring to light the things hidden in the darkness and disclose the motives of men's hearts."* Such exposure of our hearts is not just so God can punish that which is wrong, but also so He can praise that which is right—for the verse goes on to say, *"And then each man's praise will come to him from God."*

Look at what you wrote concerning the painful things inflicted upon you by others. First of all, you need to go through each experience you wrote about and acknowledge that God sees. He knows what the perpetrator did, and what he/she didn't do. God is aware! Someday He will vindicate you. He will make the wrongs right in His time. But you must also acknowledge that God is sovereign. He is able to take even these injustices you have listed and use them for good and growth in your life (Romans 8:28). Write down your reflections here.

_____

_____

_____

_____

_____

_____

_____

Secondly, you need to acknowledge that God is sovereign and that He sees the impossibilities of your present circumstances. There is a purpose even in what you don't have. Yes, that sentence is a bit unclear, so let me explain. Hagar's desperate need for water was not an accident, but part of the divine plan of God. You see, God wanted her to know thirst so she could know Him as the one who could quench her thirst and meet her needs. He had to bring her to the end of herself so she could find Him as the fountain of living waters. Use the impossibilities of your present circumstances as an occasion to cry out to the God who sees and hears. Let Him show you the well He has for you. Write down your reflections on the next page.

> *"Even the darkness is not dark to Thee, And the night is as bright as the day. Darkness and light are alike to Thee."*
>
> **Psalm 139:12**

_____

_____

_____

_____

_____

_____

_____

_____

**Confession is not
for God's benefit,
but for our own.**

God sees your pain. God sees your need. And God sees your sin. Nothing is hidden from Him. Knowing this makes His love all the more amazing. He knows everything there is to know about us and loves us anyway. Perhaps the hardest concept for me to acknowledge is that God sees the sinful things that I thought I could hide from God. Nothing is hidden from His sight. When a criminal confesses to the police, often he is telling them something they did not already know. However, it is never that way with God! He already knows everything we have done before we confess. So why bother? What is accomplished through confession if God already sees, already knows? The answer to that question is one of the most profound understandings you can have about what it means to walk in fellowship with God. Confession is not for God's benefit, but for our own.

Look at what King David learned from his sin with Bathsheba. *"When I kept silent about my sin, my body wasted away through my groaning all day long. For day and night Thy hand was heavy upon me; my vitality was drained away as with the fever heat of summer"* (Psalm 32:3–4). Even when no one saw, God saw. Even when no one knew, God knew. Even before David's sin was revealed, he suffered the consequences. He went from a meaningful, rewarding life to one of mere existence. His joy was gone, and even his physical well-being was affected.

 Can you think of any consequences you have seen either in your life or in the lives of others due to unconfessed sin?

_____

_____

_____

_____

_____

_____

_____

_____

What a change confession brings! David writes, *"How blessed is he whose transgression is forgiven, whose sin is covered! How blessed is the man to whom the Lord does not impute iniquity, and in whose spirit there is no deceit! … I acknowledged my sin to Thee, and my iniquity I did not hide; I said, 'I will confess my transgression to the LORD'; and Thou didst forgive the guilt of my sin"* (Psalm 32:1–2, 5). What have you seen in your life or in the lives of others of the joy that comes from a clean heart?

_____

_____

_____

_____

_____

_____

_____

_____

The Greek word for "confess" in the New Testament is *homologeō* (from *homo,* "the same," and *lego,* "to speak"). It literally means "to speak the same thing" or "to agree." When we confess, we are not telling God something He doesn't already know. We are merely agreeing with Him that what He calls sin really is sin. Woven into the word is the idea of repentance, for we are not truly agreeing with God if we say something is wrong with our lips, but continue cherishing it with our lives. Confession does not mean we will never stumble again, but it does mean a change in the way we think about the action, and that change in thinking leads to change in behavior. The process looks something like this...

CONFESS OUR SIN
CONFESS THAT WE ARE FORGIVEN
CONFESS OUR NEED

Not only do we need to confess (or agree with God) that something is sin, but we also need to agree with God that it is forgiven. Then we need to agree with God that we need His help, His empowering, to turn from the sin.

Can you rejoice with Hagar that Jehovah is "The God Who Sees"? Can you take comfort in knowing that He sees what others have done to you? No matter what others do, they cannot mess up God's plan for you. Are you able to trust that God sees the impossible wilderness you find yourself in? Maybe it is in finances, or in relationships, or in health. God sees your need, and He waits for your cry. It is not that He is unable to help you until you cry to Him, but that He knows if He helps you before you cry to Him, you will not be able to see that it was He who helped. "The God Who Sees" is the God who hears. You must cast your cares on Him. Finally, you can rejoice that God sees your sin too. Maybe that doesn't seem joyful, but to know that He sees and still loves you—now that is a powerful thing indeed! Knowing that God sees your sins makes you accountable to Him but also serves to liberate you. For in spite of the fact that God knows everything about you, He still loves you! You don't have to dread telling Him something He doesn't already know.

Spend some time in prayer with the Lord right now,

Dear Lord, what freedom there is in knowing that You see! I thank You that You have seen what others have done to me. You will judge . . . You will vindicate. Thank You that You see the impossibilities that face me. Help me to cry to You. Help me to bring my thirst to You so You can show me the well You offer. And Father, thank You for loving me even though You have seen my every sin. Empower me to turn to You, to agree with You, and to be liberated by You. Amen.

Use the space provided to write your own prayer to the Lord.

_____

_____

_____

_____

_____

_____

_____

_____

_____

Notes

Notes

Lot's Wife

REMEMBERING GOD'S JUDGMENT ON A SELF-SEEKING LIFE

Sometimes, Jesus was a man of few words, but those few words always contained a wealth of insight and instruction—words so profound that their echoes ring into eternity. In one of the shortest verses in the Bible, Jesus spoke three words that serve as a warning, as wise counsel, and as a word of hope to those who heed His command. In Luke 17:32, Jesus said, *"Remember Lot's wife."* It is a command, a present tense command. In other words, we are to start remembering and to continue remembering Lot's wife. In the context, Jesus was speaking about His return. Christ said that in the end times, there would be those living their lives in carefree fashion—eating, drinking, buying, selling, planting, building, and so forth. Christ's return will find them unaware and unprepared—but judgment will surely come upon them. Lot's wife was warned, but on the verge of escape from judgment, she turned to look at her heart's desire, the city of Sodom—and God's judgment struck! She became a lifeless pillar of salt, the picture of a misspent, self-centered existence.

Jesus warned those who would listen—do not be caught unaware, unprepared. Be ready to meet the Lord. Surrender your life to Him. If you try to

> *"Remember Lot's wife. Whoever seeks to keep his life shall lose it, and whoever loses his life shall preserve it."*
>
> *Luke 17:32–33*

WHERE DOES SHE FIT?

2200 B.C.	1950	1700	1450	1200	950	600	100 B.C.	A.D. 1	A.D. 100
HAGAR 2100?–2040?						Daniel 619–534?	ELIZABETH 75 B.C.?–A.D. 10?		
REBEKAH 2040?–1915?				Solomon 991–931			WOMEN of the Gospels 10 B.C.?–A.D. 50?		
LEAH 1948?–1885?		Judges Rule 1385–1051	David 1041–971						
LOT'S WIFE 2100?–2066	RACHEL 1943–1899	Joshua 1495–1385	ABIGAIL 1036?–976?	Nehemiah 480?–400?	Jesus Christ 4 B.C.?–A.D. 30?	THE SUBMISSIVE WIFE Ephesians 5; 1 Peter 2—3			
Isaac 2065–1885	Moses 1525–1405	BATHSHEBA 1016?–961?							
Abraham 2165–1990	Jacob 2005–1858	Samuel 1105–1022	JEZEBEL 889?–841		WOMAN at Well 10 B.C.?–A.D. 50?				

"save your life" by selfish, sinful, self-seeking ways, you will lose it, but if you **"lose your life"**—if you give your life to Jesus Christ to follow and obey Him, you will preserve your life, not just for time but for eternity.

What can we learn from Lot's wife? What was she like? How did she think? What was she thinking when she turned to look back on her beloved city of Sodom? What about her life and tragic death does Jesus want us to remember? Whatever it is, it matters for eternity. In this lesson, we will seek to understand the heartbeat of this woman of the city of Sodom and hopefully hear the message her life and death speaks these thousands of years later. As we listen carefully, we will doubtless hear the call of Jesus, **"Follow Me."**

MEET LOT, NEPHEW OF ABRAHAM

Families were often very close and tightly knit in the ancient world. Much of the daily routine of life during that time often connected with another family member in some way—the family business, family worship, and where the family lived. Often, when one family member moved, the rest of the family moved with him. We see a family like this in the eleventh chapter of Genesis. There, we are first introduced to Terah and his sons Abram, Nahor, and Haran. Lot and Milcah were the son and daughter of Haran, both born in Ur. Their father, Haran, died while they were living in Ur. After Abram married Sarai and Nahor married Milcah, Terah led them all, including Lot, in moving from Ur to the city of Haran. What a mix of events that occurred in this family! What can we discover about this family? Where does Lot fit in? How, when, and where does Lot's wife enter the picture?

📖 Genesis 12:1–3 reveals that God spoke to Abram and told him to go the land He would show him. What do you discover in Genesis 12:4–9? Where is Lot in this journey?

_____

_____

_____

Abram and Sarai moved from Haran to Canaan when Abram was seventy-five years of age. When they moved, Lot moved with them. Abram journeyed through the land, going first to Shechem and from there, south to the area between Bethel and Ai. From there he traveled to the Negev in the south. Lot was with him all this time, watching as Abram worshiped the Lord and followed His guiding hand.

📖 Genesis 12 tells us that Abram and his family traveled to Egypt because of a famine in the land of Canaan. Lot went with him to Egypt and returned to Canaan with him. What do you discover about Lot in Genesis 13:1–5?

_____

_____

_____

Did You Know?
WHO WERE THE CANAANITES?

There were several groups that made up the people of Canaan, and they are all labeled under the term Canaanite. These groups include Hittites, Girgashites, Amorites, Perizzites, Hivites, and Jebusites, as well as the Amalekites, Arkites, Arvadites, Sidonians, Sinites, and Zemarites. (Deuteronomy 7:1; Numbers 14:43).

When we read about Abram returning to Canaan with his family and flocks, we also learn that Lot had accumulated several *"flocks and herds and tents"* and supported several herdsmen. With Lot owning several tents, it is possible that Lot had married during this time period. However, we cannot be sure of the precise time when he married. We will look at Lot's marriage further as we proceed in our study of Lot's Wife. For now, let's gain a clear picture of the husband of this woman known to us only as "Lot's wife."

📖 What further insights about Lot and Abram are found in Genesis 13:6–11?

_____

_____

_____

_____

_____

Lot's herdsmen and Abram's herdsmen grazed their flocks together for some time, but they came to a point where they began quarreling over grazing land because of the size of both herds. Abram sought to settle the dispute by allowing Lot to choose where he would like to settle with his flocks and possessions. Lot chose the valley of the Jordan in the eastern part of Canaan, a valley that was *"like the garden of the LORD,"* well watered and fertile. From that point, Abram and Lot began living separate lives. Lot moved near the city of Sodom.

📖 The next time we see Lot, he and his household are in trouble. Genesis 14:1–12 describes the invasion of Sodom and capture of the town and its people, including Lot. Where was Lot living when all this happened? What happened next? Read Genesis 14:13–15?

_____

_____

_____

_____

_____

Lot was no longer living **near** Sodom; he was now *"living in Sodom."* After the battle and subsequent capture of Sodom and several of its citizens, a fugitive escaped and came to Abram telling him the whole story of how Lot and all his possessions were captured. Abram gathered his trained men, 318 strong, and pursued the army of the four kings, overtaking and defeating them north of Damascus.

📖 What do you discover in Genesis 14:16? Who is included with Lot?

_____

_____

_____

_____

Did You Know?

❓ "THE CITIES OF THE VALLEY"

"The cities of the plain" or *"the cities of the valley"* (Genesis 19:29) can be translated literally from the Hebrew language as "the cities of the circle (Hebrew—*kikkar*)," a designation for the cities lying in a broad valley near the south end of what is now called the Dead Sea. The cities that were destroyed included Sodom, Gomorrah, Admah, and Zeboiim. A fifth city in the valley, Zoar, was spared as a place of escape for Lot and his family. (See Genesis 19:20–22; Deuteronomy 29:23.)

After this victory, Abram recovered Lot, his possessions, and *"also the women, and the people."* Lot and his family and servants had the opportunity to see how the God of Abram, God Most High, gave Abram and them victory and escape from their enemies. They had the opportunity to recognize the true God and His power and care, if they would. Time would tell.

It is possible, even likely, that among *"the women"* who were rescued were the wife of Lot and perhaps his young daughters. If that is the case then Lot could have married one of the women of the land of Canaan, perhaps even a woman of Sodom. What would she have been like? What do we know about the Canaanites or the people of Sodom? We will see in Day Two.

Lot's Wife DAY TWO

MEET LOT'S WIFE AND HER CANAANITE NEIGHBORS

Lot and his family and servants had the opportunity to see how the God of Abram gave them victory. They had the opportunity to recognize the true God and His power and care, if they would.

We hear nothing of Lot's marriage and are only introduced to his wife when the two angels travel to Sodom to announce its doom in Genesis 19. This event occurred approximately twenty-five years after Abram, Sarai, and Lot had journeyed from Haran to settle in Canaan. We do not have all the details about when Lot and his wife married, but we know they had daughters old enough to be married in Genesis 19. We do not know the name of the woman Lot married, but we have several clues about the kind of woman she was. We will see her specific responses to the things of God in Days Three and Four, but first let's look at the people around her. What were they like? Perhaps she was one of them.

📖 We saw in Day One that Lot separated from Abram and moved near the city of Sodom. What was life like in this place? What insights do you gain from Genesis 13:12–13?

_____

_____

_____

_____

_____

Lot settled in the cities of the valley, moving his tents near Sodom. The men of Sodom *"were wicked exceedingly and sinners against the LORD,"* according to Genesis 13:13. The Hebrew word translated *"wicked"* is *"ra"* and refers to anything that is bad or of inferior quality. It points to anything that fails to come up to a good or right standard, and thus, never benefits anyone. The word *"sinner"* pictures a person who practices a lifestyle of sin. The root idea is of one who continually comes short of the right target, or continually gets off track and wanders in the wrong direction. Such a person makes sin his (or her) habit of life and is continually offensive to God. A sinner's life is consumed with self and, unless he turns to God in repentance and mercy, is fitting himself to be an object of the wrath of God. Lot moved near a city where the people were characterized by just such attitudes and lifestyles.

Think of the following truths as we consider the questions of what the Canaanites were like and what Lot's wife could have been like. What did Abraham think of the people of the land or of marriage to a Canaanite? We hear from him in Genesis 24:3 that under no condition was his son Isaac to marry a Canaanite. Years later, after Isaac and his wife Rebekah had raised Esau and Jacob, we read that Esau married two Hittite women (part of the Canaanites). Genesis 26:35 says, *"They brought grief to Isaac and Rebekah."* Literally, that verse can read, "They were a bitterness of spirit to Isaac and Rebekah." When Rebekah advised Jacob to go to Haran to her brother's house for a while, one of her concerns was the possibility of Jacob staying in the land and marrying a Canaanite. She told her husband Isaac, *"I am tired of living because of the daughters of Heth [Esau's wives]; if Jacob takes a wife from the daughters of Heth, like these, from the daughters of the land, what good will my life be to me?"* (Genesis 27:46). Clearly, the people of Canaan were not marked by the kind of character God wanted in His people. Years later, we find the Lord giving clear warnings about the Canaanites. What did He say?

📖 The Lord spoke clearly about the customs of the Canaanites, the people of the land of Canaan. Read Leviticus 18:1–5. What does God say about what was done in the land of Canaan?

_____

_____

_____

_____

_____

God warned Moses that the sons of Israel were not to do any of the things done in the land of Egypt or in the land of Canaan. Their laws and customs, culture and ways, were forbidden; *"you shall not walk in their statutes."* Rather, God's people were to walk in His judgments, His decisions about what is right or wrong, good or evil. They were to guard their lives so that they followed God and His statutes, the things engraved on His heart and in the Law He gave to Moses.

📖 What are some of the practices found in Canaan according to Leviticus 18:20–30? What did God say about these practices?

_____

_____

_____

_____

God pointed to the abominations practiced by the peoples of Canaan, things He wanted none of His people practicing. God strictly prohibited any kind of sexual relations other than between a husband and wife. Adulterous relations (sexual relations with someone else's spouse), homosexual relations, and acts of bestiality were never to be practiced by God's people. The Israelites were to never offer a child in the fires as a sacrifice to the detestable god, Molech. The Canaanites practiced all these things, practices that were an abomination to God, things that defiled them and defiled the land. These practices brought the judgment of God on these people—they would be

ABRAHAM AND THE CANAANITES

Abraham made sure that his son Isaac did not marry a Canaanite woman. Some forty years after Sodom was destroyed, Abraham made his servant, Eliezer, swear that he would not take a woman of Canaan as a wife for his son, Isaac (Genesis 24:2–9). Perhaps this was because of what he had seen in the destruction of Sodom and Gomorrah some forty years earlier or because of his own lengthy experience in dealing with Canaanites.

Word Study

LAWS, JUDGMENTS, AND STATUTES

In the Old Testament a "statute" (Hebrew: *choq*) refers to a regulation, decree, or boundary. It is from the root word *chaqaq* which means to cut or engrave. These statutes or laws were often cut or engraved into stone. They were meant to be long-term laws of the land. "Laws" (*torah*) refer to direction, teaching, or instruction. The root idea means to throw or shoot like an archer shooting an arrow. Laws are the standard that guides one in the right direction. "Judgments" (*mishpat*) refer to formal verdicts or decrees of what is considered right or law. It has to do with what is decided as the right course or action. God wants His people to follow His engravings, His standards, and His decisions—not those of the Canaanites or any other group that opposes His will.

> ## "Thus you are to be holy to Me, for I the Lord am holy; and I have set you apart from the peoples to be Mine."
>
> ## Leviticus 20:26

spewed out of the land like someone vomiting over some disease infecting the body. The people of Sodom faced an even more startling judgment (Genesis 19).

📖 Look at God's description of the customs of the Canaanites in Leviticus 20:1–21, 27. What is God's directive in Leviticus 20:22–23?

_____

_____

_____

_____

The Lord repeated listing some of the abominations He had already revealed. He added the practices of consulting mediums and spiritists, the disrespectful acts of children cursing their own parents, and the detestable practice of incest. These practices marked the peoples of Canaan. *"They did all these things,"* the Lord declared, and He *"abhorred them."* The people who followed God were told, *"you shall not follow the customs"* of Canaan. Literally, He said, *"you shall not walk in the statutes* [things engraved]" of Canaan. The things the Canaanites approved, the things they considered appropriate customs of the culture, were an abomination to God, and He wanted no such behavior to exist among His people.

📖 But what **did God want** for His people according to Leviticus 20:24–26? (For additional insight, look at Deuteronomy 26:16–19, especially verse 18, to see how the Lord describes His people and their relationship to Him.)

_____

_____

_____

God called His people to be separated **from** the people of the land and to be separated **to Him**. He wanted them to be clean in every detail of life, even in the food they ate. He set them apart to be holy. They were to walk with Him in a unique relationship. They belonged to Him. Deuteronomy 26:18 adds that they were to be *"a treasured possession,"* a picture of the great value He placed on them, the great care He showed them, and the great love He had for them.

 Did you know that every child of God is a treasure to God? We were purchased not with silver and gold, but with the precious blood of Jesus (1 Peter 1:18–19), and 1 Peter 2:9 speaks of the followers of Jesus as being *"God's own possession."* What value He places on us! Are you living in that reality? Pause and think, then thank God for how much He values and cares for you.

_____

_____

_____

_____

Was Lot's wife characterized like the Canaanites, or was she different? We will see in Days Three and Four.

THE LURE AND LEGACY OF SODOM

The Scripture has some interesting things to say about the cities of Sodom and Gomorrah. What was it about these cities, particularly Sodom that was so attractive? What enticed Lot and his wife so much that they would want to move there and raise their children and grandchildren there? What can we learn from this city and the experiences of both Lot and his wife?

📖 Read Genesis 13:5–13 once again. Describe the land around Sodom, the land of the Jordan River? Why would Lot choose that land?

_____

_____

_____

_____

When Lot looked at the land of Canaan to choose where he would settle with his flocks and herds, he saw the Jordan Valley as ideal. It was *"well watered everywhere."* Genesis 13:10 even adds that it was *"like the garden of the LORD"* (the Garden of Eden), or like the rich, fertile area near Zoar. Here was a land that had everything—an abundant and fresh water supply; rich, loamy soil; fields of lush green grass; fruit trees; and an ideal climate year-round. Lot, like many others in his day, chose this garden-like area and moved near the cities of the valley, particularly near Sodom, the predominant city.

📖 We have seen one of the characteristics of Sodom in Genesis 13:13—*"the men of Sodom were wicked exceedingly and sinners before the LORD."* What else can we learn about this city? Look at Genesis 18:16–21. What does the Lord say about Sodom and Gomorrah? How does it compare with the expression of His will in 18:19?

_____

_____

_____

_____

The Lord said the sin of the cities of Sodom and Gomorrah was *"exceedingly grave."* Was this a description of Lot's wife? The Hebrew word translated *"grave"* is *kabad*, which literally means "to be heavy." In verse 20 it refers to something very grievous and burdensome focusing on the heaviness, the weight of the sin and guilt of these cities. In contrast, the Lord spoke of Abraham, his children and his household, as those who should keep *"the way of the LORD by doing righteousness and justice."* God was fully aware that Sodom and Gomorrah had not kept the ways of the Lord, and He was prepared to deal with them and their sin. He would not hide this reality from Abraham; the Lord wanted Abraham to know the kind of nation God desired, the kind of people God wanted as His followers. He wanted Abraham to know the gravity of sin and its consequences: in this case judgment on the people of the valley with a scorched land as a daily reminder. Of which sort was Lot's wife—weighted down with guilt or walking in the way of the Lord?

Did You Know?

❓ THE CLIMATE OF SODOM

The Sea of Galilee in northern Israel is about 700 feet below sea level. Out of that lake, the Jordan River flows south to the Dead Sea, an area about 1300 feet below sea level. In all likelihood the area of Sodom and Gomorrah (most likely situated near the confluence of the Jordan River and the Dead Sea) was about the same elevation in the days of Lot and his wife before the cities were destroyed. Because the cities were situated well below sea level, the area likely was blessed with a sub-tropical climate. The climate, coupled with the abundant waters of the Jordan flowing from the Mount Hermon area, produced a garden spot, *"like the garden of the LORD."* Obviously, Sodom was a very pleasant locale and an area of rich trade and commerce, since it is described as a place of *"abundant food, and careless ease"* (Genesis 13:10; Ezekiel 16:49).

Did You Know?

❓ THE WICKEDNESS OF SODOM

The city of Sodom is mentioned several times as an example of unrighteousness and the judgment of God. The references include: Deuteronomy 29:23; Isaiah 13:19–20; Jeremiah 20:16; 50:40; Lamentations 4:6; Zephaniah 2:9; Matthew 11:24; Luke 17:28–29; 2 Peter 2:6–12; and Revelation 11:8.

📖 What request did Abraham make of the Lord according to Genesis 18:22–33?

_____

_____

_____

_____

When Abraham was made aware of how God saw the wickedness of Sodom, he began pleading with the Lord to spare the city, doubtless very concerned about his nephew Lot and his family. He then asked God to spare the city if just fifty righteous people could be found. God agreed to honor this request. Then Abraham bargained to have the city spared for just forty-five righteous people, then forty, thirty, twenty, and finally ten. God's answer was the same for each plea and agreed to spare the city—even if only ten righteous people were found there. What was this city like? What impact did Lot, Lot's wife, and their family have on this community? What did the two angels find?

📖 What do you find about the people of Sodom in Genesis 19:1–13?

_____

_____

_____

_____

_____

_____

_____

_____

The men of Sodom came to Lot's house to demand that his guests be given to them so that they could have sexual relations with them. As they interacted with Lot, he urged them against acting wickedly, yet unbelievably offered his two daughters to these men. They, however, mocked Lot and threatened to harm him and began to come against him. The angels rescued Lot and struck the men with blindness. Then they warned Lot to gather his family and flee the city and the judgment about to be brought upon it.

📖 What was at the heart of the people of this city? Ezekiel 16:49–50 speaks about Sodom and gives several characteristics of that city and its people. Are these characteristics an apt description of the heart and life of Lot's wife? What do you find in those verses? List the characteristics.

_____

_____

_____

_____

The focus of Ezekiel 16:49–50 is upon the guilty hearts of the people of Sodom. Sodom _"and her daughters"_ (the citizens) were marked first by _"arrogance,"_ a proud, self-sufficient mindset. This attitude is sickening to God because it refuses to honor God, His ways, or His Word and fails to acknowledge His

Word Study
THE "DAUGHTERS OF SODOM"

Ezekiel 16:48–49 refer to the "daughters" of Sodom. The "daughters" of a city refer to the citizens of that place or the people who express the nature of that place, much like a daughter expresses the nature of her father and mother. Scripture also speaks of _"the daughter(s) of Zion_ [Jerusalem]" (Isaiah 1:8; 4:4; Micah 4:8–10; Zephaniah 3:14; Matthew 21:5 [compare to Isaiah 62:11]; Luke 23:28; John 12:15 [compare to Zechariah 9:9]), as well as the "daughter of Egypt" (Jeremiah 46:11), the "daughter of Edom" (Lamentations 4:21–22) and the "daughter of Babylon" (Jeremiah 50:42; Zechariah 2:7) among others.

many gracious gifts. Along with their arrogance, they had *"abundant food"* and *"careless ease,"*—in other words, a booming economy and lots of leisure time. Yet, in the midst of all this prosperity, the people had no heart to help others— *"she did not help the poor and needy."* The heart attitude of haughtiness marked their actions, and therefore they *"committed abominations"* before the Lord. In God's eyes, the way they were living was sickening. The citizens of this region made God full of grief and wrath. However, even with the need for judgment, the Lord was ready and willing to show mercy, as we have seen with the Lord's response to Abraham's prayer in Genesis 18. How would Lot, his wife, and the rest of his family respond to the Lord's messengers?

 Do you find any of the characteristics of Ezekiel 16:49–50 in your life? Pause and talk to the Lord. Ask Him to reveal any sin. Confess and forsake it and come back to fellowship with the Lord. If you have never surrendered your self (your sin, your life) to Him as Lord and Savior, now is the time to do that. (See "How to Follow God" section on p. 207 of this book.) God was willing to show compassion on Lot, Lot's wife, and their family. He is ready to do the same for you.

What did Lot and his family do with the warning of destruction to come? What choices would each of them make? What influence did Lot and his wife have on their family? How will their children respond to the messengers from God and the message they bring? We will address all these questions in Day Four.

WHEN MERCY AND JUDGMENT ARE AT THE DOOR

The two angels came to the home of Lot and his wife to warn them and their family of the judgment to come. They urged them to gather all who would join them and escape the city and the valley in which it lay. This was a brief breeze of mercy blowing before the fierce, tempestuous winds of judgment struck. How would each family member respond?

📖 What do you find about Lot and his wife in Genesis 19:1–3?

_____

_____

_____

_____

Lot was sitting in the city gate of Sodom when the two angels came to the city. Lot paid them great honor and respect, bowing to them with his face to the ground. It was evening and Lot invited them, even insisted that they stay at his house and feast with him. They agreed to come. Lot (and presumably his wife and daughters) prepared a meal for them, which included unleavened bread (there was not time for leavened bread to rise and bake), meat, and drink. This action shows a measure of hospitality on the part of Lot, his wife, and family.

Lot's Wife  DAY FOUR

"He saved us, not on the basis of deeds which we have done in righteousness, but according to His mercy...."

Titus 3:5

SITTING AT THE GATE

In ancient times one entered a city through a gate. Upon entering through the gate, there were meeting areas on either side of the entryway, which opened into another large area leading into the markets. City gates like the one in Sodom were places where business transactions, government decisions, and social interaction occurred every day. Lot was most likely an influential businessman, possibly a government or judicial official, sitting in the city gate of Sodom.

The angels urged Lot to gather any and all of his family to escape the coming destruction. In verse12, the angels questioned Lot about a son-in-law, sons, and daughters, and any others whom he could convince to escape in addition to his wife and the two daughters mentioned in verse 15. It is possible that in this warning we can deduce that there were other family members besides Lot, Lot's wife, and the two daughters. If so, then the influence of Lot and Lot's wife was even less significant; not only did they fail to influence their neighbors, but they also failed to influence the very members of their family.

According to Genesis 19:14, what kind of people were Lot's future sons-in-law?

Put Yourself In Their Shoes

THE POTENTIAL INFLUENCE OF ONE FAMILY

Abraham prayed the city of Sodom might be spared if ten righteous were found there. Was Abraham thinking of Lot's family members? Consider this: it is possible Lot and his wife had as many as six children and two sons-in-law (perhaps ten people, counting Lot and his wife). Genesis 19:12 mentions the likelihood of other family members living in the city, including *"sons"* (plural, at least two) and *"daughters"* (at least two). Lot spoke to at least two sons-in-law (19:14) who were possibly already married or at least engaged to Lot's daughters (not necessarily the same two daughters mentioned in 19:15). Think of the potential influence of a family of approximately ten righteous men and women—yet, sadly, most (if not all) of Lot's family members were unrighteous, and their influence was unrighteous. However, the influence of Abraham and his praying is noteworthy— *"God remembered Abraham, and sent Lot out of the midst of the overthrow"* (Genesis 19:29).

These sons-in-law (either already married to two other daughters or engaged to his two daughters at home [v. 15]) listened to Lot's impassioned plea to flee the doomed city. They thought he was joking with them. Unfortunately, Lot could not convince them to leave. These men apparently did not see the sin of the city as God saw it, nor did they view this place as worthy of destruction. They were insensitive to any word about sin and judgment even from their own father-in-law. They laughed and ignored Lot and his plea.

In light of the supernatural power of the two angels, their judgment on the men of Sodom, and the warning of these two men to Lot and his family, what should have been the attitude of Lot, his wife, and their daughters toward the Lord and His message through these two men? What does the silence of Lot's wife say to you in all these events?

The seriousness of the situation should have gotten the attention of the family in Lot's house. The silence and inactivity of Lot's wife suggests she had a callous attitude toward the Lord—at least toward His messengers and toward the message they brought. The angels had to continually urge the family to leave, not just the night they arrived, but again *"when morning dawned."*

📖 Look at Genesis 19:16. What does the family's hesitancy to obey and leave tell you about them?

_____

_____

_____

_____

With all the urging of the angels, with the reactions of the men of Sodom, and with the mocking refusal of Lot's sons-in-law to listen to Lot, it is evident no one in the family was really convinced of the seriousness of the sin of the city. No one thought they were really deserving of judgment or that God would indeed bring judgment. Sadly, the influence of Lot and his wife upon the society was nil. They had convinced no one to follow God, and now they were failing to follow Him when He was reaching out to them in great compassion.

Think of this. Lot was a rich businessman, a leader at the city gate of Sodom. He was a relative of the rich and honored Abraham, the leader who once rescued the people of Sodom from the conquering kings, from captivity and from almost certain slavery. Lot was a man of great riches with flocks, herds, and herdsmen as well as male and female servants. He was a man of influence in business. Lot's wife would have been known in the city, in the marketplace, and in the neighborhood. However, Lot was a failure as a man of God and a failure in influencing his family or his neighbors toward following the Lord. Lot's wife had the potential to influence her family and those around her toward the Lord as well, but she failed miserably to do so. Instead, it appears Sodom was the dominating influence over her and her children.

📖 According to Genesis 19:16, what was the attitude of the Lord toward Lot? How did the Lord show that attitude to Lot, his wife, and the two daughters mentioned in verse 15?

_____

_____

_____

_____

_____

God's compassion was focused on Lot. The angels seized the hands of Lot, his wife and his daughters. In spite of the hesitancy of Lot, God showed His great compassion. We see here God's tender mercy and His loving affection in action. The word translated *"compassion"* can also be rendered as God's "merciful sparing" or His "sparing mercy." God was willing to rescue His people and bring them to safety instead of judgment. Lot's wife was the recipient of God's great mercy that morning. The angels brought Lot's wife, her two daughters, and Lot through the city to a place outside the city.

"Just as Sodom and Gomorrah and the cities around them, since they ... indulged in gross immorality and went after strange flesh, are exhibited as an example, in undergoing the punishment of eternal fire."

Jude 7

Word Study
COMPASSION

Genesis 19:16 says, *"The compassion of the LORD was upon"* Lot. The word translated *"compassion"* (*chemiah*; only used here and in Isaiah 63:9) speaks of the mercy of God willing to spare the life of someone and can be translated *"the merciful sparing of the LORD."* It pictures God actively sparing His people, delivering them out of judgment because of His mercy.

What commands and warnings were given in Genesis 19:17? What happened outside the city according to Genesis 19:26? What does this incident tell us about Lot's wife?

_____

_____

_____

_____

_____

The Lord commanded Lot and his family to *"Escape for your life!"* and then added, *"Do not look behind you."* Lot asked permission to go to the town of Zoar in the valley rather than flee all the way to the mountains. God graciously granted that request. Then, as they were fleeing from the city, fire and brimstone rained down on Sodom and the other cities of the valley. Lot's wife lingered behind Lot and *"looked back."* She turned around to look at the city and instantly *"became a pillar of salt."*

Lot's wife reluctantly left the city with Lot and their two daughters, mercifully dragged away by the two angels. She physically left the city of Sodom; however, her heart never left Sodom, nor did Sodom ever leave her heart. As the heart of Lot's wife was joined to Sodom and its sin, so she was joined to its judgment, destruction, and doom. A lifeless pillar of salt stood as a monument to her lifeless, hardened heart.

APPLY What do the actions and attitude of Lot and his family, especially his wife, say to you about your own attitude toward sin? Toward the Word of the Lord? Toward His messengers to you? Is there something about which God has been speaking to you? Are you obeying Him, or are you "looking back" in disobedience?

_____

_____

_____

_____

_____

Lot's Wife **DAY FIVE**

FOR ME TO FOLLOW GOD

"*R*emember Lot's wife!" (Luke 17:32). Jesus wants us to be fully aware of the life and death of Lot's wife. He wants us to see her choices in the light of both time and eternity. He wants us to make wise choices—especially the choice to follow Him every day in every detail of life. When Jesus spoke these words, *"Remember Lot's wife,"* He was warning and preparing. The words are a warning to those of us who will heed it that we should not be caught unprepared when Christ returns. Since we don't know the day nor the hour of Christ's return (Matthew 25:13), then we should have our hearts and minds in the right place to follow Him every day. Immediately after He spoke these words, He gave us a choice—the path to disaster **or** the way to experience the full life He wants for us. Knowing these two paths can guide us away from the wrong choices Lot's wife made. Remembering her can help us follow Him rightly.

📖 What was the focus of Lot's wife even on the day she left Sodom? The verses preceding Luke 17:32 give us some clues. Read Luke 17:28–29. Where is your focus? Check the things that are taking most of your thoughts, affections, and time. What is the Lord saying to you about your walk?

- ❏ eating, dieting—physical focus

- ❏ drinking, enjoying life—leisure/pleasure focus

- ❏ buying, shopping—material focus

- ❏ selling, business—money focus

- ❏ planting, investing—future focus

- ❏ building houses or businesses—society focus

- ❏ relationship with God, devotion to His Word and prayer—eternity focus

- ❏ caring for others, giving to meet others' needs—relationship focus

- ❏ gratefully using money and things as tools to fulfill God's purposes—kingdom focus

📖 What did Jesus say immediately after the command to "remember Lot's wife"? Look at Luke 17:33.

_____

_____

_____

_____

Jesus pointedly told His disciples, *"Whoever seeks to keep his life shall lose it, and whoever loses his life shall preserve it."* The word translated "life" is *psuche,* referring to the soul or psyche, the sum total of what one thinks, chooses, and feels. The idea of seeking to keep one's soul paints a picture of one looking for various ways to gain for his self. Such a person searches only to please self, to protect self, to promote self, and to enrich self—the focus, of course, is self. People absorbed with self inevitably lose out in life. On the other hand, the one who "loses" his life does not seek only his or her will and way. This person releases his life into the hands of the Lord to follow Him and His will. As a result the soul-life is preserved. The word translated "*preserve*" literally pictures the birth of a new life, life on a new level, and the kind of life only God can give. The one who will give up and give in to the Lord and His way, will discover His gift of new life.

In the context of Luke 17:32–33, it is evident that Lot's wife was one of those who sought to keep her life for herself, and she lost it. How can we avoid her error? How can we lose our life in order to preserve or keep it? Jesus made this same statement at other times in His ministry. One of those occasions gives us clear light for the path ahead, whatever or wherever that path might lead and shows us **how to follow Him and find life.**

THE SOUL OF LOT'S WIFE

Second Peter 2:7–8 tells us that Lot was a righteous man who *"felt his righteous soul tormented day after day"* with the lawless deeds of the people of Sodom. What he saw and what he heard *"oppressed"* his soul as he lived viewing *"the sensual conduct of unprincipled men."* There is no mention of the righteous soul of Lot's wife, nor of her being "oppressed" by what she saw and heard. Though nothing is said of her soul, the implication is that she did not have a righteous soul. Though given the opportunity to receive mercy and escape judgment, she disobeyed, looked back, and met destruction just outside the city.

Did You Know?
THE TESTIMONY OF ANCIENT WRITINGS

The author of *The Wisdom of Solomon,* one of the books of the Apocrypha, written around 100 B.C., comments on all that happened with the destruction of Sodom. *"When the ungodly perished, she [wisdom] delivered the righteous man who fled from the fire which fell down ... Of whose wickedness even to this day the waste land that smoketh is a testimony, and plants bearing fruit that never come to ripeness; and a standing pillar of salt is a monument of an unbelieving soul"* (Wisdom 10:6–7). Verse 8 says Lot's family *"left behind them to the world a memorial of their foolishness...."*

Read Luke 9:23. What does Jesus say about following Him?

_____

_____

_____

_____

_____

Anyone can follow Jesus if he or she comes in surrender to Him to follow Him His way. It is a simple concept, but one not always easy to implement.

Anyone can follow Jesus if he or she comes in surrender to Him to follow Him His way. It is a simple concept, but one not always easy to implement. First, Jesus tells us to deny ourselves—in other words, we are to say "No!" to self. In addition to denying self, one must take up a cross, an instrument of death to self. That must be done "daily," literally, "according to the day," however the day measures up, whatever the day holds. Whatever or whomever one is dealing with, one must take his place on the cross—one must release life and seek to depend totally on the Lord for His resurrection power to handle the day. That is what it means to "follow" Christ. We follow Jesus when we walk together with Him, listening, obeying, and trusting Him wherever He may lead. Lot's wife did not want to trust God and obey Him; so she went the way she wanted to go.

What is the result of following Jesus as opposed to trying to save one's own soul-life according to Luke 9:24?

_____

_____

_____

_____

_____

_____

_____

Jesus promised that those who try to save their own lives will lose out, but each one who willingly loses his life **for Jesus' sake** will find the life He alone can give, a saved life, a rescued life—rescued from the destruction of self-centeredness. He repeated this promise to His disciples when He spoke of Lot's wife. She lived for her own sake, not for the sake of the Lord.

What counsel does Jesus give each of us in Luke 9:25? How would you apply that to the life and choices of Lot's wife?

_____

_____

_____

_____

_____

_____

_____

_____

There is nothing more important than the salvation of one's soul. The world and all it can give is a useless and fruitless treasure when it comes to the things that really matter, the matters of the heart. Someone has well said, "The things that really matter aren't things." Lot's wife thought the things of Sodom were the truest treasure and risked her life for one more look. Of course, she was very wrong, and she forfeited her very life.

 How we live truly matters! Following Jesus matters forever. Look at Matthew 16:27 along with 1 John 2:28–29 and 3:1–3. Of what can we be certain as we gaze into the future? What did Jesus promise and how should each of us live in light of what He said?

_____

_____

_____

_____

_____

Word Study
FORFEIT

The word translated "forfeit" (*zēmióō*) in Luke 9:25 refers to suffering loss or harm and is rooted in the word *zemia,* referring to damage of some sort. It was used in speaking of the damage that comes with a shipwreck. (Acts 27:10, 21). One who keeps pursuing ways to gain the "world" for himself will soon find his life shipwrecked, forfeited, and lost.

The Son of Man, our Lord Jesus, will come in the glory of His Father along with His angels. When He does, He will render to every man according to the deeds he has done—judgment for wicked deeds done by those who never surrendered to Jesus as Lord and Savior and reward for obedience to those who followed Him as their Lord. His call is to attentive obedience today, to a continual walk of holiness and purity, to a constant guard against the tempting lure of the world—all in preparation for His return. The warning or Luke 17:32 still rings clear, *"Remember Lot's wife."*

APPLY How are you following? Are you trying to gain your soul-life for yourself and your selfish purposes, or are you daily releasing your life into the Lord's hands to follow Him and walk in His purposes? In what way (or ways) is the Lord speaking to you about denying yourself—saying "No!" to yourself? Is He calling you to take up your cross for the circumstances of this day? What do you need to do to follow Him in this moment? Whatever you do, **follow Jesus!**

_____

_____

_____

_____

_____

_____

_____

Everyone will be remembered for something. Jesus will remember each of us for our choices. What will you be remembered for? It all depends on what you choose to remember day by day. Remember Lot's wife. Remember her influence on others—for unrighteousness. Remember the merciful warnings given her. Remember her lingering that morning, her longing to stay, then longing to go back which led to her look back. Remember her ending, a lifeless pillar of salt. Finally, remember Jesus' promise in light of His sure return—*"For whoever wishes to save his life shall lose it, but whoever loses his life for My sake, he is the one who will save it"* (Luke 9:24).

Spend some time with the Lord in prayer right now.

Lord, I know that Your judgment and Your mercy are both very real. I am grateful for the mercy You have shown me time after time. Thank You for making me aware of the deadly dangers of a self-seeking life. I want to heed the warning found in this remembrance of Lot's wife. I want to follow You as my Lord and Savior and not get trapped in the rapids of the world around me. Thank You that *"the grace of God"* has come *"bringing salvation," "instructing us to deny ungodliness and worldly desires and to live sensibly, righteously and godly in the present age."* I am grateful that because of Your work in my heart I can live *"looking for the blessed hope and the appearing of the glory of our great God and Savior, Christ Jesus; who gave Himself for us, that He might redeem us from every lawless deed and purify for Himself a people for His own possession, zealous for good deeds"* (Titus 2:11–14). May I be remembered as one who followed You faithfully and as one who never "looked back." In Jesus' Name, Amen.

Remembering Lot's wife and the lessons of her life and death, write your own prayer to the Lord or make a journal entry of what the Lord is saying to you about following Him.

_____

_____

_____

_____

_____

_____

_____

_____

_____

_____

_____

_____

_____

_____

_____

_____

_____

_____

Notes

Notes

Rebekah

THE PERIL OF
BEING PARTIAL

Years of waiting for Abraham and Sarah were finally rewarded with the arrival of their long-expected son of promise, Isaac. This child was the joy of their hearts. Yet somewhere along the way, their joy turned to concern. For the promises of God to be realized, not only must they have a son, but their son must also have children. After Sarah died, Abraham determined that his son could not marry from among the wicked and idolatrous Canaanites, so he sent his servant back to find a wife from among his relatives. The story of Rebekah's marriage to Isaac is one of the most romantic and comforting pictures in Scripture of God sovereignly bringing a couple together. In this study, you will see that God's providential hand guided every step in the process of their matrimony.

Sadly, the story of Rebekah's lengthy marriage with Isaac does not contain a "storybook ending," for it bears the heartache and scars of barrenness, costly parental mistakes, and sibling rivalry among their children. Like almost all of the portraits of Bible characters, we see both faith and flaws, strength as well as stumbling. While there is much commendable in Rebekah's biography, the main principle we observe in her is the damaging effects of parental partiality and the consequences of striving instead of trusting God.

While there is much commendable in Rebekah's biography, the main principle we observe in her is the damaging effects of parental partiality.

WHERE DOES SHE FIT?

2200 B.C.	1950	1700	1450	1200	950	600	100 B.C.	A.D. 1	A.D. 100

HAGAR
2100?–2040?

Daniel
619–534?

ELIZABETH
75 B.C.?–A.D. 10?

Solomon
991–931

REBEKAH
2040?–1915?

WOMEN of the
Gospels
10 B.C.?–A.D. 50?

LEAH
1948?–1885?

Judges Rule
1385–1051

David
1041–971

LOT'S WIFE
2100?–2066

RACHEL
1943?–1899

ABIGAIL
1036?–976?

Nehemiah
480?–400?

Jesus Christ
4 B.C.?–A.D. 30?

THE
SUBMISSIVE
WIFE

Joshua
1495–1385

BATHSHEBA
1016?–961?

Isaac
2065–1885

Moses
1525–1405

Ephesians 5;
1 Peter 2—3

JEZEBEL
889?–841

Abraham
2165–1990

Jacob
2005–1858

Samuel
1105–1022

WOMAN at Well
10 B.C.?–A.D. 50?

REBEKAH'S PROPOSAL

ooner or later, most every girl asks the following questions in her mind: *When will "Mr. Right" come? Where will he come from? What will he look like? How will we meet?* One can only imagine the many times Rebekah sat and pondered those same questions. While culturally, women today are working more and marrying later, it is still a reality that most women will marry, and that most, if not all women, begin thinking about the possibilities and prospects of marriage long before they ever meet their husbands. Though Rebekah was a single woman many centuries ago, she likely was no different than young women today when it comes to the issue of speculating who their future husbands might be. In Rebekah's life, there were probably times of discouragement in which she thought a husband would never come. Perhaps she was not particularly enamored with the boys in her hometown and could imagine none of them as the man of her dreams. It's not too far-fetched to surmise that she wrestled with the same doubts and feelings of hopelessness women experience today and may have cried out to God as her heart filled with longing. But while she waited, God was moving in ways she could not see nor would have expected. A caravan was making its way from Canaan. Little did she know this caravan would bring with it the fulfillment of a dream. Today we want to begin looking at how Rebekah and Isaac came together.

📖 Read Genesis 23—24:1–9.

What is Abraham's charge to his servant in chapter 24?

_____

_____

_____

What had just transpired in chapter 23 of Genesis?

_____

_____

_____

_____

In your opinion, why didn't Abraham want a wife for his son to come from among the Canaanites?

_____

_____

_____

_____

What is Abraham's concern about sending Isaac as part of the journey?

_____

_____

_____

Did You Know?
"THE BODILY OATH"

In Genesis 24:1–3, why did Abraham have his servant swear with his hand under Abraham's hip? This custom, which is only mentioned here and in Genesis 47:29, was what was known as "the bodily oath." Some commentators have associated this ritual with the ancient belief that the hip was the part from which a man's posterity issued. Genesis 46:26 in the King James Version sheds some light on this belief as it says, *"All the souls that came with Jacob into Egypt, which came out of his loins [or thigh], besides Jacob's sons' wives, all the souls were threescore and six."* Early Jewish commentators supposed "the bodily oath" to be especially connected with the rite of circumcision. It is significant that the oath was by *"the LORD [Jehovah], God of heaven and earth,"* as the God who rules in heaven and on earth, and not by *Elohim*, another name for God. This distinction indicates that this oath was not an ordinary oath, but related to a matter of great importance in relation to the kingdom of God. In this case, the issue was not just finding a wife for Isaac, but the continuation of God's promise to Isaac's father, Abraham.

What was Abraham trusting for the plan to succeed (24:7)?

_____

_____

_____

_____

It was after the death and burial of Sarah that Abraham settled in his heart it was time to find a wife for his son. In that culture, dating was an unknown concept. It was usually the decision of the parents to select a bride for the son. As Abraham reflected on the kind of daughter-in-law he would find in Canaan, he realized the potential dangers. The inhabitants of Canaan were an idolatrous people, and Abraham would not have his son's heart drawn away to other gods by his wife. So he charged his servant with the task of returning to Ur to find a wife for Isaac from among his people. While it may not be immediately apparent, there is great wisdom in his unwillingness to send Isaac as part of the party. Imagine the turmoil if a suitable wife were found who was unwilling to move to Canaan. Abraham knew God's mandate was for his descendants to settle in the Promised Land, but a desirable wife would be a great temptation for Isaac to settle back in Ur. Once Abraham's servant understood the task, he vowed to fulfill it. Abraham was entrusting the task to his servant, but trusting the outcome to the Lord. Since God had promised descendants, Abraham knew God would provide a wife for his son. He was trusting God to send an angel before them to prepare the wife and prosper the journey.

📖 Look at Genesis 24:10–14 and answer the questions that follow.

What is the plan of Abraham's servant (verses 13–14)?

_____

_____

_____

_____

What was he trusting for that plan to succeed (verse 12)?

_____

_____

_____

_____

_____

> "... may she be the one whom Thou hast appointed for Thy servant Isaac; and by this I shall know that Thou hast shown lovingkindness to my master."
>
> **Genesis 24:14b**

This plan applied by Abraham's servant was indeed a wise one. He knew where to find the eligible daughters of the city, and he knew when to find them as well. At the well, the servant would see the girl's physical beauty, observe her work ethic, and even determine the wealth of the family by the size of her flock But it is clear from the narrative that Abraham's servant was trusting God, not his logic, to prosper this mission. Notice whom he is looking for: _"the one whom Thou hast appointed for Thy servant, Isaac."_ He wasn't just looking for a pretty girl—he was looking for God's will. He was trusting God to bring the right girl to him.

When does God answer the servant's prayer (verse 15)?

_____

_____

_____

How does the servant know God had answered (verse 27)?

_____

_____

_____

How does he respond to his success (verse 26)?

_____

_____

_____

Did You Know?

❓ REBEKAH'S RING

The gift Abraham's servant gave Rebekah (Genesis 24:22) was not a ring of proposal, but rather was a nose ring, as was the custom of the east (see verse 47). This ring, along with the bracelets, was an overly generous gift of thanks for her service to Abraham's servant. Scripture states the ring weighed *"a half-shekel,"* of gold, while the combined weight of the bracelets weighed *"ten shekels in gold."* Since a shekel is almost a half-ounce, the nose ring would have weighed just under a quarter ounce of gold, and each bracelet would have weighed about four and a half ounces of gold.

Abraham's servant had not even finished his prayer when God answered it. To answer this request, God prompted Rebekah to move to the well before the prayer was even uttered. While the test of words he and she would speak gave him some measure of affirmation, it seems the matter was not confirmed by this alone (see verse 21). The final affirmation came when he learned that she was indeed a relative of Abraham just as Abraham had charged (verse 4). The servant clearly trusted God with the mission, for his immediate response to his success was to worship the Lord.

📖 Survey the rest of the chapter and answer the questions that follow.

How does the servant view the circumstances that transpired (verse 48)?

_____

_____

_____

_____

How does Rebekah's family view them (verses 51–52)?

_____

_____

_____

How does Rebekah view them (verses 57–58)?

_____

_____

_____

_____

How did Isaac respond to the process (verse 67)?

_____

_____

_____

Abraham's servant was confident he had determined the Lord's will. He knew it was God who had guided him to Rebekah. Her family affirmed this as well once they had heard of all that had transpired. It is significant to notice in verse 57, however, that they were very sensitive to her feelings in the matter, which was quite unusual for that male-dominated culture. Yet clearly Rebekah saw this arrangement as God's will and went with this servant to be Isaac's wife by choice, not by force. While our culture promotes a very different process for finding a wife, it is important to recognize that the core value taught in this Day One study applies to us today. That is, in any major decision, especially in the matter of courtship and marriage, we should ask the question, "What is the will of God?" In the story of Isaac and Rebekah, once God's will was affirmed, all parties were in harmony. Even Isaac affirmed the outcome. Once he saw Rebekah and heard the servant's story, he took her as his wife, and the text tells us, *"he loved her."* After the loss of his mother, he found comfort in this new relationship.

Word Study
"BEER-LAHAI-ROI"

When Rebekah arrived in Canaan, Isaac had just returned from going to *"Beer-lahai-roi"*—this was the well Hagar named when God met with her in the wilderness. The name means "well of the Living One who sees." It would have conjured up reminders of the providence of God. At this very point the God of providence chose to bring Isaac's bride to him.

REBEKAH'S PARENTING

Rebekah DAY TWO

A s a young woman, Rebekah found love and a husband (or better said, they found her). Like most girls her age, she surely longed for the man of her dreams to come, and finally he came. Scripture makes no mention of any lengthy time of waiting on her part, so she probably was of the normal marrying age of that era—between fifteen and twenty years old. She obviously was ready to marry, for she chose to leave home in haste even though her family wanted her to tarry a bit. She most likely had some sense she was marrying into a wealthy family from her observation of the large caravan sent with Abraham's servant and the many gifts it brought. But she knew little else of what would lie ahead for her. Though her husband would be older, he would earnestly love her, and life would be good for them. They would know prosperity, but they would also know challenge. In Day One, we looked at how God brought Isaac and Rebekah together as husband and wife. Today we want to begin looking at the marriage itself.

📖 Look at Genesis 25:19–20.

How old was Isaac when he married Rebekah?

_____

Assuming that Isaac was considerably older than Rebekah, how do you think this disparity might have affected their relationship?

_____

_____

_____

We are told here that Isaac was forty years old when Rebekah became his wife. Genesis 23:1 states that Isaac's mother, Sarah, died at the age of 127, making Isaac about 37 at her death. Since Isaac was Sarah's only son, she probably doted on him, and perhaps it wasn't until her death that he began to long for a wife. Even if Rebekah were twenty years old at the time she married Isaac, that would mean she was at least twenty years younger than her husband. We can only guess what impact this age difference could have had on their relationship, but it is interesting to note that while Scripture assures us that Isaac loved Rebekah, there is no similar statement about her love for him. This doesn't mean a lack of love on her part, but there seems to have been something exceptional about Isaac's love for her.

📖 Read Genesis 25:21.

What was the first challenge that faced Rebekah and Isaac?

_____

_____

_____

_____

_____

How long was Rebekah barren (see 25:26b)?

_____

_____

Put Yourself In Their Shoes
BARRENNESS IN THE BIBLE

While culturally, barrenness was viewed as evidence of the hand of God being against someone (as sometimes it was), Bible history also paints a different consideration. Every time in Scripture when a woman was barren and then later was blessed with a child, that child grew up to be especially significant to the plan of God. Sarah was barren before giving birth to Isaac. Rebekah was barren before giving birth to Jacob. Rachel was barren before giving birth to Joseph. Manoah was barren before giving birth to Samson. Hannah was barren before giving birth to Samuel. Elizabeth was barren before giving birth to John the Baptist. It seems that barrenness was part of God's work in the lives of these parents. Once the womb was opened, the result was significant.

In this tidbit of detail, we are told that Rebekah was barren. No cry echoes so deep as that of a woman whose longings for a child go unanswered. To the people of Rebekah's day, her barrenness would have been viewed as a matter of shame—and evidence that God's hand was not on her marriage, but against it. Her barrenness lasted for twenty years, for Isaac was forty at their marriage, and sixty when she gave birth. For twenty long years, they waited. But Isaac prayed. He cast their cares on Him who cares—and the Lord answered.

📖 Read through Genesis 25:21–26 and answer the questions below.

What challenge did Rebekah encounter with her pregnancy?

_____

_____

_____

_____

How did she respond to this challenge (verse 22)?

_____

_____

_____

_____

What did the Lord reveal to her (verse 23)?

_____

_____

_____

_____

Once Rebekah conceived, the children *"struggled together within her."* At this time she was unaware that she was carrying twins and would have likely viewed the struggle as an ill omen. She may have feared miscarriage. Her statement literally reads in Hebrew, "If this be so, wherefore am I?" (i.e., "why am I alive?"). It is a statement of despair, reflecting fear that this pregnancy would end in heartache and that no children would ever come her way. But she took her concerns to the Lord. Like Abraham's servant, whom we discussed in Day One, we see that Rebekah also had a seeking faith. She brought her cares to the Lord, and He met with her in a special way. It was God who disclosed to her that she bore more than one child, and He promised to make two nations of them. God also revealed that the older child (Esau) would serve the younger (Jacob).

REBEKAH'S PARTIALITY

Romans 2:11 states emphatically, *"There is no partiality with God."* God does not play favorites. Neither does he desire such behavior from us. In fact, James 2:9 goes so far as to say, *"If you show partiality, you are committing sin and are convicted by the law as transgressors."* Partiality always causes problems, but nowhere is it more damaging than when a parent favors one child over another. In the household of Isaac and Rebekah, partiality rears its ugly head, and the consequences outlast them both. Today we want to see the why and how of the peril of partiality.

📖 Look at Genesis 25:27–28.

How were the temperaments of the two sons different?

_____

_____

_____

_____

_____

How did the parents relate to these different temperaments?

_____

_____

_____

_____

_____

_____

The name "Esau" means "hairy," as he was hairy his entire life. He was also called "Edom," meaning "red." He became the father of the Edomites. Jacob means "trickster" or "one who supplants." He was so named because he came from the womb holding to his brother's heel. This name certainly seemed to reflect the character of Jacob's early life, as he "supplanted" Esau's birthright with a bowl of stew, and tricked Isaac out of Esau's blessing. Later, Jacob's name would be changed to "Israel," meaning "one who strives with God and prevails."

Why do you think the parents showed favoritism as they did?

_____

_____

_____

_____

Even though Jacob and Esau were twins, they were as different as night and day both in appearance and personality. Esau was the outdoor type. He enjoyed hunting and was *"a man of the field,"* while Jacob was of a quieter temperament and preferred to stay inside. We are told that Isaac loved Esau and Rebekah loved Jacob. While some reason is given for these divided loyalties, other explanations are also implied. Isaac loved Esau because he liked eating the game that Esau brought home. But he may have connected with Esau as well because the boy loved the outdoors. In the culture of Isaac's day, men usually attended to the outdoor work, while the ladies did much of their work inside. This may explain why Rebekah held such affection for Jacob. Not only did Jacob have similar desires as her, but because of those desires, he probably spent a lot more time with her than Esau did. She may have favored Jacob as a reaction to Isaac's preference for Esau. It is possible that both parents were relating selfishly. While the parents may have naturally related better with one child over the other because of common interests, this does not excuse the partiality they showed in their treatment of their children.

📖 Read Genesis 25:29–34.

How do you see the different personalities expressed here?

_____

_____

_____

_____

_____

What does Esau's behavior say about how he valued his "birthright"?

_____

_____

_____

_____

_____

In this brief vignette we see the quiet, homebody Jacob preparing a meal, while Esau, the outdoorsman had been out in the field. It appears that Esau is a man dominated by his appetites. He begs for a bowl of stew as he comes in from the field, famished. Jacob, the trickster, offers Essau soup in exchange for his birthright. It wasn't even close to a fair trade, but Esau placed so little value on his birthright that he gave it away for a meal.

Why did Jacob ask for the birthright? It seems likely he had been talking to his mother. No doubt Rebekah had previously told him of the word from God she received while he was still in the womb. He grew up understanding that Esau would serve him. But instead of waiting for God to bring that about, he began the process by an unfair trade.

God prospered Isaac and Rebekah materially. During a famine, when they sojourned in Gerar, Isaac had a particularly large harvest (see Genesis 26:1, 6, 12–14). Year after year, his wealth multiplied. But their wealth didn't protect them from family problems.

📖 Look at Genesis 26:34–35.

When and how did Esau marry?

_____

_____

_____

_____

_____

How were his parents affected by his choices?

_____

_____

_____

_____

ESAU'S WIVES

It is noteworthy that there is no indication of any role being played by Esau's parents in the selection of his brides. Perhaps Isaac spoiled his son so much that he let him have his way. What a contrast from the providential way Isaac's bride was selected by Abraham.

Esau married when he was forty years old, the same age that Isaac, his father, married Rebekah. Unfortunately, he didn't follow the same wisdom as his father, but took multiple wives, and those from the Canaanites no less. These Hittite wives probably drew Esau's heart away from the living God into idol worship. We are told that Esau's wives brought grief to his parents. Literally, they "were a bitterness of spirit" to Isaac and Rebekah (see verse 35).

📖 Read through Genesis 27:1–29 and answer the questions that follow.

What is Isaac's intention for Esau (verses 1–4)?

_____

_____

_____

_____

What is Rebekah's plan (verses 5–17)?

_____

_____

_____

_____

_____

What is Jacob's role in the deception (verses 18–27)?

_____

_____

_____

_____

_____

What blessing does Isaac give (verses 27b–29)?

_____

_____

_____

_____

Did You Know?
IRREVOCABLE WORDS

The belief of Isaac's day was that the spoken words uttered in a blessing upon children had irrevocable power. Once given, it could not be retracted. While there is no scriptural teaching that required this, clearly Isaac believed thus, and refused to change Jacob's blessing even though it was obtained by deception.

In chapter 27, we see the culminating effects of parental partiality and divided loyalties shown by Isaac and Rebekah toward Esau and Jacob. As Isaac advanced in years, he wanted to bestow a blessing on his favorite son. It was culture and tradition that the oldest son was to be favored, though this was not always the way of God. It must have been particularly painful for Jacob as Isaac's twin brother to be in a lesser position only because he was born a few minutes later. Isaac's partiality to Esau, the hunter, gave fuel to Rebekah's partiality to Jacob. When Isaac sent Esau to find him some game, Rebekah began to scheme. She had Jacob impersonate Esau, and with Jacob's willing participation in the deception, Isaac was fooled into giving Esau's blessing to Jacob. Isaac proclaimed that Jacob (who he thought was Esau) would prosper and that all his kin would serve him. We are not shown what would have resulted from Isaac's partiality if he were able to bless his godless son, Esau, as he intended; but, as we will see in Day Four, the family became fractured and relationships were greatly damaged through Rebekah's favoritism.

 DAY FOUR

REBEKAH'S PAIN

What is godliness? It is being like God. Every Christian should seek to be like God. Mankind was originally created in the image of God, but through sin that image was distorted and perverted. God could no longer be clearly seen in us. Through Christ, God is in the process of re-creating His image in us. He is working in our character to be more like Him. But we must cooperate with Him in that process. The more cooperative we are, the quicker His image is formed in us. But what does godliness have to do with Rebekah? As we will see in this Day Four study, it is her sin of partiality toward Jacob that brought great pain into her life. A Christian's life is not perfect, but we certainly don't need to add to the pains of living in a fallen world by drawing unnecessary consequences into our lives through sin. **God is not partial.** He shows no favoritism. To whatever degree we show partiality, to that degree we deviate from godliness, and we will reap the consequences of what we sow.

📖 Read through Genesis 27:30–40.

How does Isaac discover what Jacob had done?

_____

_____

_____

_____

How does Esau respond (verses 34, 38)?

_____

_____

_____

_____

What is Isaac's "blessing" to Esau (verses 39–40)?

_____

_____

_____

_____

When Esau returned from hunting and prepared the meal, he brought it to his father. It was not until then that Isaac realized he had been tricked. We see glimpses of Esau's pain in the wording of his response. We are told in verse 34, *"He cried out with an exceedingly great and bitter cry."* Again in verse 38 we read, *"So Esau lifted his voice and wept."* The only blessing Jacob could speak was that Esau would live by the sword away from blessing, and that he would serve his brother but eventually break free.

📖 Look at Genesis 27:41–46.

What is Esau's attitude toward Jacob?

_____

_____

_____

_____

What does Esau plan to do to Jacob, and when was he going to do it?

_____

_____

_____

_____

_____

"So Esau bore a grudge against Jacob because of the blessing with which his father had blessed him."

Genesis 27:41

What was Rebekah's plan to protect Jacob?

_____

_____

_____

_____

_____

What reason does she give Isaac for sending Jacob away?

_____

_____

_____

_____

What effects of parental partiality do you see in the family relationships?

_____

_____

_____

_____

_____

Not surprisingly, Esau *"bore a grudge"* against his brother. His plan was to wait until their father died, and then get his revenge by killing Jacob. This would not only punish Jacob, but would pass the blessing to him as the next of kin. Hearing of the plan, Rebekah decided to send Jacob to Haran where her family lived. She told Isaac she wanted Jacob to go there to find a wife, which seems to be partly true. Notice the family dynamic now: Esau hated Jacob; Jacob feared Esau; and Rebekah could not be honest with Isaac. It appears from her statement at the end of verse 45 that Esau had broken off his relationship with his mother. It is clear from verse 46 that Rebekah did not get along with her two daughters-in-law. The family became fractured because of favoritism. Instead of trusting God to bring about blessing, Rebekah trusted her own conniving and striving and did great harm to her family. She told Jacob that he needed to leave for only a few days, but in fact he would be gone fourteen years. The cold, hard reality was that Rebekah would die before Jacob could safely return, and she would never see the face of her favorite son again.

📖 Read Genesis 28:1–9.

What is Isaac's instruction to Jacob (verses 1–2)?

_____

_____

_____

_____

_____

_____

What does Esau do when he understands why Jacob has gone away?

_____

_____

_____

_____

What does this say about Esau's relationship with Isaac?

_____

_____

_____

As Rebekah requested, Isaac sent Jacob away with his blessings to find a wife who was not a Canaanite, but rather, one from their kin in Haran. When Esau learned that Jacob was sent away and why, he figured out that *"the daughters of Canaan displeased his father."* Notice what Esau did with this knowledge. He went to the family of Isaac's estranged brother, Ishmael, and took himself another wife. It seems apparent that Esau responded this way, not from a motive to cause his father pain, but rather from a desire to remedy the pain he had caused with his two Canaanite wives. He supposed that he could get back into his father's favor with this move, but he did not take into account that God had separated Ishmael from Abraham's house. This action only served to underscore Esau's enslavement to pleasing his parents without a heart to please God.

In lessons four and five of this Following God™ study (Leah and Rachel), we will learn that Jacob, the trickster, reaped the harvest he had sown. His treachery and trickery that brought harm to Esau was poured back on him by Laban. You see, Jacob made a deal with Laban to work seven years for Laban's beautiful daughter, Rachel. But Laban deceived Jacob and gave his homely, older daughter, Leah, instead. So Jacob ended up working another seven years for the woman he loved, Rachel, proving that we reap what we sow. When Jacob finally returned to the Promised Land, he still had not reconciled with his brother, Esau. Though he eventually did reconcile, years of needless pain and separation had been reaped through the problems rooted in parental partiality.

> *"Whatever a man sows, this he will also reap"* (Galatians 6:7). The trickery Jacob sowed among others, he eventually reaped from his father-in-law, Laban.*

FOR ME TO FOLLOW GOD

Rebekah DAY FIVE

God's final purpose in our lives is to conform us to the image of Christ (Romans 8:29) If Christ is God (and He is), and God is not partial (and He isn't), then for us to show partiality in our relationships with believers or non-believers is to miss the mark (sin). God used a vision from heaven to shake the apostle Peter from the partiality of his culture (Acts 10:9–35). He desires as well to shake us from the partiality of our culture and fleshly nature. Think about that. Maybe you don't have children, or perhaps partiality hasn't shown itself in your home, but that does not mean you are immune. All of us have the potential of being on the giving or receiving end of partiality.

APPLY Have you ever experienced the pain of someone else's partiality?

_____

_____

_____

_____

_____

In what ways was this person(s) partial?

_____

_____

_____

_____

If we are wise, we will learn from the mistakes of Isaac and Rebekah.

Probably all of us have been on the losing end of partiality in some form. Having felt its pain, it makes it all the sadder when we still show it toward others. For generations, African Americans in our nation were not afforded the same rights as white people. Although the *Declaration of Independence* declared, "All men are created equal," for a long time it seemed as if some were considered more equal than others. It is hard to imagine today that less than fifty years ago, whole groups of people were treated as inferior because of the color of their skin. The choices of where they went to the bathroom, where they sat on the bus, where they got a drink of water were all limited by the partiality of those in power. I am glad some of the partialities of racism have been abandoned in America. Martin Luther King dreamed of a day when people would be judged by the content of their character, not the color of their skin. But partiality still exists. Every race, color, or creed can be tempted to show partiality to those who look or act the same as they. God is not partial, and neither should we be.

 APPLY The example we have studied this week involved partiality in the family because of personal preferences. There are many different reasons why we show partiality, and all of them are repugnant to God. Look at your own life in light of the list below. These are some of the criteria that often lead to unbiblical distinctions. Check the ones of which you are guilty:

___ Education   ___ Looks   ___ Spirituality

___ Personality   ___ Race   ___ Talents

___ Age   ___ Position   ___ Wealth

___ Other:_____

On a scale of 1 to 10, how would you rate yourself at relating to those who are different or have nothing to offer you?

NEED IMPROVEMENT   **DOING WELL**

1 2 3 4 5 6 7 8 9 10

What specific changes need to be made in your attitudes/actions as a result of these truths?

_____

_____

_____

_____

_____

What restitution do you need to make to those you have been partial against?

_____

_____

_____

_____

Spend some time with the Lord in prayer:

Lord, I grieve with Rebekah as I see the consequences of her partiality. I grieve for her husband, for her sons, and for her. I see myself in her mistakes and I want to change. Show me where. Convict me of the partialities in my life. Give me the grace to turn from them and the courage to make wrongs right. Thank You that You are not partial. Make me more like You. Amen.

Use the space provided to write your own prayer to the Lord.

_____

_____

_____

_____

_____

_____

_____

_____

_____

_____

"If you show partiality, you are committing sin and are convicted by the law as transgressors."

James 2:9

Notes

Leah

COPING WITH REJECTION

If you have ever been unloved and rejected by a spouse or any other person, then this lesson will hopefully minister to your heart. So many wives have sought for the love of their husbands—only to be rewarded with more rejection and hurt in their lives. In fact, studies have shown that feelings of rejection among women are a common occurrence today. In this lesson, we will get acquainted with Leah, the wife of Jacob. The name Leah is a Hebrew word that means "weary" and probably refers to the "weak eyes" that Scripture says she had. Her name appears twenty-eight times in the Bible. We want to see how Leah learned to cope with the obvious rejection dealt to her by her husband, Jacob.

Perhaps you have studied the life of Jacob. If you have, then you know what a deceiver he was before God crippled him and changed his name to Israel. By the twenty-eighth chapter of Genesis, Jacob had already cheated his older brother Esau out of his birthright and then deceived Isaac, his father, out of the family blessing that technically was to go to Esau. These acts of chicanery and manipulation had caused a great rift of animosity between Jacob and Esau. In fact, so great was the hatred of Esau for his brother that Genesis 27:41 says:

Leah's life reveals a heart seeking to follow God, even in the trials of a disappointed husband and a disrupted home.

WHERE DOES SHE FIT?

2200 B.C.	1950	1700	1450	1200	950	600	100 B.C.	A.D. 1	A.D. 100

HAGAR 2100?–2040?

Daniel 619–534?

ELIZABETH 75 B.C.?–A.D. 10?

REBEKAH 2040?–1915?

Solomon 991–931

WOMEN of the Gospels 10 B.C.?–A.D. 50?

LEAH 1948?–1885?

Judges Rule 1385–1051

David 1041–971

LOT'S WIFE 2100?–2066

RACHEL 1943?–1899

ABIGAIL 1036?–976?

Nehemiah 480?–400?

Jesus Christ 4 B.C.?–A.D. 30?

THE SUBMISSIVE WIFE Ephesians 5; 1 Peter 2—3

Joshua 1495–1385

BATHSHEBA 1016?–961?

Isaac 2065–1885

Moses 1525–1405

JEZEBEL 889?–841

Abraham 2165–1990

Jacob 2005–1858

Samuel 1105–1022

WOMAN at Well 10 B.C.?–A.D. 50?

So Esau hated Jacob because of the blessing with which his father blessed him, and Esau said in his heart, "The days of mourning for my father are at hand; then I will kill my brother Jacob." (NKJV)

Jacob, in his "take-matters-into-my-own-hands" attitude, had now brought much sadness to his family. The saddest thing about Jacob's attitude is that God had promised Jacob's mother, Rebekah, that Jacob would receive the blessing, but nothing would stop Jacob from getting it his own way. Well, in the twenty-eighth chapter of Genesis, Rebekah, fearing the wrath of Esau upon her favored son, Jacob, easily convinces Isaac that the time had come for Jacob to seek a non–Canaanite wife back in her homeland and near her kinsmen. Her solution seems to be "get Jacob out of there, and maybe he will escape Esau's wrath."

So, in Genesis 28:1–2, Isaac called Jacob and. . . .

blessed him and charged him, and said to him, "You shall not take a wife from the daughters of Canaan. "Arise, go to Paddan-aram, to the house of Bethuel your mother's father; and from there take to yourself a wife from the daughters of Laban your mother's brother.

Paddan-aram was the "plain of Aram." It was located in upper Mesopotamia and was near Haran to the northeast of Canaan. It was on the way to Paddan-aram that God assured Jacob that He was directing him all the way. God revealed Himself to Jacob and confirmed the Abrahamic Covenant with him in all three of its promises: a land, a seed, and a nation. Verses 12–14 of Genesis 28 state:

And [Jacob] had a dream, and behold, a ladder was set on the earth with its top reaching to heaven; and behold, the angels of God were ascending and descending on it. And behold, the LORD stood above it and said, "I am the LORD, the God of your father Abraham and the God of Isaac; the land on which you lie, I will give it to you and to your descendants. "Your descendants shall also be like the dust of the earth, and you shall spread out to the west and to the east and to the north and to the south; and in you and in your descendants shall all the families of the earth be blessed.

God goes on and says in verse 15, *"Behold, I am with you, and will keep you wherever you go, and will bring you back to this land; for I will not leave you until I have done what I have promised you."*

Jacob was now headed toward Paddan-aram under the divine direction of God, and this journey sets the table for our lesson as we study Leah.

 DAY ONE

A DESTINED WOMAN

When something is done outside of God's will, there are consequences that are difficult at best to bear up under. As a result of the sinful deception of her father Laban, we will see the hurt that is brought to bear on Leah, his oldest daughter. However, there can be no other conclusion but that she was destined to be the mother of six of the sons of Jacob. This would make up six of the tribes of Israel promised to Jacob. God was leading her even through the deception of her father and the sinful result of his unwise choices.

📖 In verses 1–4 of Genesis 29, what do you discover about the sovereign hand of God in directing Jacob's life?

_____

_____

_____

As we continue to establish background, read verses 5–18 and write out what you learn. In what verse is Leah first mentioned? What is the relationship between Jacob and Rachel in verse 18?

_____

_____

_____

_____

Now, very significant to our study is the difference between Rachel and Leah in verse 17. What is the difference that is brought out in the Scripture?

_____

_____

Rachel was beautiful to look at on the outside, or as one translation puts it, *"beautiful in every way, with a lovely face and shapely figure"* (NLT). But *"Leah's eyes were weak"* (NASB). Interpretation on the subject of Leah's eyes is varied. The Hebrew word translated "weak" in some translations is the word, *rak*. It can also mean "gentle," "tender," "delicate," and "responsive." Some believe that the term "weak eyes" might imply that Leah had an eye disease that made her unlovely to look at. Yet others believe that verse 17 is actually paying a compliment to Leah's eyes, as some versions of the Bible translate *rak* as *"tender-eyed," "delicate," "tender," "pretty,"* and even *"lovely"* (NRSV). But regardless of how we interpret the appearance of Leah's eyes, the main point of verse 17 is quite clear—overall, Leah's appearance paled in comparison to her younger sister, Rachel. However, as we continue, you will see indisputable evidence that Leah was a lovely person on the inside.

In verses 20–25, How many years did Jacob labor for the prize of marrying Rachel? When the morning after the wedding came, who was it that he had actually married?

_____

Go behind the scenes with me and let your mind imagine what took place. Imagine Laban telling Leah that she was to be married to Jacob and not Rachel. The Scripture is silent about the details, but one can't help but imagine what went on in the minds of both Rachel and Leah.

How did Jacob feel about this obvious deception? (verse 25).

_____

_____

_____

_____

Imagine Leah's father, Laban, telling her that she, not Rachel, was to be married to Jacob!

We must understand the obvious hurt and disappointment Jacob suffered when he had labored long and hard for seven years to marry Rachel only to awaken the morning after his marriage had been consummated and discover that it was not Rachel he had slept with—but Leah. But we must also understand that Leah must have expected this disappointment. She knew what Jacob did not know. How long must that night have been for her waiting on the morning light to reveal her identity to Jacob. The consequences of Laban's sin would continue to reap hurt and bitterness in this triangle of love that had been created.

Now, it might be interesting to note that this deception, of Jacob's marrying the wrong girl, was made possible because of their wedding practices. They veiled the bride and brought her to her husband when it was at night. Men and women didn't "date" as they do in our culture, and their customs of marriage were so different from ours today. If we understood the way courtship and marriage was handled during that ancient, oriental culture, we could easily explain why Jacob did not know that he had actually married Leah instead of Rachel.

Knowing that God was with Jacob, it is also interesting to note that God allowed Laban to deceive Jacob. This is rather ironic, for Jacob was the "poster child" for deception as his own name indicates. Jacob lived and benefitted from deception as we have seen in his actions with his brother Esau and his own father. It appears that God used Laban to teach Jacob a valuable lesson.

Now, verse 27 must be viewed very carefully. *"Complete the week of this one, and we will give you the other also for the service which you shall serve with me for another seven years."* Many people think that Jacob worked another seven years before he could marry Rachel. That might be true. But, there is another way of looking at this situation. The seven days spoken of in this verse was most likely the seven-day wedding feast. It had to be completed and then he could also have Rachel. So, it could be that within seven days, Jacob had two wives. But, he still had to serve the evil Laban for another seven years. Regardless which view you take, the fact still remains that Laban had the hard-working Jacob as cheap labor for another seven years.

📖 Was polygamy God's will? Did God ever have in mind a man being married to more than one wife? Look at Genesis 2:24 and Leviticus 18:18. What do you find?

_____

_____

_____

_____

_____

Nothing thwarts the purposes of God—not even the sinfulness and deceitfulness of man.

Though polygamy was **tolerated** in the early history of God's people, and obviously here in our text, it was never God's preferred system of marriage, and it often resulted in tragedy, as we will see in Leah and Jacob's relationship. But, God, in His infinite mercy and grace, allowed this circumstance of polygamy to be the foundation of the twelve tribes that would form the nation chosen of God to bring the Messiah into this world. Nothing thwarts the purposes of God—not even the sinfulness of mankind.

According to verses 30 and 31, how did Jacob feel towards Leah?

_____

_____

_____

Jacob did not realize that Leah was just as destined as Rachel in the plan of God to give him the twelve tribes of Israel. In spite of man's sin, God continues to work His plan, and Leah was a part of that plan. She too was a woman of destiny. A discussion of our own opinions as to how the situation among Jacob, Leah, and Rachel should have been handled is irrelevant. The Bible is silent as to whether Jacob was wrong for rejecting Leah, and sharing such thoughts only ends up in shared ignorance. The point is that, as a result of Laban's deception, Leah was unloved and rejected by Jacob. Nonetheless, she was destined to be the mother of six of the sons of Jacob.

A DESPERATE WOMAN

Leah **DAY TWO**

The tragedy of the situation is revealed in the conclusion of Genesis 29. The cry of a woman wanting to be loved is heard loud and clear. Leah was lonely and desolate in this "love triangle" among Rachel and Jacob and her.

📖 In verse 31, what was it about Leah that moved God's heart?

_____

_____

_____

The Lord saw that Leah was unloved! This should be so comforting to those who feel unloved. God never overlooks the cry of the unloved. God knows, and God cares. In Leah's case, He allowed her to conceive, but in every case, He cares and demonstrates His care in ways that we cannot understand. Yet we must look for those evidences of His love for us. They may not appear in the way we might expect.

Who do we learn is in charge of pregnancy and birth from verse 31?

_____

The phrase in verse 31, "_He opened her womb,_" tells us what we need to know. God is in charge of pregnancy and birth. It is not just an event that happens because of things we do. God is the One who totally controls the outcome of any physical relationship that a man and a woman may have. This truth can bring great comfort as well as cause some distress depending on your perception of God. He is a God of love, and whatever He chooses is always right. Children are His to give or not to give. He knows what we don't know and can always be trusted.

The fact that He initially chose to give Leah a child and not Rachel caused quite a conflict between the sisters. Why was the birth of a son significant? In Luke 1:25, we see the story of Elizabeth when she became pregnant with

GIFTS OF THE LORD

Genesis 29:31 informs us that the Lord opened the womb of Leah, and she gave birth to Reuben. Later she gave birth to five more sons and a daughter named Dinah. Psalm 127:3 says, "_Behold, children are a gift of the LORD...._" He gives them. We receive them.

John the Baptist. In this verse, Elizabeth muses, *"This is the way the Lord has dealt with me in the days when He looked with favor upon me, to take away my disgrace among men."*

How did Leah respond to the birth of a son in verse 32?

_____

_____

_____

She praises God for His blessing of a son, but she sees this son as a way for Jacob to finally love her. You really cannot help but feel empathy for Leah and her hurt feelings and heartfelt longing for Jacob to love her.

📖 Again, in verses 33 and 34, Leah exhibits the same hope when these next two children were born. Read the verses below and then write out what you hear her saying from these verses.

"Because the LORD has heard that I am unloved, He has therefore given me this son also. . . ." And she conceived again and bore a son and said, "Now this time my husband will become attached to me, because I have borne him three sons."

_____

_____

_____

_____

_____

It is so obvious that Leah begs for the love of her husband and thinks that bearing him another son will cause him to love her.

 Do any aspects of this lesson so far relate to you and your life?

_____

_____

_____

_____

_____

In verse 35, however, Leah changes her response. What does she do here that is different from the previous times? Read the verse below and then answer the question.

And she conceived again and bore a son and said, "This time I will praise the LORD." Therefore she named him Judah. Then she stopped bearing.

_____

_____

_____

You see, every time the Lord had opened Leah's womb, she saw that as a way to get to her husband's heart. But she missed the point. God loved her all the time. How? By giving her children. It appears that she finally saw this. You see, God loved Leah. He loves you, too! He constantly loves you! Praise Him and enjoy that love!

A DELIGHTED WOMAN

Children are not just the consequence of a man's sexual involvement with a woman whether the relationship is moral or immoral. The psalmist says in Psalm 127:3, *"Behold, children are a gift of the LORD; The fruit of the womb is a reward."* A precious child is the result of God "opening" the mother's womb. A child is a gift—not a consequence. You see, God was loving Leah through the children that He gave to her. Even though bearing children for Jacob didn't seem to change his feelings towards her, the children were still a blessing that could and would capture **her** heart. Through the children she was **much loved.**

Leah bore six sons and one daughter to Jacob, and their names are very significant. In our study today, we will take a look at these children.

Genesis 29:32–35 records the birth of Leah's first four sons. In the names of these sons, we see the heart cry of Leah for Jacob to love her. In verse 32, what is the name of the firstborn?

_____

The name Reuben means "behold a son." Can you see her wish in the name Reuben that Jacob would look upon her with favor and exclaim, "Behold, a son!"?

In Genesis 29:33, what is the second son's name?

_____

The name Simeon means "hearing," or "God has heard me." In other words, Leah was implying that *Jacob pays no attention to me, but God has heard me.* The interesting thing about Leah is that she continues to trust God and to give Him the glory for the children that He gave to her.

In Genesis 29:34 what is the third son's name?

_____

The name Levi means "joined" or to "adhere to." In Leah's heart it appears that she believed that surely now Jacob's heart would be one with hers. Again, we see the desperate cry of an unloved woman.

In Genesis 29:35 what is the name of the fourth son?

_____

The name Judah means "praise." The name originated in Leah's words of praise to the Lord on account of his birth: *"This time I will praise* [Heb. *odeh*]

> *Even though bearing children for Jacob didn't seem to change his feelings toward Leah, the children were still a blessing that could and would capture her heart. Through the children, Leah was much loved.*

the LORD,' therefore she named him Judah [or in Hebrew, Yehudah]" (Genesis 29:35). Little did Leah know that it would be through the line of Judah that the promised Messiah would one day come. This child would receive the birthright that passed over Reuben, Simeon, and Levi because of their sins. Every generation would praise the name of Judah. Through Leah, the unloved one, the Savior of the world would come.

There is an interesting conflict between Leah, the older sister, and Rachel the younger. It is seen in verses 1–13 in Genesis 30. We will look at this in more detail in our lesson concerning Rachel. But, in Genesis 30:14, we find Reuben going out into the fields and finding some mandrakes. This is a fruit that was superstitiously believed to cause one to be fertile. They were a rare find, and he brought some to his mother Leah. This made Rachel quite angry and she demanded some for herself. Verse 14 shows the contention between the two women. Write out what you see.

_____

_____

_____

In verse 15 of chapter 30, notice the controlling character of Rachel and the bargain she strikes with Leah. Do you see the place into which Leah is constantly being forced?

_____

_____

_____

According to Genesis 30:16–18, what is the name of Leah's fifth son?

_____

Verse 16 shows Leah telling Jacob when he came home that night that she had "hired" him by giving some of the mandrakes to Rachel. Perhaps you can feel much of her own humiliation. Her more beautiful sister had given her Jacob **for one night.** Wow! Thanks a lot!

Well, approximately nine months after Leah "hired" Jacob away from Rachel for the night in exchange for mandrakes, a fifth son is born to Leah, and she named him Issachar. The name Issachar means "there is recompense" or "there is a reward." The idea seems to be that God honored her even though she had been placed in the most contemptible of situations.

In Genesis 30:19–20 what is the sixth son's name?

_____

The name Zebulun means "dwelling." The idea seems to be that of God's dwelling with Leah and honoring her with another son. Again Leah gives all praise to God.

By now, Leah had given birth to six sons. Reuben, Simeon, Levi, Judah, Issachar, and Zebulun. But then she also gave birth to a daughter. What is her name according to Genesis 30:21?

_____

Did You Know?

WHAT IS A MANDRAKE?

A mandrake is a very rare fruit that in ancient times was thought to enhance fertility. Both Leah and Rachel believed this "old wives' tale" to be true.

This daughter's name was Dinah. Dinah also appears in a rather unfortunate account in Genesis 34. In this chapter, it is reported that she was raped by Shechem, the son of Hamor, who was the prince of the land. Shechem took her by force. He asked his father to get her for him as a wife. Hamor was willing to work out a deal with Jacob for Dinah to marry Shechem. But, Dinah's brothers, Simeon and Levi, could not stomach the fact that Shechem had taken her by force, so they killed Shechem and all the male Shechemites and looted their city. The name Dinah means "judged or avenged."

So we see that Leah bore a total of seven children to Jacob. Her six sons comprise half of the twelve tribes of Israel. Throughout Leah's life, God honored her crying out to Him. She praised Him, and over time, her love for the Lord actually surpassed her love for Jacob. The love that God bestowed upon Leah provided her the stability she would need for the rest of her life.

 What situation are you in that you cannot change. Is it that your spouse does not love you? Is it that you are mistakenly looking for your identity in your spouse? Have you discovered your identity in Christ, and have you realized that He and He alone cares for you the way you need to be cared for?

_____

_____

_____

_____

_____

> *Throughout Leah's life, God honored her crying out to Him.*

A DEVOTED WOMAN

Leah DAY FOUR

We must see that Leah, though rejected by Jacob, truly loved Jacob. Her looks were not in the same league as Rachel's. But inwardly, her beauty showed through. She adored Jacob and loved God with all her heart.

Turn to 1 Peter 3. Read verses 1–3 and write out what God's Word has to say about beauty. Is it the outward appearance that is important to God or is it the inward appearance?

_____

_____

_____

_____

One cannot miss the fact that God is interested in the "inward" beauty of a woman. The word "behavior" is important in 1 Peter 3:1: *"In the same way, you wives, be submissive to your own husbands so that even if any of them are disobedient to the word, they may be won without a word by the <u>behavior</u> of their wives."* The Greek word that is translated *"behavior"* in this verse is anastrophé. It refers to the inward progression of behavior, from nagging to not saying a word, that catches the husband's attention. Instead of nagging the husband, the submissive wife quietly submits to him and allows God to do the work of conviction in his heart.

Then in verse 2, Peter continues to enlarge the picture so that we can better grasp the concept of submission. He says that unrepentant husbands may be won *"as they observe your chaste and respectful behavior."* The word "chaste" is translated from the Greek word *hagnós,* which refers to a person's body and behavior being innocent and free from sin or impurities. The Greek word translated "respectful" is the word *phóbos,* which, in this context, implies reverence toward God that causes a woman's behavior toward her husband to be pleasing to God.

Finally, Peter makes it crystal clear in verses 3 and 4 that this inward beauty of a woman stems from a respectful and holy behavior within. 1 Peter 3:3 says, *"And let not your adornment be merely external—braiding the hair, and wearing gold jewelry, or putting on dresses."* In this verse, Peter isn't denouncing a woman for looking nice on the outside, but is stressing that physical beauty is not nearly as important as inward beauty. Grooming and taking care of ourselves is a must, but we shouldn't obsess about our outward looks. Outward beauty or physical attractiveness is fleeting, but inward beauty is long lasting and far more valuable. Verse 4 really brings this point home: *"but let it be the hidden person of the heart, with the* **imperishable quality** *of a gentle and quiet spirit, which is precious in the sight of God."* We will expound further into a study of 1 Peter 3 in our final lesson on "The Submissive Wife."

In light of the truths we have learned about inward and outward beauty, how would you compare Rachel and Leah? Which one shows us the inward qualities of what God calls "imperishable" beauty?

_____

_____

_____

_____

It is obvious that Leah was the one who had the inward qualities that God honored. Even though Jacob rejected Leah, God loved her. Go back through chapters 29 and 30, to 30:21 and write out Leah's response each time God opened her womb to bear children. Also, write out God's response to her.

_____

_____

_____

_____

_____

_____

_____

_____

> **"Let ... your adornment be ... the hidden person of the heart, with the imperishable quality of a gentle and quiet spirit, which is precious in the sight of God."**
>
> **1 Peter 3:3–4**

Now, from this detailed listing, what are the characteristics of Leah that you can pinpoint are beautiful to God. Remember that man looks on the outside, but God looks on the heart (see 1 Samuel 16:7).

_____

_____

_____

_____

_____

_____

_____

Leah was loyal and loving to Jacob and especially to her Lord. God honored her by giving her six sons and one daughter. The descendants of one of her sons, Judah, was God's chosen line through whom Jesus came to this earth.

Read Genesis 49:29–33 below. Where was Leah buried? What does this say in regards to Jacob's eventual appreciation for Leah for who she was?

> *Then he charged them and said to them, "I am about to be gathered to my people; bury me with my fathers in the cave that is in the field of Ephron the Hittite, in the cave that is in the field of Machpelah, which is before Mamre, in the land of Canaan, which Abraham bought along with the field from Ephron the Hittite for a burial site. "There they buried Abraham and his wife Sarah, there they buried Isaac and his wife Rebekah, and there I buried Leah—the field and the cave that is in it, purchased from the sons of Heth." When Jacob finished charging his sons, he drew his feet into the bed and breathed his last, and was gathered to his people.*

It is obvious in verse 31 that Leah was eventually honored by Jacob, for he had her buried in the family cemetery.

Did You Know?

THE DEATH OF LEAH

Jacob honored Leah in her death, burying her in the family burial cave (in the field of Machpelah) with Abraham and Sarah and Isaac and Rebekah. Jacob was buried there also (Genesis 49:29–32; 50:12–13).

FOR ME TO FOLLOW GOD

Now, today we are going to allow what we have studied to become extremely personal.

 What circumstance are you having to bear that is the direct result of someone else's sin?

_____

_____

_____

_____

_____

_____

> **We all have to bear up under the consequences of others' sins from time to time. Leah is just one of millions of people who have had to endure the consequences of the poor decisions of others.**

Isn't it interesting how we all have to bear up under other's sin from time to time? No one is exempt—especially in a personal relationship. Don't beat yourself up! You are no different than so many others who face similar circumstances and consequences. Leah is just one of millions of people who have had to endure the consequences of the poor decisions of others.

What form of rejection are you experiencing in your life?

_____

_____

_____

_____

What are you doing to cope with this rejection?

_____

_____

_____

_____

Always the thing to do in coping with rejection is to turn to Christ and allow His life in you to replace your flesh. Paul said in Galatians 2:20, *"I have been crucified with Christ; and it is no longer I who live, but Christ lives in me; and the life which I now live in the flesh I live by faith in the Son of God, who loved me, and delivered Himself up for me."* Christ is in you, fulfilling the areas of your life that are impossible for you in your own power to handle. When you turn to Him, and yield to Him and to His Word, He replaces the deficiencies and the shortcomings in your life with a godly character that only His Spirit can produce within you. This Spirit will be seen by those around you and will be a witness and testimony to others of the grace and enabling power of Almighty God. All praise be to His name!

If you had the choice to be beautiful and shallow like Rachel, or to be more comely but precious in spirit like Leah, which would you choose? Why?

_____

_____

_____

_____

_____

> **You are loved! God loves you! Never allow your circumstances to cloud this truth.**

Do you realize that God loves you in spite of the fact that others don't seem to? Romans 8:38–39 says, *"For I am convinced that neither death, nor life, nor angels, nor principalities, nor things present, nor things to come, nor powers, nor height, nor depth, nor any other created thing, shall be able to separate us from the love of God, which is in Christ Jesus our Lord."* You are loved! God loves you! Never allow your circumstances to cloud this truth. Ephesians 3:17b says, *"And that you, being rooted and grounded in love."* The "roots" of a plant are the way in which the plant receives nourishment. The nourishment of your life is in the love that God has for you! The word *"grounded"* refers to the strengthening that the root system gives to the plant. Winds cannot blow it over! It stands tall and erect because of its root system that not only nourishes but also gives the plant stability.

What have you learned from Leah that will help you cope as you deal with being "unloved"?

_____

_____

_____

_____

_____

APPLY Write out what Ephesians 3:17 personally says to you.

_____

_____

_____

_____

_____

_____

Spend some time in prayer right now.

Lord, thank You for Your endless love in my life! Thank You for Christ who so loved me that He gave His life for me and now gives His life to me in the person of His Spirit. Thank You that we are "rooted" and "grounded" in Your love and that no person or thing can separate us from Your love. Thank You for making us beautiful in Christ. Thank You for allowing us to find our identity in You! May we be the vessels through which Your character and purity may be seen! In Christ's wonderful name we pray, Amen.

In the space provided, write out your own prayer or journal entry.

_____

_____

_____

_____

_____

_____

_____

_____

_____

_____

_____

_____

_____

_____

_____

"...that you being rooted and grounded in love, may be able to comprehend with all the saints what is the breadth and length and height and depth, and to know the love of Christ which surpasses knowledge, that you may be filled up to all the fullness of God."

Ephesians 3:17–19

Notes

Rachel

BEAUTIFUL BUT BITTER

"Beauty is skin deep" is an old saying that rings true even in today's world when speaking of outward beauty. True beauty is from within and is produced by God the Holy Spirit. There are many truly beautiful women in this world on the outside, but inside, many of their hearts are full of bitterness, jealousy, and hatred. We will take a surprising look at one such person in our study this week.

Her name is Rachel. It is an unusual name in Scripture. It means "ewe" or "little female lamb." As far as we can tell, this is the first time in Scripture that a person is named after an animal in creation. Laban apparently felt it was a fitting name for his youngest daughter. Tender care had to be taken for the precious little lambs, and maybe this is where the name originated.

The story of Rachel is a story most will never forget. It began as a storybook romance in Genesis 29. Jacob had been told by his father Isaac to go into the land of Paddan-aram, which was where Haran was located. There He was to take a wife from the family of Laban, who was his mother's brother. It was in Haran that Laban lived. This is according to Genesis 28:1: *"So Isaac*

Though beautiful on the outside, Rachel faced many heart struggles with bitterness and jealousy.

WHERE DOES SHE FIT?

2200 B.C.	1950	1700	1450	1200	950	600	100 B.C.	A.D. 1	A.D. 100

HAGAR 2100?–2040?						Daniel 619–534?	ELIZABETH 75 B.C.?–A.D. 10?	
REBEKAH 2040?–1915?				Solomon 991–931			WOMEN of the Gospels 10 B.C.?–A.D. 50?	
LEAH 1948?–1885?		Judges Rule 1385–1051	David 1041–971					
LOT'S WIFE 2100?–2066	RACHEL 1943?–1899	Joshua 1495–1385	ABIGAIL 1036?–976? BATHSHEBA 1016?–961?		Nehemiah 480?–400?	Jesus Christ 4 B.C.?–A.D. 30?	THE SUBMISSIVE WIFE Ephesians 5; 1 Peter 2—3	
Isaac 2065–1885		Moses 1525–1405		JEZEBEL 889?–841				
Abraham 2165–1990	Jacob 2005–1858		Samuel 1105–1022			WOMAN at Well 10 B.C.?–A.D. 50?		

called Jacob and blessed him and charged him, and said to him, 'You shall not take a wife from the daughters of Canaan. 'Arise, go to Paddan-aram, to the house of Bethuel your mother's father; and from there take to yourself a wife from the daughters of Laban your mother's brother.' "

📖 Jacob obeyed, and Genesis 29:1–12 tells us the story. Read this passage and write out the details of how Jacob met Rachel. What did Jacob do to allow Rachel to water her sheep?

_____

_____

_____

_____

_____

_____

God is an awesome God. There is no way anyone can miss the fact that Rachel was divinely led to water her sheep at that well on that day at that time! It was a divine appointment! God led Jacob and Rachel to that well, on that day, at that particular time. Jacob fell in love with Rachel upon first sight of her.

The story begins here, and we will look deeply into it throughout the week as we see a beautiful woman who was not so beautiful on the inside. Many of the things we will discover are ever so subtle, so we must look at the text very carefully.

A BLESSED WOMAN

In the world we all live in today, pop culture and media influences place an undue amount of pressure on women to be physically beautiful. In the world's view, a woman is truly blessed if she has the perfect figure with the perfect face. You see, the world's view of beauty is pictured by what one sees on the outside. It should be no surprise then that many women who are not so naturally blessed spend countless hours trying to attain what is naturally given to others. Eating disorders abound by those trying to be what the world says is "beautiful." But to be beautiful is not the only goal to which a majority of women aspire. **To be loved** would likely take a close second to the goals of the average woman who is honest with herself. Beautiful and loved! In our world's way of thinking today, there seems to be nothing a woman could want more than to be beautiful and to be loved.

📖 Well, in our study, we have a woman who is both beautiful and loved. Read Genesis 29:17, and write out what description of Rachel the Scriptures give us.

_____

_____

_____

_____

It was a common practice for unmarried daughters to tend the flocks along with the sons, going out at sunrise and staying with the livestock until sunset. This practice included taking sheep to pasture land and watering them once a day, since sheep require drinking only once each day. Jacob met Rachel when she was at the well, preparing to water the sheep.

Beautiful and loved! In our world's way of thinking today, there seems to be nothing a woman could want more than to be beautiful and to be loved.

The phrase *"beautiful of form and face"* tells us all about her appearance. Her face was fair and beautiful, but so was her figure. She had it all as far as outward appearance.

How does Genesis 29:17 contrast Rachel with her older sister, Leah?

_____

_____

_____

_____

Rachel was beautiful to look at on the outside, or as one translation puts it, "beautiful in every way, with a lovely face and shapely figure" (NLT). But "Leah's eyes were weak" (NASB). Interpretation on the subject of Leah's eyes is varied. The Hebrew word translated "weak" in some English translations is the word, *rak*. It can also mean "gentle," "tender," "delicate," and "responsive." Some believe that the term "weak eyes" might imply that Leah had an eye disease that made her unlovely to look at. Yet others believe that verse 17 is actually paying a compliment to Leah's eyes, as other English translations of the Bible translate *rak* as "tender-eyed," "delicate," "tender," "pretty," and even "lovely" (NRSV). But regardless of how we interpret the appearance of Leah's eyes, the main point of verse 17 is quite clear—overall, Leah's appearance paled in comparison to her younger sister, Rachel. However, as we continue, you will see indisputable evidence that Rachel was not so lovely on the inside.

📖 Rachel was not only beautiful to behold, but she was also loved very much by Jacob. What does Genesis 29:18–20 tell us of Jacob's love for her?

_____

_____

_____

_____

What was Jacob willing to do for Rachel?

_____

_____

_____

_____

The word *"serve"* is the word also used for one who is a slave. It is used of someone who is willing to do hard labor. The only prize Jacob wanted for his seven years of hard labor was Rachel. Now, we must notice something here. It was not Laban who imposed the seven years on Jacob. It was Jacob that came up with that figure. Remember that Jacob was on the run from Esau. It would serve his own purpose to stay a long time with Laban. Remember that Jacob, as indicated by his very name, is a deceiver. This may cast some doubt as to the true integrity of Jacob's love for Rachel to work for her for seven years. But, the Scriptures say decidedly that "Jacob loved Rachel."

So, Rachel was truly blessed. She was beautiful, and she was loved. Jacob so loved Rachel that he was willing to pay a great price to have her as his wife.

Did You Know?

THE BRIDE PRICE

In Jacob's day, the groom would pay a price for his bride, a price agreeable to the groom and the father-in-law. This price could be paid in goods or services (as was Jacob's seven years of labor), and the amount paid often depended on several factors, including the father's financial status, the perceived value of the bride's beauty (the groom would often pay more for a woman of superb beauty), her overall usefulness, or any combination of these factors. Some considered this payment by the groom as compensation for the loss of that daughter's labor toward the family's responsibilities or business. (Genesis 29:15–20, 27). This price or a portion of it could also be given to the bride for her use within the marriage or to save in the event she became a widow. Leah and Rachel mentioned that their father spent all he received. He *"has sold us, and has also entirely consumed our purchase price [our money]."* In their case, they saw they had no *"portion or inheritance"* remaining in their father's house. (Genesis 31:14–16)

_____

_____

_____

_____

Rachel **DAY TWO**

A BARREN WOMAN

On the surface one might think that Rachel had it all, especially the way the world views things. But, the scriptures tell us that inwardly Rachel was not very beautiful. In fact, the story of Rachel brings new light to the phrase "beauty is skin deep." To give her benefit of doubt, the roots of this bitterness came from her own father. Laban had deceived Jacob. Jacob fulfilled his promise to work for her for seven years. But, on the day after the marriage was consummated, Jacob awoke to find that he was in bed with Leah, the older and much-less-beautiful sister. Rachel was forced from day one to have to share Jacob with her sister. Polygamy was not God's perfect will, but was the result of her own father's deception. She could not help the circumstance, but she could have changed her reaction to it.

This is what we must see. Life does not work out the way we want it to sometimes. We all suffer from **orginal sin** which has caused much sorrow to be in this world. We all suffer from our own **personal sin** which, when committed, causes much sorrow to ourselves and to others. But, from time to time, we suffer because of **other's sin.** In this case, Laban's sin of deception put Leah and Rachel into a very uncomfortable triangle with Jacob.

📖 Read Genesis 29:18–28 to refresh your mind with the story of how Laban deceived Jacob. Remember that Jacob was the "great deceiver" himself. You might wonder if God didn't allow this to reveal to Jacob what he himself was like.

The problem was immediate between the two sisters. There are at least two interpretations of Genesis 29:21–25. One interpretation is that Jacob had to wait seven more years to marry Leah. Another interpretation is that Jacob married Rachel after the seven-day marriage feast. If the view is correct that Jacob had to wait seven more years to marry Rachel, still Rachel had to live daily knowing that Leah had borne Jacob many children during that time. Seven years of waiting and knowing that Leah was bearing Jacob several children would have been agonizing for Rachel. However, it is likely that Jacob married Rachel after the seven-day celebration concluded for his marriage to Leah. It appears this last view is correct, because Genesis 29:31 says, "Now the Lord saw that Leah was unloved, and He opened her womb, but Rachel was barren." It seems unlikely that Genesis would mention Rachel's barrenness if she were not already married to Jacob. The fact that Leah was unloved **at the same time** that Rachel was barren makes it fairly evident that Jacob was married to both women at this time. Whatever the case, the ordeal must have been a trying and confusing time for all parties involved. During these first years of the Rachel-Jacob-Leah triangle, we begin to see the root of bitterness deepen in Rachel, especially towards Leah. Yet even though

We all suffer from original sin in this world, from personal sin in our lives, and from others' sin that can sometimes affect us with pain and sorrow.

Rachel thought her bitter feelings were directed only towards Leah, they were primarily directed towards God. All bitterness is indirectly aimed at God.

According to Genesis 30, Rachel was barren—not because she and Jacob had never tried to have children—but because God had not opened her womb.

📖 Read Genesis 29:32–35. Leah had borne four sons to Jacob. What were their names?

_____

_____

Leah and Jacob's firstborn son was named Reuben. The other three sons were Simeon, Levi, and Judah born in that order. For more information on the names of Leah's sons, see Lesson Four, "Leah—Coping with Rejection."

📖 Read Genesis 49. According to Jacob's blessing of Judah, what was the lasting significance of Judah's birth?

_____

_____

_____

_____

_____

Little did Leah and Jacob know how significant the birth of Judah was! Many years later, as Jacob was on his deathbed in Egypt (Genesis 49), he officially bestowed upon all his sons the appropriate blessing that was due to each of them. Normally, the firstborn child would have received a double portion or share of the father's inheritance, hence—the greatest blessing. However, because of the heinous and detestable sins of Reuben (see Genesis 35:22), Simeon, and Levi (see Genesis 34), the greater blessings were passed down to Judah, and to Joseph and his two sons, Ephraim and Manasseh (see Genesis 49:8–12, 22–26). As Jacob prophesies in Genesis 49:8–10, every generation would praise the name of Judah. Genesis 49:10 is one of the most significant prophetic passages of the Old Testament, for its words foretell the coming of the Messiah, Jesus Christ: *"The scepter shall not depart from Judah, Nor the ruler's staff from between his feet, Until Shiloh comes, And to him shall be the obedience of the peoples."* This verse indicates that the messianic line would run through the descendants of Judah. Matthew 1:2–16 traces the lineage of Christ all the way back to Judah.

Write out your thoughts on why "Judah," the line through whom Christ came, was born to Leah and not to Rachel. Could this tell us how God viewed Leah, the unlovely one?

_____

_____

_____

_____

_____

_____

"...but Rachel was barren."

Genesis 29:31

It certainly seems that God honored Leah, the unlovely one, by choosing to make "Judah" the line through whom Christ came. God could have easily chosen to bring His messianic line through one of the sons of Rachel, but He did not. If you are studying this and feel you are not the "radiant beauty" that Rachel was, but perhaps the "unlovely [or unloved] one" on the outside, always remember that God honors the beauty of the heart.

📖 In the culture of Rachel's day, it was important for women to bear children, especially sons. Barrenness was considered to be divine punishment. Look at Genesis 16:2. What does Sarah say that the Lord had done?

_____

_____

_____

Sarah believed with all her heart that the Lord prevented her from having children. Though God had plans for Sarah to conceive, she grew impatient and took matters into her own hands, prompting her husband, Abraham, to have sexual relations with her servant, Hagar. (See Lesson One of this study, "Hagar—Trusting That God Sees.)

In Genesis 30:23, what does Rachel say regarding the issue of barrenness?

_____

_____

The Hebrew word for "reproach" used in Genesis 30:23 can also be translated "disgrace." As evidenced by Genesis 16:2 and chapter 30, it was a great affront for a woman of that era not to have children. But let's not confuse the times of the patriarchs with our own situations. To all who are taking this study: if God has not blessed you with children, this is no "disgrace" to you. We are now in Christ and are His vessels through whom He does His work. What He chooses for us is right, and we can rest in Him and in His will for us. Romans 12:2 tells us that His will is good, acceptable and perfect. So, don't make the mistake of thinking that it is a disgrace not to have children.

So far, we have learned that Rachel was a beautiful woman but also a barren woman.

A Bitter Woman

N ow, we must approach this part of the study carefully. We do not in any way want to make Rachel appear as something she was not. But, if you will look carefully at the Scripture, you will likely see many inconsistencies in Rachel that lead to only one conclusion. Rachel was filled with anger and bitterness. When it began, no one can say for certain. In Hebrews 12:15 we read, *"See to it that no one comes short of the grace of God; that no root of bitterness springing up causes trouble, and by it many be defiled."* The anger inside someone, if not allowed to be changed by the grace of God, will boil over when that person is put under pressure.

Put Yourself In Their Shoes
ABOUT
BARRENNESS

Consider the struggle of barrenness. Sarah faced the scorn of Hagar in her barrenness and complained to Abraham about it (Genesis 16:5). Leah spoke of her *"affliction"* (Genesis 29:32). Rachel told Jacob, *"Give me children, or else I die"* (Genesis 30:1). Hannah wept often over her condition. She was *"greatly distressed"* and *"oppressed in spirit"* (1 Samuel 1:5–18). Childlessness was sometimes the judgment of God on a couple (Leviticus 20:20–21), though this was not the case with Elizabeth in the New Testament. However, Elizabeth still struggled, calling her barrenness a *"disgrace"* or a reproach (Luke 1:25). Rachel considered her barrenness a reproach as well.

📖 Let's see if we can find the source of Rachel's bitterness. First of all, we must address a very important fact. Read chapters 29 and 30 of Genesis and see if you can find where it says that Rachel "loved Jacob." What did you find?

_____

_____

_____

There is no reference that tells us that Rachel loved Jacob. In verses 18 and 30 of chapter 29, it says that Jacob "loved" Rachel, but nowhere does it say that Rachel loved Jacob. That is so interesting! Perhaps this is why Scripture makes no mention of her complaining when her father, Laban, deceptively switched Leah in place of Rachel on what was supposed to be Rachel's wedding day. Surely Rachel knew about the switch, but Scripture is silent about any response whatsoever. There seems to be a darker side to this person than meets the eye. We see much more of it in chapter 30.

Genesis 30:1 says two things about Rachel. What are they?

_____

_____

Genesis 30:1 tells us that Rachel was barren and jealous of her sister, Leah. Don't make the mistake of continuing to feel sorry for Rachel because of her father's sin and miss the fact that she could have responded differently. All of us have a choice to make when we get into adverse circumstances. We are not products of our own environment, but of our own choices. We must learn to trust God in all circumstances of our life. Jealousy is a trait of our flesh. In Galatians 5:20, Paul lists jealousy as one of the works of our sinful flesh.

In Genesis 30:1, what does Rachel demand of Jacob?

_____

_____

Rachel "put the screws" on Jacob with her demand that he give her children? What does this tell you about her understanding of childbirth? Does she think that Jacob can give her children on his own effort, or does she understand that God has to open the womb?

_____

_____

_____

Obviously, Rachel's ability to think rationally was pretty limited at this point, since she actually thought that Jacob had the power to give or produce life. Only God has this power, and instead of pointing an accusatory finger at Jacob, she should have gone before God and sought His answer.

How is Rachel's attitude toward God different from Leah's? (Genesis 29:31–35)

_____

_____

_____

All of us have a choice to make when we get into adverse circumstances. We are not products of our own environment, but of our own choices.

Leah focuses on God in verse 32, as she says, *"Because the LORD has seen my affliction."* In verse 33, she says *"Because the LORD has heard that I am unloved, He has therefore given me this son also."* In verse 35, Leah says, *"This time I will praise the LORD."* Even though Leah was frustrated with Jacob because she felt he did not love her, her mind was still focused on the fact that only God can give life.

How does Jacob respond in Genesis 30:2 to Rachel's demand?

_____

_____

_____

Jacob became angry with Rachel—the woman he deeply loved—for her unfair and unreasonable demand. He rebuked her for not realizing that only God has the power to allow a woman to become pregnant. It is apparent that both Jacob and Leah understood something about the providence and power of God Almighty!

What does Rachel do out of jealousy of Leah in verse 3?

_____

_____

_____

Like Sarah did with Abraham in Genesis 16, Rachel implored her husband, Jacob, to have sexual relations with her servant, Bilhah, in order that Rachel could claim the children officially as her own. Rachel and Sarah both acted impetuously and improperly in their requests. Sarah's actions were improper because she did not trust God's promise to her and to Abraham that they would have a son. We have no knowledge that Rachel was ever promised a son by God, but her plan of having a child through Bilhah was clearly inspired by her insatiable desire to avenge herself of her reproach and to "get even" with Leah.

What one phrase in the verse tells us that she is jealous of Leah?

_____

_____

"That through her I too may have children." It is interesting to note, that in that culture and time, a child born by a maid of a master woman, was considered to be the master woman's child—not the maid's. Who was born out of the relationship between Jacob and Bilhah, the maid of Rachel in Genesis 30:5?

_____

Rachel named this son Dan. The name "Dan" means "judge." How is God intervening in this upside-down situation to accomplish His promise to Abraham and then to Isaac and then to Jacob?

_____

_____

_____

_____

It is important to realize that even though God was constantly dealing with sinful men and women like Jacob and Rachel, He was still accomplishing His own purpose of building the twelve tribes of Israel. All sons born to Jacob through Leah, Leah's maid, Rachel's maid, and, eventually, Rachel herself, make up the twelve tribes. The sons born to Leah and her maid, Zilpah, that we studied in the previous lesson, along with the sons born to Bilhah, Rachel's maid, were the first to be born into this "nation of Israel" promised to Abraham.

📖 Go back to Genesis 28:13–15 and review the promise made to Jacob in a dream as he was journeying to Paddan-aram. Write down what you find.

_____

_____

_____

_____

God promised a land where Jacob's descendants (Israel) could dwell and call their own. God also said that the descendants of Jacob would multiply rapidly to innumerable proportions and become a great nation that would bring blessing to "all the families of the earth," a veiled messianic prophecy, for through the nation of Israel came our Lord and Savior, Jesus Christ, who will one day rule as King of kings and Lord of lords.

📖 In Genesis 30:7–8 what is the name of the second son born to Bilhah?

_____

_____

_____

Naphtali means "my wrestling." With whom has Rachel been contending or wrestling (verse 8)?

_____

_____

_____

It is obvious that Leah is a major source of contention with Rachel. What does this word "wrestling" tell us about Rachel and her motives towards her sister? The Hebrew word translated "wrestling" in verse 8 means to contend with cunning. It seems to mean to be crafty in trying to be better than someone.

What does this "wrestling" cause Leah to do (verses 9–13)?

_____

_____

_____

_____

_____

Leah had her own flesh to contend with, so she offered her maid to Jacob when she believed it was no longer possible for her to have any more children.

Word Study
"WRESTLING"

The Hebrew word translated "wrestling" is *naphtuwl* which is akin to the name Naphtali. *Naphtuwl* comes from the word *pathal*, whose root idea is "to twine." It points to two people in an intense struggle or to someone twisting another like strands of rope. The word can also refer to cunning in wrestling. The phrase *"with mighty wrestlings"* found in Genesis 30:8 can literally be translated "wrestlings of God," possibly pointing to Rachel's struggle with God along with her struggle over circumstances involving Jacob and her competition, Leah.

What was the result? What was God doing in spite of the power struggle taking place between Rachel and Leah?

_____

_____

_____

_____

So far, eight sons had been born to Jacob: four by Leah; two by Rachel's maid, Bilhah; and now, two by Leah's maid, Zilpah. God continued to build the nation of Israel and used the contention and ill will of two sisters for His glory.

_____

_____

_____

_____

In verses 14 and 15 of Genesis 30, what does Rachel do to further belittle her sister Leah?

_____

_____

_____

Rachel told Leah that if she would give her some of the mandrakes, then she could sleep with Jacob that night. What does this say of Rachel's love for Jacob? Can you see the contentious attitude that is manifested?

_____

_____

_____

_____

In verses 17–19, 21 how did God bless Leah in spite of her humiliation?

_____

_____

Did You Know?
RACHEL'S TENT

In an age when polygamy was common-place, it was customary for each wife to have her own tent where she and her children stayed. In Jacob's family, there was a tent for Jacob, a tent for Leah, a tent for Rachel, and a tent for the two maids, Bilhah and Zilpah. Other servants of Jacob tents had their own tents as well. (Genesis 31:33–34).

God blessed Leah with two more sons, Isaachar and Zebulun, and a daughter, Dinah. Now, go back through what we have studied and list the children that Jacob had through Leah, Bilhah, the maid of Rachel and Zilpah, the maid of Leah.

_____

_____

_____

_____

_____

At this point (Genesis 30:21), Jacob had six sons and a daughter by Leah. These are Reuben, the firstborn, Simeon, Levi, Judah, Issachar, and

Zebulun. He had a daughter by Leah named Dinah. He had two sons by Zilpah (Leah's maid) who were Gad and Asher. He had two sons by Bilhah (Rachel's maid) who were Dan and Napthali. These children total ten sons and one daughter.

Yet, how many children did Rachel have at this point?

_____

Absolutely none! Rachel was still a beautiful, barren, and bitterly jealous woman. But God continued to build the nation of Israel.

A BROKEN WOMAN

Now, God loves us all, even with our darker sides. He is always working in our behalf. He is not a respecter of persons. God loved Rachel as much as He loved Leah. The fact that God is not a respecter of persons sometimes disturbs some of us who think we deserve His love. You see, in reality, no human being that has ever lived deserves God's love. Some people once asked a great man of God, "Doesn't it bother you that God could hate Essau?" He answered, "No, that has never bothered me." They asked, "Then what does?" He said, "What bothers me is how He could ever love Jacob." We can take that anecdote one step further to say that it is mind boggling that God could love any man and woman that has ever lived, including you and me.

But let's move on with our study of Rachel. The question I am sure some of you are asking at this point is, "Does God ever open Rachel's womb so that she can bear children?"

📖 Read Genesis 30:22–24. Write down in your own words the highlights of what you find.

_____

_____

_____

_____

_____

Rachel, by God's grace, finally conceived and gave birth to a wonderful son whom she named Joseph. Now that God has finally allowed Rachel to bear a son, what is her immediate response towards God after she named her son "Joseph"? (Some Bible translations don't bring this out. The New American Standard Bible [NASB] sheds more light on this response.) Genesis 30:24 states, *"And she named him Joseph, saying, 'May the LORD give me another son."*

Do you see the selfishness in Rachel? It is an attitude that says "Give me! Give me! Give me!" She wanted a son, and before she even had time to enjoy the one God had finally given to her, she asks for another. She gives her son the name, Joseph, or "the Lord increases." What does this say to you about her competitive spirit towards her sister Leah?

"Then God remembered Rachel, and God gave heed to her and opened her womb. So she conceived and bore a son and said, 'God has taken away my reproach.' And she named him Joseph, saying, 'May the LORD give me another son.'"

Genesis 30:22–24

_____

_____

_____

Rachel was blinded by her jealousy of Leah to the gratitude she could have had for the wonderful son God gave to her. Joseph was to stand out above all of the sons of Jacob. But, we need to see another dark side of Rachel to fully grasp how one can be beautiful and wicked at the same time. She was also an idolatrous woman.

📖 Read Genesis 31:1–34. Jacob had announced that God told him to go back to his homeland. Both wives are getting ready for the journey. What does Rachel do in verse 19?

_____

_____

_____

_____

Verse 19 says that Rachel stole the idols that belonged to her father. Why do you think she did this?

_____

_____

_____

It could be that Rachel knew that her sudden departure with Jacob, Leah, and their servants would deny her from enjoying her father's wealth. So she may have wanted to take some items of value with her. She took the idols and hid them in the saddle on the camel and then sat on them so that Laban would not find them.

According to verse 32, what did Jacob do, not knowing that it was Rachel, his beloved, who stole the idols from her father?

_____

_____

_____

_____

Jacob unwittingly pronounced a death sentence to the one who stole the idols. What does this whole secret act of theft on Rachel's part tell you of her relationship with Jacob? Was it close and intimate? If you say it was close and intimate, then why did she keep the fact that she had stolen the idols from him?

_____

_____

_____

_____

GOOD ADVICE FROM A WIFE

When Jacob informed Rachel and Leah that the Lord had instructed him to leave Laban and Haran behind and return to Canaan, Rachel and Leah told him, *"Do whatever God has said to you."* (Genesis 31:16). That is good advice anytime!

Did You Know?

② HOUSEHOLD IDOLS

The idols that Rachel stole were not merely family treasures. Possession of these idols usually went hand in hand with being the head of the family's estate, along with all rights pertaining to that position. This included prime rights to the inheritance. If he wished, a man could appoint his son-in-law as the chief recipient of the inheritance by giving him those small household idols. The transfer of idols from one to another symbolically notarized the transfer of the inheritance. It appears Rachel was trying to make sure headship belonged to Jacob and with it the family inheritance of her father Laban. Not only did she steal the idols, but she was also even willing to lie to her father and to her husband to guarantee that she kept them and thus fulfill her desire. Laban went to great expense chasing Jacob, trying to retrieve these idols. He ended up making a covenant with Jacob, part of which was the promise that Jacob would not return to Haran to do him any harm. This would insure that Laban's inheritance stayed with his son, since, if Jacob had the idols hidden somewhere, by virtue of this covenant, he could not bring them back and claim any inheritance. (Genesis 31:19, 22–55).

It is most interesting how Rachel kept her sin to herself, thinking probably that no one would ever find out. But, God always knows! Sin will take you further than you ever wanted to stray. It will keep you longer than you ever wanted to stay, and it will cost you more than you ever dreamed you would pay!

📖 Read Genesis 35:16–19. What happened? What other son was born to Rachel? What happened to Rachel upon this son's birth?

_____

_____

_____

_____

_____

Rachel could have had a wonderful and happy life with Jacob. She experienced sentiments similar to those any one of us could experience when we are in difficult circumstances, particularly when we endure trials that are beyond our control. In spite of Rachel's adverse circumstances, she still had options as to how she could turn those circumstances to her advantage. But because of jealousy and bitterness, she forfeited all that could have been hers. Bitterness is like the acid you have inside that you want to spew on others, but before you get the chance it will eat you alive. Rachel was a beautiful, barren, and bitter person for most of her life that we have recorded for us in Scripture. She died giving birth to Benjamin, the father of the last of the twelve tribes of Israel.

FOR ME TO FOLLOW GOD

L ife doesn't always work out the way we would like for it to work. But, we are not to react to our circumstances. We are to respond to the God who is in charge of our circumstances.

📖 Read James 1:2–4 and write out the response God expects out of His followers.

_____

_____

_____

_____

_____

James wants his readers to understand that God is always in charge of all events in our life. We are to *consider it all joy . . . when* [we] *encounter various trials.* The Greek word here that is translated "consider" is the word *hegeomai*, which means "to make it a priority." An understanding of priorities is essential as a believer learns to view life from God's point of view. We must put this attitude that James is about to reveal as a top priority in our thinking. *"Consider it all joy, my brethren, when you encounter various trials."* Wow! We are to realize that life works for us—not against us. Notice that

Word Study
WHAT'S IN A NAME?

Rachel named her second son **Ben-oni,** meaning "son of my sorrow," pointing to her sorrow over her life that was ebbing away as she gave birth. Jacob changed the name to one of great honor and blessing— **Benjamin,** or "son of my right hand." (Genesis 35:16–18). Benjamin was a treasured child to Jacob since he was born of Rachel. Another likely reason for Jacob favoring his youngest son was the fact that it had been at least sixteen years since the birth of Rachel's first son, Joseph.

Rachel   DAY FIVE

"Consider it all joy, my brethren, when you encounter various trials."

James 1:2

James 1:2 says *"when* [not if] *you encounter . . . trials,* revealing the inevitability of hardship in our lives. Life is not always going to work the way we want it to. The Greek word for "encounter" (*peripipto*) means "to fall or stumble into" something. We cannot plan the uncomfortable events that are going to occur in our lives. Trials are going to befall us before we have the luxury to plan for them. So, we should go ahead and make it a priority to brace ourselves for any unseen but certain pitfalls that loom over the horizon. We need to choose to believe that no matter what happens—God is in control and is working in our behalf!

The Greek word translated "various" is the word *poikilos*, which literally means "multicolored" or "variegated." I guess you could say that our trials are color-coded! Another way of putting it is that the trials that befall us come in various shapes, sizes, patterns, and colors, and are definitely not a one-size-fits-all, vanilla ice cream-like, uniform phenomenon. But *poikilos* is also the word used in 1 Peter 4:10, when Peter says, *"As each one has received a special gift, employ it in serving one another, as good stewards of the **manifold** grace of God.* The Greek word for *"manifold"* here is *poikilos*. Not only are the "trials" color-coded and complex, **but so is the "grace" of God.** Grace is the "enabling power of God." With every trial there is matching "grace" to bear up under and to respond properly to whatever uncomfortable circumstance may come upon us. But *poikilos* is also the word found in Ephesians 3:10: *"in order that the **manifold** wisdom of God might now be made known through the church to the rulers and the authorities in the heavenly places.* So we have seen that trials are color-coded and sophisticated, and that God's grace is as well—but so also is the "wisdom of God" color-coded. Do you see it? Whatever trial we endure is equally matched with the enabling power of God (grace) and the wisdom of God so that we might walk through and bear up under anything that comes our way. God is in control!

📖 Read Romans 8:14–35 and write out what you discover about how God is in control of our circumstances.

_____

_____

_____

_____

_____

In Romans 8:14, Paul says, *"For all who are being led by the Spirit of God, these are sons of God."* Since the Greek word used here for sons (*huios*) refers to mature sons, then it would read, at first glance, all the "mature sons" are consciously being led by the Spirit of God. But, since in the context (verse 16), Paul uses the word *teknon* for children, one cannot force the "mature" part of the meaning of the word "son" in verse 14. So, with this in mind, all the children of God are being led by the Spirit of God. The "mature" ones are conscious of this, but, regardless, all believers are being led. God has a plan for His children. He had a plan for Leah, and she responded well. He had a plan for Rachel, but Rachel fought Him all the way to the end.

A pastor friend of mine has a son with a serious heart problem. Recently, my wife and I called him to see how his son was doing. His office said that he was at the hospital with his eleven-year-old son and we could call him there. As we talked with him during this very difficult time, my friend told me

We can rest assured that for each color of trial we face, God has color-coded His grace and His wisdom to match it.

that he had been studying Psalms 23. He said to me, "do you know that Psalm 23:3 could be translated 'He leads me in the right paths'?" He said, "This path of suffering that our family is going through is the 'right path.' Pray for us that we will respond properly to the grace of God, so that we might grow and mature through this no matter how it turns out!" What a profound statement! God is always leading us! He is always leading us in the "right paths." He is our Shepherd, and He knows what we need.

APPLY So how are you responding to the circumstances of your life?

_____

_____

_____

_____

_____

_____

_____

If you are married, how would you rate your marriage, and how are you handling it?

_____

_____

_____

_____

_____

_____

_____

_____

What has this study done to help you in your walk with God—even in the midst of circumstances you have not chosen for yourself?

_____

_____

_____

_____

_____

_____

_____

Is your beauty surface deep?

_____

_____

_____

_____

_____

_____

"The LORD is my Shepherd. . . . He guides me along right paths."

Psalm 23:1, 3 NLT

How do family members (spouse, children, brother/sister, grandparents, etc.) see you?

_____

_____

_____

_____

_____

_____

_____

_____

Remember, physical beauty is a temporary, fleeting quality, but spiritual beauty is an eternal blessing!

I speak on behalf of all the authors of this study in saying it is our prayer that you will discover how God sees you in such a different way than man does. God looks on the heart. I don't think anything can be more beautiful to God than our unconditional surrender and submission to Him. And this is the beauty that His Spirit produces through our lives that shines before others. Remember, physical beauty is a temporary, fleeting quality, but spiritual beauty is an eternal blessing!

Let's spend some time with the Lord in prayer right now.

Father, thank You for making "something beautiful" out of our lives as believers. Thank You for sending Your Spirit to live in and through those who love You and have trusted Your Son for their salvation. Help us to experience the joy of surrender to Your will and ways! Educate the ones who are taking this course who do not think of themselves as beautiful. May they bask in the joy of who they are in You! Thank You, Father, for sending Your Son to live in us in the presence of Your Spirit, Amen.

Write out your own prayer in the space provided.

_____

_____

_____

_____

_____

_____

_____

_____

_____

_____

_____

_____

Notes

Notes

Abigail

A WOMAN MARKED BY BEAUTY AND WISDOM

You will not find many people in Scripture that will win your heart more than the lovely woman named Abigail. Her story is found in the twenty-fifth chapter of 1 Samuel and will warm your heart as you study her life. She was not only a beautiful woman but a very intelligent woman who knew God and therefore knew how to live with a foolish man.

So many books and articles are written in these days concerning men being fools. Granted there are many who qualify. But few books or even articles are written on how godly women can live with them. Abigail rises above others because she demonstrates a rare poise and behavior—in the midst of the worst possible marriage. She was married to a rich, drunken fool. His name was Nabal.

God Himself will deal with fools. But when life forces us to live with them, God intervenes with His enabling power and ability to allow us to do what must be done. Life may have dealt you this kind of circumstance. I'm speaking of the kind of circumstance that you would have never chosen intentionally. So often we must deal with circumstances that come into our lives

ABIGAIL

Abigail was marked by both beauty and wisdom—the wisdom of God that allowed her to deal with the foolishness of others.

WHERE DOES SHE FIT?

2200 B.C.	1950	1700	1450	1200	950	600	100 B.C.	A.D. 1	A.D. 100

HAGAR
2100?–2040?

Daniel
619–534?

ELIZABETH
75 B.C.?–A.D. 10?

Solomon
991–931

REBEKAH
2040?–1915?

WOMEN of the
Gospels
10 B.C.?–A.D. 50?

LEAH
1948?–1885?

Judges Rule
1385–1051

David
1041–971

LOT'S WIFE
2100?–2066

RACHEL
1943?–1899

Joshua
1495–1385

ABIGAIL
1036?–976?

Nehemiah
480?–400?

Jesus Christ
4 B.C.?–A.D. 30?

THE
SUBMISSIVE
WIFE
Ephesians 5;
1 Peter 2—3

BATHSHEBA
1016?–961?

Isaac
2065–1885

Moses
1525–1405

JEZEBEL
889?–841

Abraham
2165–1990

Jacob
2005–1858

Samuel
1105–1022

WOMAN at Well
10 B.C.?–A.D. 50?

uninvited. Learn from Abigail that whatever is over your head—is under His feet. Since marriages were for the most part arranged by the parents, Abigail was more than likely forced into nuptials with Nabal. He was a rich man and seemed industrious, so it's likely that Abigail's parents felt that Nabal would be a good catch for their daughter. But, oh, the horror that lurked beneath what on the outside looked so good.

 **DAY ONE**

THE DILEMMA OF ABIGAIL

In the setting of our story found in 1 Samuel 25, David had not yet taken the throne, although he was the anointed king.

📖 Read 1 Samuel 16:1–13 and see how David was anointed king by Samuel. Write out what you learn from verse 7.

_____

_____

_____

_____

Isn't it awesome that God does not see things as we do? He does not look on the "outside" as men look; He looks upon the "heart." Don't you love how Samuel asks if he had seen all of Jesse's sons and they reluctantly said, "Well, there is one left." David went from being a shepherd to being a king-in-waiting that day! God saw a king in this shepherd boy.

 What do you think God sees in you?

_____

_____

_____

_____

_____

 **Did You Know?**

DAVID'S CARE

First Samuel 25:16 says David and his men were *"a wall . . . by night and by day"* to Nabal's men and the flocks they tended. Here is the picture of a city wall protecting all within. The care and protection David and his men provided reveal both the heart and the skill of David.

At first, Saul liked David. But, it didn't take long before Saul was jealous of him, particularly when David slew the giant Philistine in chapter 17. So David became something akin to a pariah or outlaw as far as Saul was concerned, and he was forced to live in the hills. He had a true covenant friend in Jonathan, the son of Saul, and chapter 18 describes the covenant that they entered into with one another. As a result of this covenant, Jonathan saved David's life from Saul's wrath on more than one occasion.

David had about six hundred men in his little army. It is right after Samuel's death that the subject of our lesson is mentioned in chapter 25. Here, David's men are in need of food. He hears that Nabal is in Carmel, shearing his sheep. Now, if you read 1 Samuel 25:7, 15, and verse 16 you will see how David had protected Nabal's herdsmen on many occasions. So, naturally, David thinks he has a friend in Nabal. David naturally thinks that Nabal would be willing to share. He even uses the term "your son David" in verse 8.

📖 Now, enter Nabal. Let's see what God's Word says about Nabal. Read 1 Samuel 25:2–3 and write out what you find out about Nabal.

_____

_____

_____

_____

The word Nabal means "fool." The Hebrew word used here for *"harsh"* is synonymous with the English words "hard," "mean," or "cruel." The Hebrew word used for "evil" is evil in its worse sense. It can also mean "malignant" or "malicious." It is evil that is harmful to others. This man was a fool marked by a malicious attitude.

After reading verses 5–9 write out David's request in your own words. Was this request forceful or uncalled for in any way?

_____

_____

_____

_____

_____

_____

What was Nabal's response to this peaceful request from David (verses 9–11)?

_____

_____

_____

_____

Now, what may not surface immediately is Nabal's rude, blunt, and degrading reply. In this curt reply, Nabal degrades David:

> *"Who is David? And who is the son of Jesse? There are many servants today who are each breaking away from his master. Shall I then take my bread and my water and my meat that I have slaughtered for my shearers, and give it to men whose origin I do not know?"*

News of David being the king-in-waiting was common knowledge throughout the country. Nabal knew good and well who David was. His herdsmen knew him. But Nabal was a proud and selfish man. He was not about to help David, so he masked this unwillingness by degrading David as a vagrant who has run away from his master.

📖 Read verse 11 and then write down the number of times Nabal uses the word "I" and "my."

_____

_____

Did You Know?
FESTIVE DAYS

The term *"festive day"* in 1 Samuel 25:8 was used as a term that identified a special day of celebration. The celebration was for the abundance of wool that would come from the sheep. On these occasions, much food was provided for those celebrating.

Word Study
NABAL

There are several Hebrew words that can be translated "fool," ranging from being simple or silly (*pethi*) to being wicked and crooked (*nabal*). The words include *pethi*, one who is simple, easily led astray, or silly; *kasal*, one who acts stupidly or is dull in thinking; *sakal*, one who continually strays from the good and right; *evil*, one who acts rashly without seeking wise counsel or clear understanding; and *nabal*, one who acts foolishly, even immorally or with wickedness or impiety. There is a greater degree of wicked intent in *nabal*, and the word carries with it a certain moral deficiency. The root idea of *nabal* is "to wither" or "to fall" like withered leaves, flowers, or fruit. This kind of foolishness is as withered, fallen fruit—lifeless and useless. This type of foolishness aptly describes Nabal, Abigail's husband.

📖 Well, you might guess how David, the warrior, received that reply. Read verses 12 and 13. What did David do?

_____

_____

_____

_____

How many men armed with swords did he take with him?

_____

Now, we must stop here and think. David at this point is acting just as foolishly as Nabal. David is the anointed king of Israel. He was a servant of God, and his outburst of passion was inappropriate. The fact that Nabal did not feed David's army and even insulted David and his family did not give David the right to kill Nabal. But David's temper had flared, and now he was on his way to kill Nabal.

📖 One of Nabal's men came to Abigail, Nabal's wife, and told her what had happened. Read 1 Samuel 25:14–17 and write out what you learn. Especially note how the man who reported to Abigail actually defended David and his men. Also, note how the herdsman speaks of Nabal. In what ways do this herdman's comments shed more light on Nabal's foolish character?

_____

_____

_____

_____

_____

_____

God gave Abigail the wisdom to know what to do in the instant a decision had to be made.

Well, here you see the dilemma of Abigail. She is caught between a fool, and a king who is acting like a fool. What is she to do? David has set out to kill her husband. Now what? Isn't it amazing that we have the Scriptures that tell the entire story! We can see what Abigail could not see. God also planned to use Abigail to protect His king from doing something very foolish and costly. Yet God was also using Abigail to protect her own husband from a savage death. This story is all about God! And it's also about a woman who knew God and was willing to be used by Him. God gave Abigail the wisdom to know what to do in the instant a decision had to be made. No matter how you are threatened and no matter how you are pushed to make a decision, God will answer you! He will use you to accomplish His divine plan.

 **DAY TWO**

THE DECISIVENESS OF ABIGAIL

The Scriptures do not speak of Abigail crying out to God, but in our study we will see that her whole life was lived in submission to Him. Some things are implicit when they are not immediately explicit.

Abigail, led by God, who was protecting His king, intelligently and promptly jumped into action.

📖 Look at 1 Samuel 25:32 to make certain you understand that God is directing these events. Then go back to verse 3 and write out what God's Word says about Abigail.

_____

_____

_____

In responding to the critical situation God had led her into, what does verse 18 say that she did?

_____

_____

_____

What do you think was her intent?

_____

_____

_____

_____

It seems pretty obvious that Abigail intends to disarm the anger of David with the food she brings for his men. What does she do concerning Nabal in verse 19 that shows she was acutely aware and conscious about what she was doing?

_____

_____

_____

Abigail quickly prepared food for David's men. She knew if Nabal found out that she had done this, there could be severe consequences for her servants and for herself. So she sent the servants ahead, so that they might avoid any trouble that might befall her. Though her actions may be interpreted by some as insubordination to her husband, she did this for his own good—to keep him from being slaughtered by David and his army.

Now, in verse 20, we see the most miraculous thing happen. Here comes Abigail riding her donkey, laden with foodstuffs, through the hollow of the mountains; and here comes David and his men at exactly the same time. What does this tell you about the timing of the Lord? Who is in control here?

_____

_____

_____

_____

_____

"THE HIDDEN PART OF THE MOUNTAIN"

First Samuel 25:20 records that Abigail rode her donkey *"coming down by the hidden part of the mountain."* This verse simply means that Abigail rode her donkey in a hollow between two peaks, most likely to avoid calling attention to her actions.

Verses 21 and 22 are important. David not only feels that Nabal has insulted him, but that Nabal has insulted God. Therefore, David appeals to God to enable him to bring justice on Nabal: *"May God do so to the enemies of David, and more also, if by morning I leave as much as one male of any who belong to him."*

Isn't it amazing how when we are offended we think we have the right to react, sometimes even more harshly than the one who has offended us? Sure, Nabal was wrong, but so was David. Standing between these two, one about to do a foolish thing, the other an outright fool, was Abigail.

Imagine the scene. Abigail, alone, coming down the mountain pass and running right into David who is bent on killing every male in Nabal's household by daybreak.

What proper respect does Abigail pay to the "anointed king" of Israel? According to verses 23–24, how do her actions help in disarming this potentially volatile situation? What does she do to take David's eyes off her foolish husband Nabal?

_____

_____

_____

_____

_____

_____

In our world today, most would defend themselves and let the "fool" get what he deserves. But here we have a beautiful woman who is filled with godly wisdom. She knew what a fool Nabal was and it seems that she understood how foolish David was acting. Yet she took the blame for the entire conflict and put it on herself, hoping that David would not avenge his anger on her. Abigail very decisively moved into action and, piece by piece, disarmed the otherwise unresolvable situation.

 Abigail was a godly woman! Her godly intuition helped her handle the fools that God had placed in her life. But how are you handling the "fools" God has put into your life? Is your heart in tune with God's, or are you acting foolishly like Nabal did, as evidenced in the revenge and spite that you harbor in your heart?

_____

_____

_____

_____

_____

_____

_____

Is your heart in tune with God's, or are you acting foolishly like Nabal did, as evidenced in the revenge and spite that you harbor in your heart?

The Discernment of Abigail

We have seen that God is the one who orchestrated the events of Abigail's life. Abigail was a willing vessel that God used to protect His king and also to protect her foolish husband. God always has a way. The key for us is to always be willing in our hearts to be a part of what He is doing!

Now, in verses 26 and following of 1 Samuel 25, Abigail shows a tremendous discernment of "the bigger picture" that David evidently had not seen. Verse 26 states:

> *"Now therefore, my lord, as the LORD lives, and as your soul lives, since the LORD has restrained you from shedding blood, and from avenging yourself by your own hand, now then let your enemies, and those who seek evil against my lord, be as Nabal."*

Turn to Genesis 20:6. According to this passage, what did God do to protect Abimelech the same way He protected David?

_____

_____

_____

_____

_____

_____

God came to Abimelech in a vision and prevented him from unwittingly committing adultery with Sarah, Abraham's wife. Through Abigail, God also prevented David from murdering Nabal.

Did Abigail see herself as God's instrument in protecting David?

_____

_____

_____

By the phrase *"now then let your enemies, and those who seek evil against my lord, be as Nabal,"* Abigail seems to be saying, "Let your enemies act like the fools they are, but don't you act like them because you are the king." Wow! What discernment! Nabal has enough enemies that will act accordingly.

In verse 27 she offers the food to David and to his men. In verse 28 what does she say to David about a "house"?

_____

_____

_____

This is prophetic. In 2 Samuel 7:11 in the Davidic Covenant, God says to David almost the very same words. Do you see how Abigail is being led of God to speak to David?

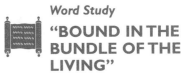

Word Study
"BOUND IN THE BUNDLE OF THE LIVING"

First Samuel 20:29 says, *"And should anyone rise up to pursue you and to seek your life, then the life of my lord shall be bound in the bundle of the living with the LORD your God."* The phrase *"bundle of the living"* comes from the custom of binding up precious and valuable items in a bundle so that they would not come to harm. Abigail acknowledged the Lord's protection and care of David as one of His valuable possessions. The Lord providentially cares for each of His children as a treasure.

When Abigail met David, she spoke about *"all the good"* God had promised concerning David and about His plans for David (1 Samuel 25:28–31). In 1 Samuel 13:14 and 15:28, God speaks of the then-yet-future rulership of Israel and the kingdom being given to another—to David—as 1 Samuel 16:1, 12–13 reveal. These things are more fully declared later in the Davidic covenant (2 Samuel 7:8–16).

In verse 29, look at the phrase *"bound in the bundle of the living with the LORD."* This phrase has to do with the promise that God binds us in His love for all eternity. We have in Him eternal life and no one can take it from us. But, in a narrow way and certainly contextual to what we are studying, it means that David will be protected by God from his enemies. God would not allow David's enemies to do to David beyond what His grace would enable him to endure. What a promise! Romans 8:38–39 tell us, *"For I am convinced that neither death, nor life, nor angels, nor principalities, nor things present, nor things to come, nor powers, nor height, nor depth, nor any other created thing, shall be able to separate us from the love of God, which is in Christ Jesus our Lord."*

Abigail was so evidently led of God. She continues in verses 30 and 31 to show extraordinary understanding that could only have come from God. She may have had times of sharing with the prophets, but whatever the case, there is no other way she could have known these things unless God had shown her.

📖 In verse 30, what event does Abigail describe that had not yet happened? Remember that Samuel has anointed David, but this is the Lord that sets him apart in front of all Israel.

_____

_____

_____

_____

In verse 31, she tells David that he will be glad one day for the mercy shown to Nabal once he becomes the ruler of Israel.

God was using this beautiful woman to tell David what He wanted David to hear. Had it not been for this meeting in the hollow of the mountains, David would have done something very foolish. As we follow God and are sensitive to His leading in our lives, we may never know how He will use us in eternal ways.

📖 What was David's response in verses 32–35? Write it all out in your own words! Especially notice how David saw the divine providence in Abigail's actions and words.

_____

_____

_____

_____

_____

_____

_____

_____

_____

_____

_____

Now, what does Abigail do in verse 36? What condition does she find Nabal in when she arrives at home? What discernment does she display with Nabal, the fool?

_____

_____

_____

_____

We must note that she kept going back home to the old drunk. Society and the world today would say, "Divorce him! You deserve better." But, she was faithful to God and to this wretch of a man. Nabal never knew what value he had in Abigail. In verses 37–38, we see an amazing thing take place. Abigail finally tells Nabal what she had done.

📖 What do the Scriptures say happens to Nabal?

_____

_____

_____

_____

_____

_____

What does this tell you about taking matters into your own hands and not allowing God to do what only He can do?

_____

_____

_____

_____

WHATEVER HAPPENED TO NABAL?

When Abigail revealed to Nabal the details of her meeting with David, he became very distraught to the point of illness. First Samuel 25:37 says that Nabal's *"heart died within him so that he became as a stone."* Apparently, Nabal suffered a stroke and was paralyzed until he died ten days later.

God had already ordered Nabal's death. Abigail was faithful to God and faithful to her husband until "death" parted them. Her willingness to honor God protected David from killing Nabal out of vengeance. Her willingness to trust God and to honor Him allowed God to put an end to her suffering at the hands of Nabal. God had it all under control. Surrender to God and to Nabal allowed Abigail to experience God's inner workings in her life.

 Write out what God is saying to you in your circumstance.

_____

_____

_____

_____

_____

So far, we have studied the **dilemma**, the **decisiveness**, and the **discernment** of Abigail. In Day Four, we will study one more aspect of Abigail.

THE DEVOTION OF ABIGAIL

Haven't you been blessed in just observing through the text how God used this precious woman to accomplish His divine purposes? The Scriptures have proven to us how Abigail was devoted to God first, then to her husband, even to a drunken husband.

As a result, God protected her and even removed the biggest obstacle in her life. There is no telling how Nabal had treated her during his periods of drunkenness. The Scripture is silent about the verbal and even possible physical abuse she lived with daily. But, God was watching over her. When David met her and heard what she had to say, it dawned on him how God had used Abigail to keep him from doing a foolish thing.

📖 Read verse 39. In your own words, write out what David realized.

_____

_____

_____

_____

_____

Isn't this a wonderful chapter in God's Word? What did David do when he discovered that Abigail was now free of Nabal? Does this help you more fully understand God's justice and God's intervention in Abigail's life?

_____

_____

_____

_____

_____

Do you think that Abigail ever thought she would be the wife of a king? She was beautiful, intelligent—but more than that—she was faithful to God. God was now honoring her in a way she would have never thought possible.

📖 What is Abigail's response to the proposal of David? (Read verses 40 and 41.)

_____

_____

_____

_____

Verse 41 says, *"And she arose and bowed with her face to the ground and said, 'Behold, your maidservant is a maid to wash the feet of my lord's servants.' "* Do you see the obvious humility of Abigail here? She was not only willing to wash his feet, but his servants' feet. She saw herself as lower than the servants.

> "All of you, clothe yourselves with humility toward one another, for GOD IS OPPOSED TO THE PROUD, BUT GIVES GRACE TO THE HUMBLE. Humble yourselves, therefore, under the mighty hand of God, that He may exalt you at the proper time, casting all your anxiety upon Him, because He cares for you."
>
> I Peter 5:5b–7

What about Nabal's riches? He was very rich. So, then, aside from the riches of her character and beauty, Abigail brought with her a fortune. David at this time had nothing and was living in caves with his men. What does this say of God's hand in the situation?

📖 Turn to 2 Samuel 3:3 and write out the name of the child who was born to Abigail and David.

_____

Abigail was devoted to God. This devotion led her to be devoted to her drunken husband as well. Her devotion to Nabal led her to protect him, and in protecting his life, she met David and spared him from doing a foolish thing. Then Abigail lived the rest of her life as the wife of the king and was devoted to him until death.

📖 Now turn to 2 Samuel 2:2–4. What is Abigail privileged to see in verse 4?

_____

_____

_____

When God looked at David, a shepherd boy, He saw a king. When God looked at Abigail, the wife of a drunk, he saw a queen. Have you ever wondered what God sees in you?

_____

_____

_____

_____

_____

FOR ME TO FOLLOW GOD

Abigail   DAY FIVE

There are many things that God must have used in this story to speak to you. Why not write down some of the things you learned from this lesson? First of all, write out what you learned about the pre-eminence that God must have in your life.

_____

_____

_____

_____

So often in my own life, I make the mistake of choosing my own way instead of God's and miss out on the divine encounters that God has orchestrated for me. When we choose to trust God, then there can be no other option. Faith allows no other choice. We can put no confidence in our flesh whatsoever. Had Abigail not totally trusted God and been willing to obey

Had Abigail not totally trusted God and been willing to obey Him, she would not have been in the right place at the right time.

Him, she would not have been in the right place at the right time. I heard a phrase a long time ago that stuck with me. It is "hinging on the unreasonable lies the unexpected." When we are willing to do what God tells us no matter how much our minds cannot fully process it, then we enter the unexpected blessings of God.

 Now, write out how different a situation is when you view it from God's perspective.

_____

_____

_____

_____

_____

Abigail would never have understood her circumstances had it not been for the divine perspective that God only gives to those who are willing to trust Him. Even though her husband was a fool, God loved him as He loves us all. God opened Abigail's eyes to see what she could not have seen if she had not been trusting Him. Paul writes in Romans 8:28, *"And we know that God causes all things to work together for good to those who love God, to those who are called according to His purpose."* Paul says, *"we know."* The word "know" is translated from the Greek word, *oida*. It means an "intuitive perception." Paul includes himself in the "we." But whom else does he describe with the word "we"? He describes those who love God and those who are called according to His purpose. The verb "love" is in the present active tense, so the verse literally says "to those **who are loving** God." Jesus said in John 14:21, *"He who has My commandments and keeps them, he it is who loves Me."* To love God is to obey God and trust Him so much that you surrender to Him and to whatever He says.

So, who is it that has the divine perception of any given situation in life? It is those who, like Abigail, trust and obey God. God then opens our eyes so that we might see the way He wants us to see. Maybe you need to bow before Christ and say yes to Him and to His Word so that He might open your eyes and give you a different perspective.

To love God is to obey God and trust Him so much that you surrender to Him and to whatever He says.

 What is going on in your life? Do you need to be more obedient to God's Word or more trusting of his ways?

_____

_____

_____

_____

_____

The beautiful thing about failure, if there can be anything beautiful in failure, is that God uses it to teach us and to draw us to Himself. Don't beat yourself up if you have not been allowing God to give you the right perspective towards your situation. Instead, confess it before God and ask Him to so direct your life that He would open your eyes to see your husband or circumstance the way He wants you to see it. Grace is a beautiful thing! It doesn't erase the consequences of doing things wrongly, but it does provide the mercy to bear up under those consequences and allows you to see from God's perspective.

Are you living with a "fool"?

_____

_____

_____

The choices a person makes can lead him to a foolish lifestyle. Thus, he is characterized as a fool. But, always remember, that it all starts with a choice. You must understand from God's perspective that God has allowed you to be in the circumstance you're in and that He has a plan to allow that "fool" to be the instrument that He uses to change you and to conform you into His image. Life and all its characters work for us, not against us.

Have you allowed God to love this "fool" through you?

_____

_____

_____

_____

Life and all its characters work for us, not against us.

When you are willing to admit that there is nothing to love in the "fool" you are living with, then you are a candidate for God to do a work through you. If you think about it, there is nothing to love in any of us but God loved us in spite of us and sent His Son to die for us. This same love is resident in you in Christ and when we realize how inefficient we are to respond properly to the "fool," then we become desperate and ask God to do what we have discovered we are totally incapable of doing. God produces a love in us for the "fools" around us that we never thought possible. The fruit of His Spirit is love (see Galatians 5:22)!

Are you consistently in the Word of God?

_____

_____

_____

_____

_____

_____

When you choose not to be in the Word of God, then there is no way you can say you are trusting God. God's Will is found in His Word! Without His Word in your heart and mind you cannot know whether or not you are walking in the Way He has for you! You must *renew your mind* with the Word of God. God's ways are not our ways! His thoughts are not our thoughts! His Word contains His ways and thoughts! He doesn't ask our opinion! We must understand His way of thinking, or the "fools" in our lives will be the targets of our anger and critical remarks rather than the object of God's love through us.

We must understand His way of thinking, or the "fools" in our lives will be the targets of our anger and critical remarks rather than the object of God's love through us.

Do you realize that receiving wisdom from God is God's way of giving you the ability to properly apply the knowledge that you have gained by your study in God's Word?

_____

_____

_____

_____

The Greek word for wisdom is *sophia*. It is a divine insight into the knowledge you have of God's Word. You are not given such insight by God until you know God's Word. When you know God's Word, God takes your knowledge and makes it into practical direction and application for how you should live. Without wisdom we are totally helpless to apply God's Word. If you are living with a "fool," then you need God's wisdom more than ever. You must start with learning God's Word.

What is God telling you to do as a result of this study in His Word?

_____

_____

_____

_____

_____

_____

Spend some time with the Lord in prayer.

Lord, thank you for the "Abigails," who are sensitive enough to You that they can be used as Your vessel to speak to Your servants and for Your service. Thank You for the encouragement I have just received from this Bible study that I can also be sensitive to Your leading in my life and be used in ways to promote your kingdom work. I love you. Amen.

_____

_____

_____

_____

_____

_____

_____

_____

_____

_____

> If you are living with a "fool," then you need God's wisdom more than ever. You must start with learning God's Word.

Notes

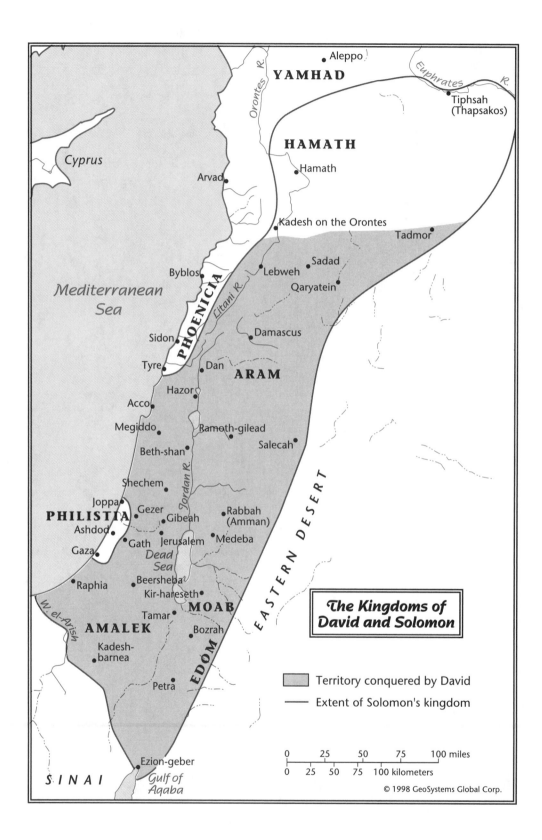

Aleppo
YAMHAD
Euphrates R.
Orontes R.
Tiphsah
(Thapsakos)
HAMATH
Hamath
Cyprus
Arvad
Kadesh on the Orontes
Tadmor
Byblos
Lebweh
Sadad
PHOENICIA
Qaryatein
Mediterranean
Sea
Litani R.
Damascus
Sidon
Tyre
Dan
Hazor
ARAM
Acco
Megiddo
Ramoth-gilead
Beth-shan
Salecah
Jordan R.
Shechem
EASTERN DESERT
Joppa
Rabbah
(Amman)
PHILISTIA
Gezer
Gibeah
Ashdod
Jerusalem
Medeba
Gath
Gaza
Dead
Sea
Raphia
Beersheba
Kir-hareseth
Tamar
MOAB
AMALEK
Bozrah
Kadesh-
barnea
EDOM
Petra
W. el-Arish

*The Kingdoms of
David and Solomon*

Territory conquered by David

Extent of Solomon's kingdom

Ezion-geber
SINAI
Gulf of
Aqaba

0   25   50   75   100 miles
0 25 50 75 100 kilometers
© 1998 GeoSystems Global Corp.

Bathsheba

FINDING FAITH AFTER FAILURE

What hope does life hold after failure? What can you do when you have failed royally (if you'll pardon my pun)? Bathsheba is one of the best-known characters of the Old Testament, but not for reasons she would want to be known. She is most remembered for the sin she shared with another well-known and highly-cherished character of the Bible, King David. Their adulterous affair rocked a nation and held consequences for decades. Yet, in the shadow of this very public sin, is a private story of hope and redemption. Though their marriage was established with sin and built on a lie, God would choose Bathsheba, of all David's wives, to continue the kingly line that would lead to Christ. She was the mother of Solomon, and all the kings of Judah descend from her all the way to the Lion of Judah, Jesus Christ. Though she stumbled in sin, she didn't stay there, and we can find hope and encouragement in her example, for whether big or small, we all stumble. We all find ourselves in need of forgiveness. We all need to learn that life can hold joy again after failure, if we will but cling to our faith. As the prophet Joel said of God's dealings with wandering Israel, *"I will give you back what you lost to the . . . locusts,"* (Joel 2:25 NLT) if we will but repent and return to Him.

BATHSHEBA

The name "Bathsheba" (or "Bath Shua") was a Canaanite name (possibly meaning "daughter of the oath") suggesting that she was not a Hebrew. Her husband, Uriah, was a Hittite (one of the Canaanite tribes). Her father served as one of David's officers, and, probably, this was how she met her husband who served in the king's army. Since both her father and her husband served King David, apparently they were Canaanite converts to Judaism.

WHERE DOES SHE FIT?

2200 B.C.	1950	1700	1450	1200	950	600	100 B.C.	A.D. 1	A.D. 100

HAGAR
2100?–2040?

Daniel
619–534?

ELIZABETH
75 B.C.?–A.D. 10?

Solomon
991–931

REBEKAH
2040?–1915?

WOMEN of the
Gospels
10 B.C.?–A.D. 50?

LEAH
1948?–1885?

Judges Rule
1385–1051

David
1041–971

LOT'S WIFE
2100?–2066

RACHEL
1943?–1899

Joshua
1495–1385

ABIGAIL
1036?–976?

Nehemiah
480?–400?

Jesus Christ
4 B.C.?–A.D. 30?

THE
SUBMISSIVE
WIFE

BATHSHEBA
1016?–961?

Isaac
2065–1885

Moses
1525–1405

Ephesians 5;
1 Peter 2—3

JEZEBEL
889?–841

Abraham
2165–1990

Jacob
2005–1858

Samuel
1105–1022

WOMAN at Well
10 B.C.?–A.D. 50?

A WRONG RELATIONSHIP

"Mankind is feeble and frail and prone to falling"
—Charles H. Spurgeon

What kind of woman was Bathsheba, the object of David's affections and affair? Today we want to get to know her, to understand more about her relationship with David and her role in his stumbling. It is a very human portrait we will paint of both, without airbrushing and glamorizing. One of the things that sets the Bible apart from every other religious book is its abject refusal to hide the flaws of its personalities. Humanity and human nature are portrayed clearly and honestly, warts and all. But that is its great strength. Often it is the failures of the heroes of faith with which we can most easily relate. Charles Spurgeon was right in his assessment of humanity: "Mankind is feeble and frail and prone to falling." Yet as we see in the life of Bathsheba, failure doesn't have to be final. On the other side of failing we can find faith. Christianity is not a religion for the perfect—for it is sinners (and only sinners) who need a savior.

📖 Read 2 Samuel 11:1–2a.

What was going on in David's life at this point?

_____
_____
_____

What was the normal activity for a king at this time of year?

_____
_____
_____

What principles do you see about how this contributed to David being vulnerable to temptation?

_____
_____
_____
_____

When did David get out of bed, and what does this tell you?

_____
_____
_____
_____

David was probably in his mid fifties when Bathsheba entered his life. The kingdom was prospering under his reign. In the spring of the year when kings normally went into battle, David decided to take a vacation. He sent the troops out without him, and stayed home. Since normally he would have been at war, staying home meant lots of idle time. Have you ever noticed that it is when you have too much time on your hands that you have the hardest time being consistent in your walk with God? David was either staying up late and sleeping in or taking an afternoon nap, for 2 Samuel 11:2 tells us "*. . . when evening came David arose from his bed.*" The Scripture text hints that this was an extremely idle, indolent time in David's life.

📖 Look at 2 Samuel 11:2b.

What did David see from the rooftop?

_____

_____

What does it say of Bathsheba that she would bathe in the middle of the city in view of the palace?

_____

_____

_____

He went for a stroll on his roof and temptation found him in the form of Bathsheba taking a bath. We are told that she was *"very beautiful in appearance."* She caught David's eye. It does not say much for her modesty that she would bathe in such a fashion. We do not know if she intended to catch David's eye, but she certainly made it easy for him. Adam Clarke asks, "How could any woman of delicacy expose herself where she could be so fully and openly viewed? Did she not know that she was at least in view of the king's terrace? Was there no design in all this?"* Scripture does not say.

*Lockyer, Herbert. *All the Women of the Bible.* ©1988 Zondervan Publishing House.

📖 Read 2 Samuel 11:3–5.

What does David do with his desire for the woman?

_____

_____

_____

What resistance do you see from Bathsheba?

_____

_____

What is the result?

_____

_____

_____

James tells us, *"When lust has conceived, it gives birth to sin; and when sin is accomplished, it brings forth death"* (James 1:15). This progression is easy to see in the sin of David and Bathsheba. David desired her, and sent messengers to get her. It is significant that he sent messengers, not soldiers. This was no act of force, and there is no hint of resistance on her part. The result was that David committed adultery with Bathsheba, and she became pregnant. We can choose our sin, but we can't choose our consequences. We have

Did You Know?

SLEEPING ON THE ROOF

The Hebrews, like others of the Middle East, rose at daybreak and often took a nap during the heat of the day, and, afterward, they lounged in the cool of the evening on their flat-roofed terraces. Since the climate of Palestine in spring is exceedingly mild and balmy, it is probable that the custom of sleeping on the housetop may have existed among the Hebrews, as is still universal in Persia and other eastern countries. (From *Jamieson, Fausset, and Brown Commentary.* Grand Rapids, MI: Wm. B. Eerdmans, 1946, p. 241)

"When lust has conceived, it gives birth to sin; and when sin is accomplished, it brings forth death."

James 1:15

no way of knowing what David and Bathsheba would have done had she not become pregnant. It seems likely however, that they would have continued their covert relationship.

📖 Now read 2 Samuel 11:6–27 and summarize in your own words all that David does to try and hide his sin.

_____

_____

_____

_____

_____

_____

David's heart must have stopped when Bathsheba spoke those three fateful words, *"I am pregnant."* First, David called Uriah in from the war in hopes that he would sleep with his wife and all would think the child of the pregnancy was his. But Uriah was far too noble a soldier to seek wifely pleasure while his comrades were in battle, so he slept at the door of the king's house. Next, David tried getting him drunk but had no success. Finally, when all else failed, David arranged for Uriah to be placed in a military setting that insured his death. As soon as Bathsheba finished the prescribed period of mourning, David took her as his wife, probably under the guise of compassion for the widow and honor for the soldier. Their sin was hidden from everyone except God.

 *Bathsheba* DAY TWO

REAPING WHAT WE SOW

S in will take your further than you thought you'd stray, keep you longer than you thought you'd stay, and cost you more than you thought you'd pay. David and Bathsheba learned these lessons the hard way. In fact, trying to hide their sin only led to more sin. Adultery got compounded into murder—all for a few minutes of illicit pleasure. Hebrews 11:25 tells us that there is a pleasure to sin, but it is a passing pleasure, and with it comes lasting pain. Paul tells us in Galatians 6:7, *"Do not be deceived, God is not mocked; for whatever a man sows, this he will also reap."* No matter how hard we try to deceive ourselves into thinking otherwise, we cannot hide our sin from God, and He will not allow us to get away with it. He has put into life a fundamental law of sowing and reaping just as certain and having just as much power over us as the law of gravity. We may escape it for a time, but sooner or later, what goes up must come down.

📖 Read 2 Samuel 12:1–9.

Why do you think Nathan uses a parable to confront David (verses 1–4)?

_____

_____

"Do not be deceived, God is not mocked; for whatever a man sows, this he will also reap."

Galatians 6:7

What does David think of the parable (verses 5–6)?

_____

_____

_____

What all does Nathan identify as David's sins (verse 9)?

_____

_____

_____

_____

In very creative fashion, the prophet Nathan got David to look honestly at his sin and evaluate it by initially making David think he was referring to the sin of another. By doing this, Nathan helped David be objective without the need to defend himself. David rightly concluded that the guilty party of such a sin was deserving of death and must make restitution. Imagine how his countenance fell when Nathan proclaimed, _"You are the man!"_ Every one of David's sins God had revealed to Nathan. The first sin Nathan pronounced was not against Bathsheba or Uriah, but against God. David had _"despised the word of the LORD."_ Specifically, he had violated that word from God against adultery. Next, he had murdered Uriah. Notice that Nathan said, _"You have struck down Uriah. . . ."_ God did not see David's cover-up as arranging murder, but committing murder—and stealing the victim's wife! Compounding this sin even further is the fact that David allowed the swords of the Ammonites (uncircumcised enemies of God) to become accomplices in his murderous crime.

📖 Look at 2 Samuel 12:13. How does David respond when he sees his sin, and what does Nathan promise?

_____

_____

_____

When David fully understood his sin, the hiding was over. He confessed. To confess simply means to agree with God. When God showed David his sin, he responded, _"I have sinned against the LORD."_ His sin was not simply against Bathsheba or Uriah, but against God who said _"you shall not commit adultery"_ and _"you shall not murder"_ (Exodus 20:13–14; Deuteronomy 5:17–18). Nathan, knowing from God that David's repentance was genuine, announces _"The Lord also has taken away your sin; you shall not die."_ The marks of an unrepentant sinner are shown in an attempt to hide sin and blame others. The mark of one who truly is repentant is seen when that person openly confesses the sin and accepts his/her responsibility for that sin.

📖 Now read 2 Samuel 12:10–14. What consequences does Nathan prophesy will come from David and Bathsheba's sin?

_____

_____

_____

Doctrine
RESTITUTION

David prescribed rightly that the punishment for stealing another man's sheep was to restore it four-fold (Exodus 21:1). Restitution is a biblically recognized component of true repentance. In a sense, what David said was also prophetic, for the life that was taken (Uriah's) was paid for in a four-fold manner by David. Four of his sons died tragic deaths as Uriah did (the first child conceived with Bathsheba; Amnon, who was murdered by Absalom after he raped his sister; Absalom, who led a revolt against David; and Adonijah, who tried to steal the throne from Solomon).

By divine revelation Nathan knew of David's sins, and likewise, he knew of their consequences. The first consequence would be that since David used the sword to commit one of his crimes, the sword would be one of the instruments of the judgment to come upon David's family. Metaphorically, the sword of judgment would permanently linger over David's household. David himself would reap evil from his own family. David and Bathsheba's act of hidden adultery would be revealed in a public way that would be humiliating to both of them. Finally, the child conceived in sin would die. Though David was repentant and received forgiveness (verse 13), we must see that he still suffered great consequences from his sin.

📖 Read through 2 Samuel 12:15–23 and answer the questions below.

Why does David fast and pray even though he has been told the child will die?

_____

_____

_____

_____

_____

What does David do once the child dies?

_____

_____

_____

_____

Where does David say the child is (verse 23)?

_____

_____

_____

_____

THE PROPHECIES OF NATHAN

Each of the prophecies of Nathan concerning the consequences of David's sin were fulfilled:

☑ The sword never departed from David's house (war).

☑ Evil was raised against David from his own house. (Absalom, his son, tried to take the throne from him.)

☑ David's wives were taken before his eyes (also by Absalom).

☑ The child conceived in adultery died.

Even though the death of the child is prophesied, David called on the Lord to relent and show mercy. It must have been a grievous thing to see the innocent child suffer in the place of the guilty. Once the child died, David cleaned himself up and went to the house of the Lord to worship. He made one of the clearest statements in Scripture about the fate of one who dies too young to place faith in God. David says, *"I shall go to him."* In other words, he believed that the child went to heaven.

Though this passage does not speak of Bathsheba's response to the death of the child, remember, **it was also her child.** Scripture does not mention that she had any children with Uriah, so this was likely her first child. One can only imagine the anguish that must have vexed Bathsheba's spirit. You see, David and Bathsheba might have been able to pick their sin—but not their consequences. They now were reaping the consequences of death and travail that they had sown with their sins.

RETURNING TO GOD AFTER FAILURE

One of the greatest truths in Scripture is that failure doesn't have to be final. The whole panorama of Scripture illustrates over and over again that the penitent prodigal can return to their loving Father and be welcomed back into fellowship. If the story of Bathsheba and David ended with our study in Day Two, what a tragic, hopeless saga it would have been. But the story doesn't end there. Even though there were consequences to their sin, their lives held much joy and a renewed walk with God. Today we want to begin looking at the process and product of their return to the Lord.

The Bible gives us much more detail of the process of David's repentance than it does of Bathsheba's. Yet, clearly, she repented as well. We find her as the recipient of God's blessings, and we find unique affirmation to the children David had with her. We can assume that the godly example of repentance David set for us in Psalms 32 and 51 were beneficial in her life as well. It may well be that together they spent times of tearfully seeking God. Today we want to see the process Bathsheba witnessed in David and the example she followed in him.

Perhaps nowhere is David's heart for God seen more clearly than in Psalm 51. The introduction to this Psalm reads, *"A Psalm of David, when Nathan the prophet came to him, after he had gone in to Bathsheba."* As we seek to have a heart after God's heart as David did, this contrite sinner's prayer for pardon will give us a more detailed look at how a sinner can keep following God—by dealing with his/her sin. We know that Bathsheba did deal with her sin. We know David did as well as evidenced through this psalm.

📖 Read through Psalm 51. Take your time—it would even be a good idea to read it twice.

One of the marks of genuine repentance is taking full responsibility for our own choices. We see such a heart in David.

📖 Read Psalm 51:3–4. How did David view his sin?

_____

_____

_____

_____

_____

_____

_____

David took full responsibility for his sin and blamed no one else—not even Bathsheba. Even though his sin affected others, he recognized that it was God's law he had violated and that it was God he had offended. He offered no defense or excuses. An important part of repentance is agreeing with God about our sin. And as we begin to see the sin in our lives the way God sees it and repent, we will begin to see the temptations we face each day the way God sees them and learn to turn from them.

DAVID'S REIGN

David reigned over all Israel from 1011 to 971 B.C. His affair with Bathsheba happened in 980 B.C. meaning that they were married approximately eight or nine years.

📖 Look at each of the following verses in Psalm 51. What was David asking God to do in his life?

Verse 2

_____

_____

Verse 7

_____

_____

Verse 10

_____

_____

Verse 11

_____

_____

Verse 12

_____

_____

It is important to see that David was not merely asking that his sin be forgiven. In verse 2 he asked to be washed thoroughly and "cleansed." In verse 7 he requested the priestly purification of hyssop and literally says, "may You wash me." Verse 10 is most significant, for he called on God to create *"a clean heart"* in him. David was not merely looking for removal of the consequences; he wanted his heart changed to what God wanted it to be.

In verse 11, he sought the presence of God in his life, and in verse 12 he asked God to sustain in him *"a willing spirit,"* pliable to God's work in his life. David wanted a restored relationship with God, and he knew his sin was a barrier to that relationship. But he also knew that God in His abundant mercy could restore and sustain that relationship.

📖 Identify from verses 16–19 the kind of sacrifice God desires for our sin.

_____

_____

_____

_____

_____

God is not interested in religious compensation for our sins. He wants brokenness. When our hearts are made right, then and only then do our offerings and sacrifices—and our works of service—have any meaning to God.

Did You Know?
HYSSOP

Hyssop was used to dip the blood of the Passover lamb out of the basin and to place it on the lintel and doorposts of Israelite homes on the night of the first Passover in Egypt (Exodus 12:21–28). The priests in the cleansing ceremony used it for a healed leper (Leviticus 14:1–9). It was part of the mixture burned with the red heifer to create the ashes used for cleansing (Numbers 19:6), and its leafy branch was also used for sprinkling that ash mixture mixed with water for ceremonial cleansing (Numbers 19:18). David knew that hyssop spoke of cleansing.

📖 Read Micah 6:6–8. What does the Lord require of us?

_____

_____

_____

_____

We will not win God's heart with mere acts of service, but with a heart that loves what He loves (justice and kindness) and humbly seeks His presence. A heart after God's heart—that is the goal. It is this kind of heart that God desires, and only God can make this kind of heart. This is why we see David calling on God to *"create in me a clean heart."* If we are going to find hope after failure, we are going to have to find faith after failure. Following God is not an arrival where the journey is completed. It is a pursuit we keep returning to, and each time our hearts are stained with sin, we must call on God to recreate His heart in us. That is what David and Bathsheba did.

MINISTRY IN SPITE OF MISTAKES

Failure doesn't have to be final. We can find hope, faith, and even useful ministry after failure. When you think about it, every ministry is after failure, for all of us have sinned and fallen short of the glory of God. I do not mean by this that sin doesn't matter or that there are no consequences. Some sins can close the door permanently on certain ministries. But we can still walk with God, and if we do, He can still work through us in other's lives. Bathsheba and David sinned greatly—David more than Bathsheba—but God still chose to use them in His plans. We have that same potential to be used by God, even if we have failed.

Charles Colson was a success story. A noted attorney, his talents landed him the enviable position as Special Counsel to the President of the United States. He had definitely arrived! But a short time later, news of a certain "little" scandal, forever known as "Watergate" began to leak out to the press. As more and more evidence regarding "Watergate" was collected, pointing to criminal activity at the highest levels of the administration, Richard Nixon was forced to resign as President, and Charles Colson ended up in prison for his involvement in the scandal. While undergoing the humiliation of prison life, God birthed a vision in him, and upon his release, he started **Prison Fellowship International**, a Christian ministry with impact around the world. By his own testimony, it was not his greatest success that gave him his ministry, but his greatest failure. We can find faith on the other side of failure, but only if we turn from our sin to God.

📖 Read Matthew 1:1–6.

What is the purpose of this list of names?

_____

_____

_____

📖 **Doctrine**
CONFESSING SIN

The Old and the New Testaments reveal the same truths. We are to agree with God about our sin. In 1 John 1:9, we find these words: *"If we confess our sins, He is faithful and righteous to forgive us our sins and to cleanse us from all unrighteousness."* The Greek word for "confess"—*homologeo*—means "to say the same thing." We are to say the same thing about our sin as God says. He says that it is wrong. It is to be forsaken. It has been forgiven. We can experience His forgiveness and cleansing.

Who was the mother of David's son, Solomon?

_____

The Gospel of Matthew begins with a genealogy showing the line of Abraham down to David, the king, and then tracing the kingly line all the way to Jesus. Most of the names featured here are men, yet in this record we see mention of Bathsheba. Think about it. The line from Abraham to Jesus runs through Bathsheba. She was the mother of all the kings of Judah down to the Lion of Judah, Jesus Christ!

📖 Look at 2 Samuel 12:24–25 and answer the questions that follow.

When did David and Bathsheba conceive this second child?

_____

_____

What was the Lord's name for Solomon, and what does it say about God's attitude toward this second child?

_____

_____

_____

_____

_____

Although the text makes it seem like David immediately resumed sexual relations with Bathsheba, we know that physically, she would not have been able to get pregnant instantaneously. The Bible is unclear on exactly how much time passed after the death of their first child until David and Bathsheba conceived their son, Solomon, but we can assume that some degree of time had passed. It is a significant statement, in light of all that has transpired, that *"the Lord loved"* Solomon. What an affirmation this word from Nathan must have been to David and Bathsheba. The name, Jedidiah, God's name for Solomon, means "beloved of the Lord."

📖 Read 1 Kings 1:5–31.

What was Adonijah trying to do?

_____

_____

_____

_____

How does Nathan intercede?

_____

_____

_____

_____

_____

"Then David comforted his wife Bathsheba, and went in to her and lay with her; and she gave birth to a son, and he named him Solomon. Now the LORD loved him and sent word through Nathan the prophet, and he named him Jedidiah for the LORD'S sake."

2 Samuel 12:24–25

What is Bathsheba's role?

_____

_____

_____

_____

What was the outcome?

_____

_____

_____

Adonijah, the younger brother of Absalom, viewed himself as the rightful heir to the throne. As David neared death, Adonijah tried to make himself king. The prophet Nathan brought the matter to David's attention through Bathsheba, and disaster was averted. In 1 Chronicles 28:5, David states that the Lord had chosen Solomon to be king. Because of Bathsheba's intervention, Adonijah's conniving did not prosper.

God used this woman, Bathsheba in many ways. In fact, many believe she was the author of the famous passage in Proverbs 31 defining the virtuous woman. It is thought that she wrote it as advice for Solomon in finding a wife. Though her relationship with David began wrongly, she repented, and sat on the queen's throne in Israel (1 Kings 2:19). The prophet Nathan exposed her sin with David, but instead of being bitter, this was something the two became grateful for. In fact, they named one of their sons, Nathan (1 Chronicles 3:5). There were many trials in their relationship, but many joys as well. They found faith after failure, and walked with God.

FOR ME TO FOLLOW GOD

Each of us sins. There is no one perfect but Jesus. Fortunately, not all of us will have our sins exposed to an entire nation and none of our sins are recorded in Scripture for all generations. Yet if you think about it, such exposure is part of Bathsheba's ministry. The example set by Bathsheba and her husband, David, is a model for us of what to do with our own failures. It was not God's will that they should sin, but when they repented, God took their sin and produced ministry opportunities from it. Everything placed on the altar is usable to God, even our mistakes. Were it not for their stumbling, we would not have Psalm 51 in the Bible. God is able to bring beauty from ashes (see Isaiah 61:3 NKJV). I think if we could interview David and Bathsheba, they would tell us it would have been better for them had they not sinned. Yet, even today, they would be able to speak of God's goodness in their lives in spite of the consequences of their sin. Their tragic story has many application-based principles for us.

As we seek to learn from the example of David and Bathsheba, there is much we can learn from their stumble into sin on how to avoid our own freefalls into sin. Think about how both of them made it easy for each other to stumble. Think of David taking a vacation from leadership, hanging out

If we are wise, we will learn from the mistakes of David and Bathsheba.

on the rooftop with too much time on his hands. Think of the beautiful Bathsheba bathing in full view of the palace. Think of David lusting and then pursuing the woman. We do not know when he decided to commit adultery, but probably the decision was not made all at once. He may have fooled himself into thinking he would just have her over for dinner and enjoy her company. Perhaps he crossed all the "little bridges" till he ended up in bed with Bathsheba—a final step he may not have originally intended to take. Think of Bathsheba, flattered by the king's attention, not resisting his advances. Both made it easy for the other person to sin. It's possible that both overestimated their strength and underestimated the power of temptation.

📖 Look up Romans 13:14 and write down what you learn there about how to avoid falling into sin.

_____

_____

_____

_____

 Think about the first instruction that Paul mentions in this verse. How does it apply to you today?

_____

_____

_____

_____

Do you *"put on the Lord Jesus Christ"*? Perhaps a better way of asking this question would be "Have you placed Jesus Christ as Lord of your life?" To do this means to let Christ be in control of your life. It means surrender. If Jesus is in the driver's seat of your life, He will not take you down the road to sin. The first, and most important protection is to yield our lives to His control. This is not a one-time decision—it is an everyday decision. Have you put on the Lord Jesus Christ today?

_____

_____

_____

Put Yourself In Their Shoes
TWO KEYS TO AVOIDING A FALL

☑ Put on the Lord Jesus Christ.
☑ Make no provision for the flesh.

Can you think of a time when you stumbled because you weren't walking surrendered to Christ's lordship?

_____

_____

_____

_____

_____

The second instruction Paul mentions is to *"make no provision for the flesh in regard to its lusts."* In other words, "don't make it easy for you to sin." If you are a shop-a-holic, don't browse at the mall for entertainment. If you struggle with an addiction to sweets, don't keep them in your cabinet. You cannot make your life temptation proof, but you can make it more difficult for you to sin. You can raise the hurdles higher to make them more difficult to cross over. All of us know our own propensity to sin. We know what temptations we consistently give in to. Paul tells us in Romans 13:14 to make sure we aren't making it easy for ourselves to succumb in areas where we know we struggle.

 Think of your own life. What are some ways you can "make provision" for your fleshly lusts?

_____
_____
_____
_____
_____
_____
_____

What do you need to do to make it more difficult to sin in those areas?

_____
_____
_____
_____
_____
_____

Another key to Bathsheba's and David's stumble into sin was their failure to heed a key principle taught throughout Scripture and one that Paul shared with the church at Corinth: *"Flee sexual immorality"* (1 Corinthians 6:18 NKJV). Notice that Paul doesn't say, "Fight it"; he says, "Flee it." We are not strong enough to resist temptation by standing at the edge of the line, and trying not to cross over. When we find ourselves in tempting situations, we need to get out of those situations. This is exactly what Joseph did when Potiphar's wife tried to lure him into adultery (Genesis 39). She grabbed his coat, and he immediately ran away—leaving his coat in her hands. Joseph knew that it was better for him to lose his coat than to lose his testimony.

 Can you think of a time when "fleeing" kept you from sin?

_____
_____
_____
_____
_____
_____

We are called to flee immorality, not to fight it.

Can you think of a time when you didn't flee but wished you had?

_____

_____

_____

_____

_____

_____

You may be saying, "All this talk about fleeing sexual immorality sounds well and good, but it is too late for me—I've already fallen." It is true that the easiest sin to deal with is the one you don't give in to. But when we do fall, our failure doesn't have to be final. Make sure you have followed the example of Bathsheba's husband, David. Read through Psalm 51:1–12 and see the steps below in David's prayer.

Confess your sin and repent. Confessing means agreeing with God that what He says is sin really is sin. If there is not repentance in our heart, we really don't agree that it is wrong.

_____

_____

_____

_____

_____

_____

Ask God to create a clean heart in you. Don't just ask Him to take away the consequences, ask Him to take away the sin.

_____

_____

_____

_____

_____

Ask Him to renew a steadfast (faithful) spirit in you. Ask Him to give you that desire to do right.

_____

_____

_____

_____

_____

Put Yourself In Their Shoes

TRUTHFULNESS IN THE INNER MAN

God has always wanted truthfulness in the innermost part of a man or woman. The first question posed to Adam after he sinned was "Where are you?" meaning more than location. The Lord wanted Adam to admit where he was in his relationship with the Lord. Why was he hiding and covering himself with fig leaves? God asks the same question of you, "Where are you? What is true of you, today, in the inner man?" John 4 reminds us that the Father seeks those who *"shall worship* [Him] *in spirit and in truth"*—from the heart with a cleansed conscience. That also means those who are truthful in spirit. Ephesians 6 tells us the first piece of armor is the belt of truth, which implies truthfulness—an open, honest heart. God wants truthfulness in the innermost being. David and Bathsheba understood God's desire for them to be truthful in their confession.

📖 Now read Psalm 51:13 and write what David says will result from following those steps with an earnest heart.

_____

_____

_____

_____

If we are truly repentant, God is able to create in us a clean heart, and that means that we are usable to Him again. David teaches that the result of true repentance and brokenness is ministry in the lives of others. There are more who will be affected by our returning to the Lord (or not doing so) than just us. David and Bathsheba sinned greatly. But fortunately their story didn't end there. Yours doesn't have to either.

Spend some more time with the Lord in prayer right now.

Dear Lord, lead me not into temptation, but deliver me from evil. Help me to see my path as You see it. Show me any areas where I am making provision for my flesh, making it easier to sin. Help me to flee temptation instead of trying to fight it. Create a clean heart in me and give me a steadfast spirit to follow You. And let others benefit from my repentance and brokenness. Amen.

Write your own prayer of application to the Lord.

_____

_____

_____

_____

_____

_____

_____

_____

_____

_____

_____

_____

_____

_____

_____

_____

_____

_____

_____

The Kingdoms of Israel and Judah

0 10 20 30 40 miles
0 10 20 30 40 kilometers

Beirut

Sidon

PHOENICIA

Damascus

Abana R.

Mt. Hermon

Pharpar R.

ARAM

Tyre

Dan

Litani R.

Kedesh

J. Jarmuk

Hazor

Acco

Sea of Galilee

Ashtaroth

Mt. Carmel

Mt. Tabor

Yarmuk R.

Edrei

Mediterranean Sea

Kishon R.

Mt. Moreh

Megiddo

Beth-shan

Ramoth-gilead

Taanach

Mt. Gilboa

Ibleam

Jordan R.

Jabesh-gilead?

Tirzah

Samaria

Succoth?

Penuel?

Mahanaim?

Mt. Ebal

Jabbok R.

Schechem

Mt. Gerizim

Yarkon R.

Aphek

Shiloh

ISRAEL

Rabbah (Amman)

Joppa

Bethel

AMMON

Gezer

Jericho

Ashdod

Aijalon

Mt. Nebo

Heshbon

Jerusalem

Gath

Bethlehem

Medeba

Ashkelon

Mareshah

Gaza

Hebron

Dibon

Gerar

Dead Sea

Arnon R.

Raphia

JUDAH

Beersheba

MOAB

PHILISTIA

Kir-hareseth

W. el-Arish

Besor Br.

Zered Br.

WILDERNESS

Region periodically contested by Judah and Edom

Bozrah

EDOM

WILDERNESS

Kadesh-barnea

WILDERNESS

© 1999 MapQuest.com, Inc

Jezebel

THE SIN OF BEING A STUMBLING BLOCK

In Matthew 18 Jesus said that it would be better to have a heavy millstone hung around your neck and be drowned in the depth of the sea, than to cause a child to stumble. If that be the penalty for causing a child to stumble, what would one deserve who caused a whole nation to stumble? The queen behind the scenes at the lowest point in Israel's history was a woman named Jezebel. Few parents, if any, name their daughters Jezebel anymore, and for good reason. From antiquity her name has come to be associated with sin. Though her husband, Ahab, was one of the most wicked kings Israel ever knew, much of the blame can be laid at the feet of his stumbling-block wife. The sins of previous monarchies were trivial compared to the evil Israel knew with Ahab and Jezebel. Corruption became the standard. Idolatry and pagan worship became the norm. Priests and prophets were banished from the land, replaced by pagan priests on the royal payroll. Wickedness was rampant, and justice could not be found. How could things get so bad so fast? It was not that Ahab was such a strong leader into evil, but rather, that he was a weak puppet manipulated by an evil and self-serving wife. The result was a gargantuan-sized stumbling block for the people called by God's name.

JEZEBEL

In most cases a person's name in Scripture links with his or her character and experience. Jezebel is the glaring exception to this rule. Her name means "chaste, free from carnal connection." The meaning of her name could not have been further from the queen's nature and behavior.

WHERE DOES SHE FIT?

2200 B.C.	1950	1700	1450	1200	950	600	100 B.C.	A.D. 1	A.D. 100

HAGAR 2100?–2040?

REBEKAH 2040?–1915?

LEAH 1948?–1885?

LOT'S WIFE 2100?–2066

RACHEL 1943?–1899

Isaac 2065–1885

Abraham 2165–1990 Jacob 2005–1858

Joshua 1495–1385

Moses 1525–1405

Judges Rule 1385–1051

Solomon 991–931

David 1041–971

ABIGAIL 1036?–976?

BATHSHEBA 1016?–961?

Samuel 1105–1022

JEZEBEL 889?–841

Daniel 619–534?

Nehemiah 480?–400?

ELIZABETH 75 B.C.?–A.D. 10?

WOMEN of the Gospels 10 B.C.?–A.D. 50?

Jesus Christ 4 B.C.?–A.D. 30?

WOMAN at Well 10 B.C.?–A.D. 50?

THE SUBMISSIVE WIFE Ephesians 5; 1 Peter 2—3

THE PROMOTION OF FALSE RELIGION IN ISRAEL

In Matthew 18:7, Jesus warns, *"Woe to the world because of its stumbling blocks! For it is inevitable that stumbling blocks come; but woe to that man through whom the stumbling block comes!"* If anyone was deserving of woe in the Old Testament, it was the stumbling block of a wife married to evil King Ahab—Jezebel of the Sidonians. Through her a great many stumbling blocks were established in Israel, and many people stumbled over them. One of the chief ways Jezebel introduced her stumbling influence was through the promotion of the worship she brought from Sidon based on tradition instead of truth. She wanted worship, but not the accountable worship of the one true God practiced in Israel. She would have religion so long as it placed no demands on how she wanted to live. But in her mind, these meddling priests of Jehovah would have to go. Today we will look at the role Jezebel played behind the scenes in advancing the false religions of Baalism and Ashtaroth.

What kind of king was Jezebel's husband, Ahab? Evil and wicked do not seem to be strong enough adjectives to describe his perverse reign. First Kings 16:30 tells us, *"And Ahab the son of Omri did evil in the sight of the LORD more than all who were before him."* What an overwhelming statement! There were some incredibly evil kings before Ahab: Jeroboam brought false worship to Israel; Elah spent most of his reign in a drunken stupor; Omri, Ahab's father, was called the most wicked king yet. But Ahab surpassed them all. Sadly, when a leader is wicked, everyone is stained. I think it is impossible to separate the sins of Ahab's reign, from the stumbling block he married.

Some in Israel may have argued, "Ahab is evil, but he does a good job leading the country. After all, he was an effective military leader." Others might have asserted, "Maybe Ahab's personal life should not matter as long as the country is prospering." Yet it is impossible to separate a leader's performance from his character. The character and behavior of a leader set the standards for the nation. The sins of Ahab and his wife made it easy for all of Israel to take their own personal sins lightly.

Perhaps nowhere do the sins and selfishness of Ahab and Jezebel show themselves more clearly than in worship. Israel's forefathers had established the pattern of worship given to them from the Lord. From Abraham to Moses to David, God had not only defined **whom** to worship, but also **how** He was to be worshiped. But Ahab and Jezebel wanted to worship their own way. As some have pointed out, the middle letter in "sin" and the middle letter in "pride" are the same—I.

📖 Read 1 Kings 16:29–33. What three things did Ahab do to begin and set the tone of his reign?

_____

_____

_____

What clues about Ahab's reign do you see in his marriage (verse 31)?

_____

_____

_____

_____

How did his reign compare with that of previous kings (verses 30–31, 33)?

_____

_____

_____

The idea of verse 31 is that the wickedness of Jeroboam was nothing compared to the wickedness of Ahab. In hindsight we can better understand what a terrible influence his wife, Jezebel, was to him. Since her father is identified as *"Ethbaal king of the Sidonians,"* we can draw a few conclusions.

First, since Ethbaal's name includes the word "baal," we can assume that he held a lifelong observance of this pagan religion with all of its wicked practices, including infant sacrifice. Second, we know from history that the Sidonians were among the idolatrous tribes that made up the Canaanites. Remember that it was because of the sins of the Canaanites that God removed them from the land. Third, since Jezebel was the daughter of a king, most likely her marriage to Ahab was intended to form a political alliance.

📖 Now look at 1 Kings 16:34 and compare it with Joshua 6:26. What does this incident tell you about the reign of Ahab and Jezebel?

_____

_____

_____

_____

God had made it clear in Joshua's day that Jericho was never to be rebuilt. Joshua 6:26 tells us, *"Cursed before the LORD is the man who rises up and builds this city Jericho; with the loss of his first-born he shall lay its foundation, and with the loss of his youngest son he shall set up its gates."* Not only does 1 Kings 6:34 show us that God fulfilled His promise against the man who attempted to rebuild Jericho, but it is significant that the attempt occurred while Ahab and Jezebel were king and queen.

Perhaps others also had this idea of rebuilding Jericho's walls, though Scripture does not tell us if anyone had attempted it before Hiel the Bethelite tried it. But in previous reigns, the salt and light of a God-fearing nation and God-fearing kings would have likely prevented this. That Ahab allowed this blatant violation of the revealed will of God shows his personal disregard for the Lord and His dictates. Following God was unimportant to him, and one must wonder what influence his wife, a Canaanite, had in this. The wickedness of Ahab's reign is reflected not only in the fact that he allowed this to be done, but that apparently none of the people attempted to stop this sinful act either.

THE SOURCE OF JEZEBEL'S WICKEDNESS

Jezebel's father was a man named "Ethbaal" (man of Baal). According to Josephus (*Against Apion* 1.18; cf. Ant. 8.13.1–2), Ethbaal is called Ithobalus by Menander, who also says that he was a priest of Astarte, and, having put the king, Pheles, to death, assumed the scepter of Tyre and Sidon, lived sixty-eight years, and reigned thirty-two. We see here the reason Jezebel, the daughter of a priest of Astarte, was so zealous a promoter of idolatry. (From *The New Unger's Bible Dictionary.* Chicago: Moody Press, 1988, p. 680)

WHO WAS TO BLAME FOR THE DROUGHT?

Ahab blamed Elijah for the drought and resulting famine in Israel. He even sent his representatives to the surrounding nations to find Elijah, making the people swear an oath if they said that Elijah was not there (1 Kings 18:10, 17–18). A man controlled by selfishness always looks for someone to blame for his problems. In reality the drought was brought on by Israel's sins.

Perhaps no story involving Ahab and Jezebel is more familiar than the encounter with Elijah and the prophets of Baal on Mount Carmel. We look at that story more fully in our workbook, *Following God: Life Principles from the Prophets* (AMG Publishers © 1999, Barber, Rasnake, Shepherd), as we study Elijah, but there are a few significant points to highlight here. As you probably remember, the encounter at Carmel (1 Kings 18) came at the end of a three-year drought sent from the Lord. Elijah challenged the prophets of Baal to a contest: they would call to their god, and he would call to his. The god who would answer with fire is the god Israel should worship.

Of course Baal did not answer since he was a god invented by men. When it was Elijah's turn, he prayed to the one true God, Jehovah, and was answered by fire from heaven, which consumed his sacrifice. Israel repented of their Baal worship and put to death all of the prophets of Baal. Now let's look at Ahab's role in all of this.

📖 Read 1 Kings 18:41—19:2.
Make a list of everything Ahab did.

_____

_____

_____

_____

_____

_____

What would you have expected him to do that he didn't do?

_____

_____

_____

_____

_____

What does this say about his convictions about Baal worship compared to those of Jezebel?

_____

_____

_____

_____

_____

Ahab's immediate response to the encounter at Carmel is a bit surprising. He offered no rebuke to Elijah and even seems to be following his instructions. If Ahab were truly devoted to Baal, one would expect some form of grieving or even revenge. Instead there seems to be a sense of complacency. We must realize however that the people affirmed that the LORD (Jehovah) is God (Elohim). Ahab's silence was probably motivated more by fear of the people than by fear of Jehovah. This seems evident, since he immediately ran home to inform Jezebel, who then vowed revenge.

All of this seems to suggest that Ahab had no religious convictions in either direction. His worship was simply pointed in whichever direction was expedient at the time. Baal worship in Israel was probably due not to the influence of Ahab, but to the influence of the stumbling block, Jezebel, on Ahab.

THE PERSECUTION OF RIGHTEOUSNESS

Jezebel **DAY TWO**

Because Jezebel was committed to a false form of worship, she was equally committed against the worship of Jehovah. Not by Ahab's conviction, but by Jezebel's conniving and use of his position, the national religion of Israel was being stamped out. Think about that. God made Israel a nation. He gave them a land that He had taken away from the Canaanites because of their wickedness. Now His chosen people were choosing the gods of the people they dispossessed. Jezebel was at the root of the stumbling of an entire nation. As we will see today, she was zealous against those who would worship the one true God, and she did everything she could to persecute those who stood for righteousness.

📖 Read 1 Kings 18:4 and 13.
What does Jezebel do to persecute those who are righteous?

_____

_____

_____

_____

Why do you think Scripture identifies the events of 1 Kings 18 as the act of Jezebel instead of the act of Ahab, the king?

_____

_____

_____

Things were so bad in Israel that prophets (those who speak forth for God) had to be hidden in caves.

Clearly the persecution of the righteous was Jezebel's initiative, not Ahab's. Although we are given no details of when, or exactly why, apparently Jezebel attempted to kill every prophet of the Lord that she could get her hands on. Things got so bad that prophets (those who speak forth for God) had to be hidden in caves. Jezebel was not a Jew, but Ahab was. It speaks ill of him that he would allow this atrocity to take place during his reign. This shows how much Jezebel had been used as a stumbling block in his life.

📖 Look at 1 Kings 18:5–12, and 22.
What did Obadiah say that Ahab was trying to do to Elijah (verse 10)?

_____

_____

_____

_____

What would Ahab do to Obadiah for withholding information concerning Elijah's wherabouts (verse 12)?

_____

_____

_____

Elijah was the only **public** prophet left in Israel (18:22), and Ahab was trying to do everything he could to find him and kill him. He would even kill anyone who knew anything about Elijah and didn't reveal it to the king. Although Obadiah feared the Lord greatly (verse 3), he also feared Ahab, who apparently through Jezebel's influence had by this time become zealous in persecuting prophets.

📖 Read over 1 Kings 18:19. What do you learn there about Jezebel's promotion of her religion over the worship of Jehovah?

_____

_____

_____

_____

Not only did Jezebel put the prophets of the Lord to death, but she also put 450 prophets of Baal and 400 prophets of the Asherah on her personal payroll (eating at her table). It is not just that Jezebel promoted her religion over others—she promoted it while persecuting those who tried to lead the people in worship of Jehovah, the true God.

We have already looked at Ahab's response to Elijah's successful showdown with the prophets of Baal, but what did Jezebel think of this?

📖 Look at 1 Kings 19:1–4.

How did Jezebel find out what Elijah had done?

_____

_____

_____

What was her response?

_____

_____

_____

_____

What effect did this have on Elijah?

_____

_____

_____

_____

_____

"Then Jezebel sent a messenger to Elijah, saying, 'So may the gods do to me and even more, if I do not make your life as the life of one of them by tomorrow about this time.'"

1 Kings 19:2

It seems painfully obvious, from Ahab's spineless response on Mount Carmel to his quick report to Jezebel, that she was the one who wore the proverbial pants in the family. After Ahab told her all the gory details, Jezebel sent word to Elijah, vowing to kill him within twenty-four hours. Elijah stood up to Ahab and the pagan prophets, but he ran for his life from the threat of Jezebel. His fear of her placed him in a despondent, near-suicidal state that seems out of character for Elijah. The fact that Elijah feared Jezebel more than he feared Ahab tells us one thing: Jezebel was a powerful force of persecution, not only tempting the weak away from worshiping Jehovah, but also frightening the strong from taking a stand. Truly she was a stumbling block in Israel.

PAMPERING HER HUSBAND'S FLESHLY DESIRES

One of the greatest reflections of King David's heart was his view of his possessions (and of the things he did not possess). When Saul possessed the throne after he had been rejected as king, David refused to take it by force, but waited on the Lord to give it to him. When Ornan the Jebusite offered to give David the threshing floor where Abraham had sacrificed Isaac, he refused to take it without payment, being unwilling to worship God with that which cost him nothing. When his mighty men were moved by his longing to drink from the well in Jerusalem and risked their lives to fetch water for him, instead of guzzling it down, he poured it out as an offering to the Lord in recognition of their sacrifice. When preparations were being made to build the Temple, it was David who took the lead, starting the project with a gift of one hundred thousand talents of gold and one million talents of silver as well as immeasurable quantities of bronze and iron, timber and stone (1 Chronicles 22:14). Then in addition, he gave a second offering of three thousand talents of gold and seven thousand talents of silver (1 Chronicles 29:2–5).

Obviously, David was not possessed by his possessions. In his prayer for the Temple he revealed his heart: *"Who am I and who are my people that we should be able to offer as generously as this? For all things come from Thee, and from Thy hand we have given Thee"* (1 Chronicles 29:14). What a contrast this is from the example we find in Ahab! Like David, Ahab's view of possessions reflected his heart, but, oh, what a different heart was Ahab's. Today we will see how the selfish, greedy fleshly desires of Ahab are pampered by his evil, stumbling block of a wife.

📖 Read 1 Kings 21:1–4.

What do you learn there about Ahab's desires?

_____

_____

_____

_____

The selfish, greedy, fleshly desires of Ahab were pampered by his evil stumbling block of a wife.

How did he respond when he didn't get his way (verse 4)?

_____

_____

_____

Ahab looked out his window one day and decided he wanted the vineyard of his neighbor, Naboth. Ahab did nothing wrong in making a request of the land. The price he offered was a fair one. But because of the family ties to the land, Naboth was unwilling to sell. The phrase, *"the LORD forbid"* indicates that Naboth viewed selling the land as a violation of the law and disobedience to God.

Ahab went into a tailspin, throwing another pity party followed by a king-sized tantrum. Although he lived in luxury in the ivory palace he had built for himself (1 Kings 22:39), he could not be satisfied staring at something he could not have, and hid himself in his room for a royal pout, refusing even to eat. Without contentment, the selfish heart cannot be satisfied even in abundance.

📖 Read 1 Kings 21:5–16.

How did Jezebel respond to her husband's flesh?

_____

_____

_____

How did she go about getting the vineyard over which Ahab was pining?

_____

_____

_____

Did You Know?
PROPERTY RIGHTS IN ISRAEL

Naboth would not part with his land because it was *"the inheritance of* [his] *fathers"* (1 Kings 21:3) and as such was not to be sold or traded out of his tribe. Numbers 36:7–9 clearly states that land was not to be transferred from one tribe to another. Each tribe was to hold on to its inheritance. The law in Leviticus 25:23 also said the land could not be sold permanently. Naboth saw Ahab's proposal as against the Lord (*"the LORD forbid"*) and His Word, a sin against Him.

When Jezebel saw Ahab's pouting, instead of telling him how childish and selfish he was acting, she pampered his fleshly interests. She took matters into her own hands and arranged to get Naboth out of the way. Through a conspiracy with the elders of the city, she trumped up false charges of cursing God and the king and had Naboth stoned to death.

Although the elders were participants in this evil act, that does not mean they supported it. By using the royal seal on the instructions, Jezebel made the instructions a royal mandate. Disobedience to a royal mandate from the king (she did it in Ahab's name) would probably result in death. Ahab showed no regret for this action of treachery. As soon as the dirty deed was completed, he made haste to take possession of the object of his desire.

📖 Read 1 Kings 21:17–26.

What rebuke did Elijah give to Ahab (verses 19, 25–26)?

_____

_____

_____

_____

How did Ahab view this messenger from God (verse 20)?

_____

_____

_____

_____

God revealed to Elijah the wicked thing that Jezebel had helped Ahab to do and called Elijah to confront Ahab with his sin. God pronounced judgment: Ahab would die, and the dogs would lick up his blood in the same place where Naboth died. Jezebel would suffer a similar fate in Jezreel. Judgment would also come upon their descendants, most notably their sons. The judgments that were to come upon Ahab were a harsh but fitting punishment.

Ahab's heart is revealed in how he received the messenger from God. His first response was to call Elijah his "enemy." A person who has rejected righteousness hates those who are righteous. To be confronted with his sin was a good thing for Ahab, but he did not receive it as such. What a sad commentary on his wicked life is found in verses 25–26: _"Surely there was no one like Ahab who sold himself to do evil in the sight of the LORD,_ **because Jezebel his wife incited him.** _And he acted very abominably in following idols, according to all that the Amorites had done, whom the LORD cast out before the sons of Israel"_ (emphasis mine).

📖 Read the conclusion of the story in 1 Kings 21:27–29.

What was Ahab's response?

_____

_____

_____

What did the Lord do (verse 29)?

_____

_____

_____

Ahab's response here is surprising. For the first time we see evidence of repentance and humility. Instead of pouting over this bad news, he tore his clothes, put on sackcloth, and fasted—these actions were accepted signs in that day of a godly repentance. It is difficult to determine what is more amazing here, that the wicked king Ahab would ever repent, or that God would relent of His judgment because of it. Although there were still consequences in store for Ahab, Jezebel, and their children, they were delayed for the time being.

The fact that a wicked person like Ahab can repent and find mercy with the Lord is astonishing. Remember, _"there was no one like Ahab who sold himself to do evil"_ (verses 21–25). What better proof do we need to proclaim that no prodigal is beyond the reach of the Lord's loving-kindness if he is willing to humble himself. Unfortunately, there is more hope for the one who stumbles than for the one who places the stumbling block. As we will see in Day Four, the unrepentant Jezebel will not fare so well.

A person who has rejected righteousness hates those who are righteous.

It is difficult to determine what is more amazing here—that the wicked king Ahab would ever repent, or that God would postpone His judgment because of it.

THE PUNISHMENT OF HER WICKEDNESS

"*Woe to the world because of its stumbling blocks! For it is inevitable that stumbling blocks come; but woe to that man through whom the stumbling block comes!*" (Matthew 18:7). As we stated at the beginning of this lesson, if anyone was deserving of woe in the Old Testament, it was the stumbling block of a wife married to evil King Ahab—Jezebel of the Sidonians. As we will see throughout Day Four, God dealt with her in strong fashion. Because of Ahab's repentance, her judgment was delayed until after his death, but delay did not change the outcome for Jezebel.

📖 Look at 2 Kings 9:30–31.

What did Jezebel do when she heard Jehu had come to Jezreel?

_____

_____

_____

_____

What do you think this says about her attitude?

_____

_____

_____

_____

"I ALONE AM LEFT"

When Elijah said to God, "*I alone am left*" (1 Kings 19:10, 14), God made it clear that this was not true. He told him to anoint three people (one of whom was Jehu) who would be used by the Lord, and then reminded him that He had seven thousand more who had not bowed the knee to Baal.

When Jezebel heard that Jehu the newly anointed king of Israel (northern ten tribes) had arrived to administer God's wrath upon her and her descendants, she painted her eyes and adorned her head. She did this not to allure him, but to present an imposing figure and to die with the proper adornment befitting a queen. As he entered the city, she mocked him out the window, calling him Zimri (the earlier king whose reign lasted only seven days). Although Jehu is God's instrument of judgment, there is no hint of repentance or even remorse in Jezebel's posture.

📖 Read 2 Kings 9:32–33.

How does Jehu respond to Jezebel's taunts (verse 32)?

_____

_____

_____

What part does he play in her actual death (verse 33)?

_____

_____

_____

Jehu has come to execute judgment. That is what God anointed him as king to do (2 Kings 9:6–7). When Jezebel flaunts her pride, he asks, "*Who is on my side?"* In other words, "who in the court is loyal to me instead of her?" When he finds two who are loyal, he commands them to throw her out the window, and they obey. He then tramples her wounded body under the feet of his horse until he is sure she is dead.

📖 Read 2 Kings 9:34–37 and write what you learn of Jezebel's end.

_____

_____

_____

_____

After Jehu is certain that Jezebel is dead, he goes inside for a meal. Afterward, he sends people out to bury her, but just as Elijah prophesied, dogs had eaten her body, and all that was left was her skull, her feet, and her hands. There wasn't even enough left to bury.

God dealt harshly with this stumbling block to Israel. In fact, after her death, all seventy of Ahab's sons were put to death. It is a serious thing to cause another to stumble.

FOR ME TO FOLLOW GOD

Jezebel is the antithesis of one who follows God. Not only did she fail to follow, but she got in the way of others who did follow God. First Kings 16:30 tells us of her husband, *"And Ahab the son of Omri did evil in the sight of the LORD more than all who were before him."* Ahab and Jezebel's reign was ruinous for Israel, and together they became a stumbling block for an entire nation. It is doubtful anyone of similar wickedness would have any interest in a Bible study such as this one, but there are important lessons even the most godly can learn from this negative example. If we are wise, we will learn from Jezebel's mistakes and not let them become our own. Wisdom purchased from the mistakes of others is much less costly.

Jezebel was selfish and self-centered, and she promoted a worship that appealed to her flesh, even though it ran contrary to truth. Most likely, none of us have erected altars to Baal, but, to some degree, all of us from time to time allow our worship to be stained by self-centered values away from truth. For example, I have often wondered what would happen to charitable giving if we no longer got a tax deduction for it. It might make for smaller offerings in churches and smaller monetary gifts to charities, but it would surely purify motives. Now, I am not saying that it is wrong to accept a legal tax advantage, but hopefully that is not the reason we give. When we allow our worship to be stained by self-centered values, we become a stumbling block for others.

While other gods may not show up in the rituals of our religious activity that usually take place one day out of the week in church, they may lurk in our priorities and practices the rest of the week. John identifies our temptations in 1 John 2:16 as *"the lust of the flesh and the lust of the eyes and the boastful*

If we are wise, we will learn from Jezebel's mistakes and not let them become our own. Wisdom purchased from the mistakes of others is much less costly.

pride of life." The lust of the flesh would include gods of a sensual nature such as sex and food. The lust of the eyes points toward our possessions as idols—a lust for material things such as cars, boats, houses, etc. Even these things can become our gods if we worship and serve them. The boastful pride of life speaks for itself—it is the enthronement of self above God, the lust for accomplishments and awards to tell us how great we are compared to others.

While all of us are tempted in each of these areas from time to time, one of the three major temptations likely plagues us more than the other two. As you look honestly at your own life, rate these temptations as to how difficult each one is for you (with "1" being the hardest to resist).

___ The lust of the flesh
___ The lust of the eyes
___ The boastful pride of life

Realize that self is at the root of each of these major temptations. Paul warned Timothy that in the last days people *"will be lovers of self, lovers of money. . . . lovers of pleasure rather than lovers of God"* (2 Timothy 3:2–4). How do you think God views such an idolatrous life?

We have identified Jezebel as a stumbling block. Matthew 18:7 makes an interesting statement about those who cause people to stumble. Jesus says, *". . . it is inevitable that stumbling blocks come."* In other words, they will be there in all our lives. The question for you and me is not **IF** we will encounter stumbling blocks, but what we will do **WHEN** we encounter them. Ahab and Israel didn't have to stumble through the influence of Jezebel.

📖 How can we "stumble proof" our lives? What can we do to guard against the Jezebel's who must inevitably come our way? One of the most important things we can do is what we are doing right now. Look at the verses below and write what they say will keep us from stumbling.

Psalm 119:165

_____

_____

_____

Proverbs 3:23 (see context in verses 13–23)

_____

_____

_____

Proverbs 4:12 (see context in verses 1–12)

_____

_____

_____

_____

The question for you and me is not IF we will encounter stumbling blocks, but what we will do WHEN we encounter them.

The single greatest defense against stumbling blocks in our lives is truth. What we are doing right now—Bible study—is what we need to do. David tells us in Psalm 119:165 that nothing will cause those who love the Word of God to stumble. David's son, Solomon, adds to this advice in Proverbs 3:13, 23, where he counsels us to *"[find] wisdom . . . gain understanding,"* for only then will you *"walk in your way securely, and your foot will not stumble."* He continues this theme of truth overpowering stumbling blocks in Proverbs 4. The result of a wisdom-filled life is that *"you will not stumble"* (Proverbs 4:12). The study of God's word fills us with the wisdom needed to avoid the stumbling blocks that will inevitably come. That is why what we are doing in a study such as this is so important.

Proverbs 4:12 also moves into some very practical applications that wisdom ought to produce. Verse 13 adds, *"Take hold of instruction."* This goes beyond just studying the Bible—it requires meditation and application. Simply knowing truth does not bring blessing, but applying it surely does. As you have seen, in this character-study book and perhaps the other books in this series, one entire day of homework in each of the twelve lessons (Day Five) is devoted to application. We must take this application time seriously and determine not to skim over these Day Five sections so we can receive the full benefit that God intends for us.

 Think through this lesson and write down two or three "instructions" of which you need to take hold.

_____

_____

_____

_____

_____

_____

Proverbs 4:14–15 takes us one step further. Not only must we "take hold" of the instruction God brings to us, but there is also something we must not do. *"Do not enter the path of the wicked,"* Solomon warns, *"And do not proceed in the way of evil men. Avoid it, do not pass by it; Turn away from it and pass on."* Using the wisdom we glean from our pursuit of truth, we must make choices to avoid the paths of the wicked.

 Think honestly about what avoiding "the paths of the wicked" means in your life. Look at the ideas below, and check any areas that you need to avoid.

Are you reading any magazines or other literature that are paths you need to avoid? Maybe the entire magazine or book isn't bad, yet parts of it cause you to stumble. Be specific! In other words, identify which magazines and which types of books cause you to stumble.

_____

_____

_____

_____

"Those who love Thy law have great peace, and nothing causes them to stumble."

Psalm 119:165

What about movies? Have you ever been in a cinema and watched a film that you knew you should have gotten up and walked away from, because once you became wrapped into the film's plot, you realized it contained paths leading to wickedness? I am not one to crusade against watching movies, but I cannot count the number of times my wife and I have walked out of what we thought would be a good movie because we realized that the path you had to follow to get to the main story line wasn't worth it. Can you think of any times when you did this, or wish you had? This question can be applied to watching home videos as well.

_____

_____

_____

_____

_____

_____

What about television? Are there any TV shows you watch on a regular basis that are paths you should be avoiding?

_____

_____

_____

_____

_____

What other "paths of the wicked" should you avoid in the future?

_____

_____

_____

_____

_____

> *"Do not enter the path of the wicked, And do not proceed in the way of evil men. Avoid it, do not pass by it; Turn away from it and pass on."*
>
> **Proverbs 4:14–15**

It is inevitable that stumbling blocks come. Life is strewn with "banana peels," and we all have opportunities to slip. God isn't going to remove the stumbling blocks until judgment day. In the mean time, He wants His children to love His Word so that nothing will cause them to stumble.

Spend some time with the Lord in prayer right now:

Dear Lord, no one is sinless but Christ. James tells us *"we all stumble in many ways."* Guard my life, Lord. Guide me in right paths and use the truth of Your Word and the convicting power of Your Spirit to keep me from wrong paths. Help me to learn what You desire from this lesson, and help me to evaluate my life honestly to avoid the stumbling blocks that are there. Amen.

Use the space provided to write your own prayer to the Lord.

_____

_____

_____

_____

_____

_____

_____

_____

_____

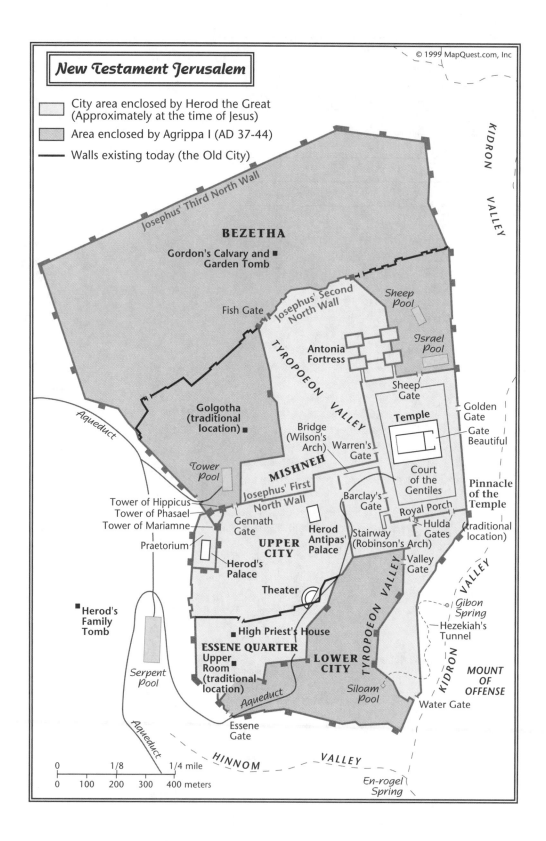

New Testament Jerusalem

City area enclosed by Herod the Great
(Approximately at the time of Jesus)

Area enclosed by Agrippa I (AD 37-44)

Walls existing today (the Old City)

© 1999 MapQuest.com, Inc

KIDRON VALLEY

Josephus' Third North Wall

BEZETHA

Gordon's Calvary and
Garden Tomb ■

Josephus' Second North Wall

Fish Gate

Sheep Pool

TYROPOEON VALLEY

Antonia
Fortress

Israel Pool

Sheep
Gate

Golgotha
(traditional
location) ■

Temple

Golden
Gate

Gate
Beautiful

Bridge
(Wilson's
Arch)

Warren's
Gate

Court
of the
Gentiles

**Pinnacle
of the
Temple**

*Tower
Pool*

MISHNEH

Barclay's
Gate

Royal Porch

(traditional
location)

*Josephus' First
North Wall*

Hulda
Gates

Tower of Hippicus

Tower of Phasael

Tower of Mariamne

Gennath
Gate

**UPPER
CITY**

**Herod
Antipas'
Palace**

Stairway
(Robinson's Arch)

Valley
Gate

VALLEY

Praetorium

Herod's
Palace

Theater

TYROPOEON VALLEY

*Gibon
Spring*

Aqueduct

■ **Herod's
Family
Tomb**

■ **High Priest's House**

*Hezekiah's
Tunnel*

ESSENE QUARTER

**LOWER
CITY**

KIDRON

*Serpent
Pool*

Upper
Room
(traditional
location)

**MOUNT
OF
OFFENSE**

Aqueduct

*Siloam
Pool*

Water Gate

Essene
Gate

Aqueduct

0		1/8		1/4 mile
0	100	200	300	400 meters

HINNOM

VALLEY

*En-rogel
Spring*

Elizabeth

SINGING THE SONGS OF SALVATION

Some days it is difficult to sing—life can be tough, circumstances can seem overwhelming, and disappointments can crowd the calendars of our lives. We find that situation when we open the Gospel of Luke. There we are introduced to Zacharias and Elizabeth, a couple who lived in Israel in the last century B.C. They were born around 70 B.C., and Israel was under Roman dominion for most of their lives. When we open the Scriptures on their lives, it is around 6 B.C., and they are living under the reign of the infamous Herod.

Zacharias and Elizabeth, like so many in Israel, longed for the day when the Messiah would be born and deliver Israel from any and all foreign enemies and establish His righteous reign. Like other Jewish families, Zacharias and Elizabeth prayed that perhaps the Messiah would be born into their home, but that could not happen, because Elizabeth was barren. That was about to change. There were some awesome surprises awaiting this godly couple; in the midst of faithfully following God they were about to be swept into the flow of the river bringing the Messiah to the world. Even more surprising were the ways God would use to bring a song to their home, and then, through their home, send that song throughout the world for all time—even into eternity.

THE SONG OF "THE FORERUNNER"

"And you, child, will be called the prophet of the Most High; For you will go on BEFORE THE LORD TO PREPARE HIS WAYS; to give to His people the knowledge of salvation by the forgiveness of their sins, because of the tender mercy of our God, with which the Sunrise from on high shall visit us, TO SHINE UPON THOSE WHO SIT IN DARKNESS AND THE SHADOW OF DEATH, to guide our feet into the way of peace."

Luke 1:76–79

WHERE DOES SHE FIT?

2200 B.C.	1950	1700	1450	1200	950	600	100 B.C.	A.D. 1	A.D. 100

HAGAR 2100?–2040?						Daniel 619–534?	ELIZABETH 75 B.C.?–A.D. 10?
REBEKAH 2040?–1915?				Solomon 991–931			WOMEN of the Gospels 10 B.C.?–A.D. 50?
LOT'S WIFE 2100?–2066	LEAH 1948?–1885?		Judges Rule 1385–1051	David 1041–971	Nehemiah 480?–400?	Jesus Christ 4 B.C.?–A.D. 30?	THE SUBMISSIVE WIFE
	RACHEL 1943?–1899	Joshua 1495–1385	ABIGAIL 1036?–976?				Ephesians 5; 1 Peter 2—3
Isaac 2065–1885		Moses 1525–1405	BATHSHEBA 1016?–961?				
Abraham 2165–1990	Jacob 2005–1858		Samuel 1105–1022	JEZEBEL 889?–841		WOMAN at Well 10 B.C.?–A.D. 50?	

In this lesson, we will read the songs surrounding the birth of John the Baptist and Jesus the Messiah. These songs picture our Savior as the light dawning, bringing the joy of a long-awaited day, the day of our salvation. As we look at the life of Elizabeth and those closest to her, we will hear those songs of salvation and experience the same joy these followers of the Messiah experienced. This couple will encourage us in following Jesus our Savior, our *"Sunrise from on high,"* as He shines His light and guides our feet into *"the way of peace"* and our hearts into the light of His song (Luke 1:78–79).

DAYS WITHOUT A SONG

When we open the Scriptures on the life of Elizabeth and her husband, Zacharias, we find them both *"advanced in years"* (Luke 1:7). What were their lives like in their early years? What kind of lives did they lead all those years? What do we find about their circumstances in the first chapter of the Gospel of Luke?

First, some basic information—Zacharias and Elizabeth lived in Judea during the reign of Herod, known in history as Herod the Great, an appointee of the Roman Senate, and not a descendant of David. In fact, Herod was an Idumean (an Edomite) from the southernmost regions of Israel. He was not the king Israel wanted, nor the promised messiah-king they longed for. Herod was the heavy-hand of Rome, oppressing the land, intensifying the longing for God's true King, the Messiah.

📖 What do you discover about Zacharias and Elizabeth as they are introduced in Luke 1:5?

_____

_____

_____

Zacharias, whose name means, "the Lord has remembered," was a priest in Israel, a descendant of Aaron and part of the priestly tribe of Levi. His wife, Elizabeth, was also from that tribe (see verse 7). Her name means, "my God has remembered." The fact that Zacharias and Elizabeth were both from the line of Aaron, the priestly line, was considered an honor and a blessing. Zacharias was part of the division of Abijah, the eighth division of twenty-four divisions within the priesthood. Each division was responsible for a one-week assignment at the Temple, twice a year.

📖 How was Zacharias' and Elizabeth's relationship with God? Read Luke 1:6. What do you find there about their daily walk?

_____

_____

_____

_____

_____

Both Zacharias and Elizabeth were *"righteous in the sight of God."* They had a personal faith in God and sought to follow Him every day. They walked with God, following all His commandments and seeking to fulfill the ordinances He had given in the Law. They offered sacrifices, observed the feast days, sought to order their diet, their daily conduct, and all their relationships the way God had prescribed. Luke 1:6 says they were blameless. The word "blameless" by no means suggests they were sinless. It simply means that there was nothing in their lives to which anyone could point as being offensive to God or man based on the Law. They followed God, trusting Him, His Word, and His ways.

What noticeable facts marked their home according to Luke 1:7?

_____

_____

_____

_____

How did the fact of barrenness affect Elizabeth? What was her testimony in the midst of these years of barrenness according to the second half of Luke 1:25?

_____

_____

_____

_____

Did You Know?

ZACHARIAS AND THE PRIESTHOOD

Zacharias was a priest of the division of Abijah. In the course of Israel's history, King David divided the priesthood into twenty-four courses to distribute the workload at the Temple (1 Chronicles 23—26). The division of Abijah was the eighth division of those twenty-four divisions, each being responsible for a one-week assignment twice a year. Estimates of the number of priests serving in Zacharias' day range from eight thousand to twenty thousand. Each day's assignment in the Temple service was determined by lot, and in Luke 1 we find Zacharias chosen by lot to offer incense during the morning and evening sacrifices, a once-in-a-lifetime privilege (since there were so many priests). That day was the highpoint of his service as a priest. Concerning the age of a priest, a Levite was required to retire at age 50, but a priest could serve several more years as long as there was no ill health or physical infirmity (Numbers 8:24–26; Leviticus 21).

Along with the sterling character and commendable testimony of this couple, we find a point of potential heartache. Elizabeth was barren. They had no children, no grandchildren, and no hope of having any children. Why? They were both well *"advanced in years,"* most likely at least sixty years of age. In their day, sixty was considered the beginning of agedness, and they were likely well past that. The barrenness they faced came with the stigma of reproach in the eyes of many. In fact, Elizabeth described her barrenness as a reproach or a disgrace; there was obviously a sense of shame that hung over their lives. In spite of the fact that they were right with God, even walking blamelessly, it is probable they faced the critical comments of others from time to time. The occasional whispers, words, and opinions of a few gossipers and busybodies in the marketplace or in the neighborhood likely added to Zacharias and Elizabeth's burden of barrenness. Their days of prayer for a child slowly became days without a song.

Luke 1:8–10 shows us that even with the circumstance of having no children all these years, Zacharias and Elizabeth remained faithful in following God day by day, year by year. They were faithful to the Lord and His call on their lives. Zacharias served as a priest year after year, and Elizabeth was by his side as a faithful wife. Luke 1:8–9 informs us that Zacharias went to the Temple to serve one week out of the two weeks his division was required to serve each year, and it was during this week that he was chosen by lot to enter the Holy Place and offer incense on the golden altar. This was a worshipful offering, given every morning at 9:00 and every afternoon at 3:00 in

BARRENNESS

Consider the struggle of barrenness. Sarah faced the scorn of Hagar in her barrenness and complained to Abraham about it (Genesis 16:5). Leah spoke of her *"affliction"* (Genesis 29:32). Rachel told Jacob, *"Give me children, or else I die"* (Genesis 30:1). Hannah wept often over her condition. She was *"greatly distressed"* and *"oppressed in spirit"* (1 Samuel 1:5–18). Childlessness was sometimes the judgment of God on a couple (Leviticus 20:20–21), though this was not the case with Elizabeth. Elizabeth still struggled, calling her barrenness a *"disgrace"* or a *"reproach* [KJV]*"* (Luke 1:25).

THE WAITING GAME

Alfred Edersheim, commenting on the waiting of Zacharias and Elizabeth, stated, "They had waited together these many years, till in the evening of life the flower of hope had closed its fragrant cup; and still the two sat together in the twilight, content to wait in loneliness, till night would close around them." (*Life and Times of Jesus the Messiah*, Book One, p. 137. Eerdmans, 1971) But that was not the end of the story. With God, waiting is weaving, weaving the full, beautiful tapestry of His will.

conjunction with the offering of the lamb as a burnt offering. As Zacharias prayed and offered this symbolic incense of prayer, God was about to reveal Himself and His will in some very unique ways.

We read in Luke 1:11–13 that as Zacharias was offering the incense, the angel Gabriel suddenly stood before him beside the golden altar. Zacharias, filled with fear, heard the angel say, *"Do not be afraid, Zacharias,"* then, *"for your petition has been heard."* What petition? The angel then announced the answer to his prayer (and what an answer it was!).

What did Gabriel announce in Luke 1:13? Look carefully at his words and think about their meaning.

_____

_____

The angel Gabriel confidently proclaimed to Zacharias that his prayer had been answered. The Greek word translated "prayer" or "petition" (*deēsis*) refers to a specific request. From what Gabriel said, a son was the answer to that request. When had he prayed? It appears Zacharias had prayed for a son for years but came to a point when it was assumed the answer from God was "No,"—yet God had not said "No." He had said, "Yes, but wait," and indeed He had made Zacharias and Elizabeth wait these many years—perhaps over forty years. However, on this day, Zacharias heard His "Yes, now," for Elizabeth would in fact bear a son, and they were to name him John—a name that means "The Lord/Jehovah has been gracious" or "to whom the Lord is gracious." That name conveyed the idea that this child was both a gift of God and the evident sign that God had chosen to be gracious not only to Zacharias and Elizabeth, but also to His people. The birth of this son was part of a bigger picture of the redemption God would provide in His Son, the Lord Jesus. John's birth would be a statement that God had chosen to pour out His grace upon His people.

APPLY What do you think it was like all those years without a child? Have you prayed about something only to think the answer was "No"? Are you waiting on God about something now? Remember, He cares about the smallest thing and is working all within the big picture of His redemptive plan—that includes **you**. Trust His timing and His goodness. His blessings may not come until they are almost too late, but God is never late—nor is He ever too early. He is always on time, working according to His timing that is always perfect.

_____

_____

_____

_____

_____

_____

_____

The angels' announcement was the beginning of a song for both Zacharias and Elizabeth. How would they respond? We will see in Day Two.

THE DAWNING OF THE DAYS OF SONG

We can call this event in the Temple "Gabriel's Good News— Zacharias' Struggle." It would not end with his struggle, but with a song. This was the next movement in the symphony of salvation that began before the foundation of the world. Gabriel's announcement to Zacharias that he and Elizabeth would have a son certainly surprised Zacharias. Did he understand all that the angel said? What did all this mean? Zacharias understood much of the Old Testament and the prophecies about salvation and God's kingdom, but there were some things that had not fully connected in his heart and mind. When they made connection, the song would sound forth from his heart, but at first we find a doubting future dad.

📖 Read the full statement of Gabriel in Luke 1:13–17. What would happen as a result of this birth according to verse 14?

_____

_____

_____

What would mark this son according to Luke 1:15?

_____

_____

_____

God promised that at the birth of John, Zacharias and Elizabeth would experience great joy and gladness and many would join them in their rejoicing. John's birth would be noteworthy not only because of the miraculous way God made Zacharias and Elizabeth parents, but because of an evident work in the infant son—the presence of God would be with him, even in him, in a unique way. This son would actually be filled with the Holy Spirit while still in his mother's womb. The one who would announce the coming of the Messiah, the bringer of the New Covenant, would experience one of the hallmarks of that New Covenant, the presence of God living in a person. This son would be *"great in the sight of the Lord,"* exalted as the one who would proclaim the coming of the Messiah. It appears that he was to live as a Nazirite, drinking no wine or strong drink.

What would he do? Read Luke 1:16–17 and record your insights.

_____

_____

_____

_____

John's ministry would be to call men and women to repentance turning them back to the Lord their God to follow Him in true faith and obedience. To call people in this fashion, he would minister *"in the spirit and power of Elijah,"* the prophet who thundered against Baal worship in the days of Ahab and Jezebel and sought to bring Israel back to the Lord (1 Kings

Did You Know?

? THE NAZIRITE VOW

Numbers 6:1–8 details the Nazirite vow, which included three elements for the person taking the vow: **1)** one must not drink wine, strong drink, or eat any fruit of the vine in any form, **2)** one must not cut his hair, and **3)** one must not touch a dead body. Samson (Judges 13:4–7; 16:17) and Samuel (1 Samuel 1:11) were under a Nazirite vow from birth. It is possible that John followed these same restrictions.

17–19). In addition, he would turn the hearts of the fathers back to their children—back to leading them to follow the Lord God as the one true God, to walk in all His ways, obeying His Word (Deuteronomy 6:1–25). This ministry as a forerunner was in fulfillment of the prophecies of Isaiah (40:3) and Malachi (3:1; 4:5–6). John the Baptist would also call those who were walking in disobedience to a righteous walk so that they, along with everyone else, would be ready to follow the Messiah with a whole heart.

📖 Describe the struggle of Zacharias found in Luke 1:18–22. What assurances do you find Gabriel giving concerning Zacharias, Elizabeth, and John?

_____

_____

_____

_____

_____

Zacharias could not get past the unlikelihood of Elizabeth having a child at her age. He doubted and questioned the angel: *"How shall I know this. . . ?"* The angel spoke on the authority given by God. He was Gabriel, who stands in the very presence of God; who was sent from God; whose message was good news from God. Two things were certain: first, Zacharias would have a sign, a way to know this would really happen; he would be unable to speak until John was born. The word translated "silent" (*siōpaō*) can mean to be dumb (unable to speak) **and** deaf, and it is possible that Zacharias was both deaf and dumb, since those at the Temple were making signs to him at John's birth (Luke 1:62). Secondly, the angel stated that events would take place *"in their proper time"* and that Elizabeth would bear a son to be named John. When Zacharias came out of the Temple he was unable to pronounce the expected benediction, and the people recognized that he had seen a vision of some sort.

Zacharias returned home to the hill country of Judea, possibly to the city of Hebron, an area allotted to the priests (see Joshua 21:10–11). There he doubtless tried to explain to Elizabeth the appearance and announcement of the angel, Gabriel. Since he could not speak, he probably wrote the details on a tablet like the one he would use at the Temple after John was born. Think of how he would tell Elizabeth about these things: the surprise appearance of the angel, the surprise announcement, even the surprise that this was an answer to prayer—the prayer they had prayed for many years before. Zacharias had responded with unbelief; then Gabriel gave him a "sign"—his inability to speak—and he went home realizing God was at work in a miraculous way. How did Elizabeth respond?

📖 Read Luke 1:24–25 and describe the response of Elizabeth to the message of God through the angel.

_____

_____

_____

_____

_____

It appears that Elizabeth received the news with a heart of belief rather than unbelief. She withdrew in seclusion when she discovered that she was pregnant. This was a treasured time for her as she saw in this news the evident work of God. This was a miracle. She saw the Lord dealing with her in a very loving way, revealing His grace. The Greek word translated *"looked with favor upon"* (*epeidon*) carries the idea that God looked upon Elizabeth in a focused, intense way, getting the full picture and gaining clear perception so that He could help meet the precise need He saw. God looked upon her with the intention of helping her, and Elizabeth recognized that. Seeing God act on her behalf, she gratefully acknowledged that her disgrace was taken away—forever removed by His gracious care.

APPLY **When God says, "No" to your request, He is always saying, "Yes" to His best.** (Read that sentence again.) That is what Zacharias and Elizabeth discovered. For years, God had seemingly said, "No" to their request, because He wanted to give them His Best—the birth of John the Baptist, the forerunner of the Messiah. Is God saying "No" or "Wait" to you about something? Trust Him that He is also saying "Yes" to His best in your life or in the life of someone for whom you are praying. Thank Him. Trust Him.

> *When God says, "No" to your request, He is always saying, "Yes" to His best.*

_____

_____

_____

_____

_____

_____

ELIZABETH AND MARY SHARE THE SONG

Elizabeth **DAY THREE**

L uke informs us that in Elizabeth's sixth month, God sent the angel Gabriel to Nazareth to speak to a relative of Elizabeth, a young woman named Mary. Read the account in Luke 1:26–38. Note the beauty and power of the angel's words in verses 30–33, 35. They were like a song to the ears of Mary.

📖 Look at Mary's question in Luke 1:34 and then the angel's answer in verses 35–37. What did the angel give as evidence of God's working? What does this tell you about Elizabeth and what was going on in her heart and mind?

_____

_____

_____

_____

_____

Unlike Zacharias' attitude of skepticism, Mary's response was not "I don't believe it," but "I don't understand how." Mary simply wanted to know how

this conception and birth could be possible. Gabriel assured her about God's holy design and plan. Then, as evidence, he told her about God's work in the life of Elizabeth, a woman past childbearing age and barren for so many years. Elizabeth was already in her sixth month of pregnancy, only three months away from giving birth. Then the angel revealed an eternal principle at work in Elizabeth's life, one that would also be at work in Mary's life—*"For nothing will be impossible with God."* Literally, that statement reads, "For no word will be without power [*dunamis*] with God." In both Elizabeth's and Mary's situations, God revealed His will through His messenger, Gabriel, sent from His very presence in Heaven. God declared His will in the word given by the angel, and His full power marked that word— the power to bring life and fruitfulness to the barren womb of Elizabeth and the power to bring the very Son of God, the Son of the Most High, to the virgin womb of Mary. Elizabeth was already experiencing the life-giving power of God fulfilling His Word. He had promised her a son, and, finally, she was carrying that son. In her seclusion, she had the opportunity to meditate on all this promise meant, living in awe of the wonder of the will of God and singing the song He had put in her heart.

📖 Mary immediately left Nazareth and *"went with haste"* to a city in the hill country of Judah (where Elizabeth and Zacharias lived), a three or four-day journey. What happened when Mary came into the house? Look at Luke 1:39–41, 44 and record your insights.

_____

_____

_____

_____

_____

Mary greeted Elizabeth as soon as she came into the house. When Elizabeth heard Mary's greeting, the baby John leaped for joy in Elizabeth's womb. Elizabeth became filled with the Holy Spirit and overflowed with joy. There was a song in her heart and in her response to Mary. What did she say to Mary?

📖 Read Luke 1:42–43 and restate what Elizabeth said. Be sure to make the connection of what she said in verses 42–43 with what happened in verse 41 and verse 44.

_____

_____

_____

_____

Elizabeth heard Mary's voice, and she was filled with the Holy Spirit. In response, she cried out with a loud, exuberant voice and declared the blessing of God upon Mary and upon the child to whom she would give birth. In humility, Elizabeth revealed the honor she felt that Mary would come to her, and even more so, that Mary would carry her Lord. In some way, God revealed to Elizabeth that Mary's child was the very Lord God of Israel. In Elizabeth's heart, God had connected the promise that her son John would be the forerunner who would prepare men's hearts before the Lord. For such a task John would be filled with the Holy Spirit—while in his mother's womb. Elizabeth knew that had just happened, and John expressed as much joy as he could—leaping in her womb—just as she had expressed her joy in the blessing she gave Mary. The rejoicing of the unborn infant John and the song of Elizabeth came forth in a symphony of blessing.

📖 Elizabeth proclaimed another word of blessing concerning Mary. Read Luke 1:45. What was the focus of Elizabeth's blessing? What does this tell you about Elizabeth?

_____

_____

_____

_____

Elizabeth had a believing heart about the birth of her own son. In the events in her life, she had seen the Lord deal with her barrenness, look upon her with favor, and now—give her a son. It appears she recognized in Mary a similar believing heart—Mary had heard the Word of God sent through the angel Gabriel, recognized it as the Word of God, and surrendered to that Word. She was a humble maidservant of the Lord, a bondservant ready to obey. As trusting followers of God, Elizabeth and Mary both knew that God would fulfill His will in each of their lives; each would give birth to a son in the *"proper time"* fulfilling *"what had been spoken . . . by the Lord"* (1:20, 45). There is in this meeting a sharing of a song of faith, not yet fulfilled but as good as fulfilled.

📖 How did Mary respond to Elizabeth's blessing? Read Luke 1:46–55. Think of how Elizabeth's words encouraged this response from Mary.

_____

_____

_____

_____

Mary immediately focused on the Lord and exalted Him as her God and Savior. She knew these events were not about her or about Elizabeth. They were about Jesus the Messiah and the salvation He would bring, the salvation promised by the Lord to Abraham and his descendants. At the same time, with humility and gratitude Mary recognized the mighty things God was doing for her and through her. This song of Mary is both a Spirit-directed song and a shared song, a song encouraged by the Spirit-filled blessings of Elizabeth toward Mary. Mary magnified the Lord for His mercy *"upon generation after generation toward those who fear Him."* This would certainly apply to the mercy He had shown to both Mary and Elizabeth, who were probably two generations apart. Most likely Mary was around thirteen or fourteen years of age, and Elizabeth was at least in her sixties; yet, God was doing *"mighty deeds"* in the lives of both. What an awesome song of praise that must have come from the heart of Mary that day, a song shared with Elizabeth. Their hearts overflowed with the joy of the Lord and His salvation, and their songs would overflow into the lives of so many more.

Word Study
FILLED WITH THE HOLY SPIRIT

The first chapter of Luke specifically mentions three people who were filled with the Holy Spirit: Elizabeth, her unborn infant (John), and Zacharias. It is evident that Mary gave evidence of the Spirit's filling as well (see Luke 1:15, 41, 44, 67). Joy and a song marked each one of these people. Exuberant joy and perpetual singing are just some of the indicators of the fullness of the Spirit noted in Ephesians 5:18–20. In addition, the Greek word for "leaped" used of the infant John (*skirtaō*) is used in the Greek Old Testament (Septuagint) of mountains and hills skipping like rams and lambs, a picture of unrestrained joy (Psalm 114:4).

MANY MORE SHARE THE SONG OF SALVATION

he songs were not finished then, nor will they be through all eternity. Mary stayed with Elizabeth a full three months until it was time for Elizabeth to deliver her son, John. It is possible, though definitely not certain, that Mary stayed through the birth of John—even helping with the delivery and first days before she traveled back to Nazareth. What is certain is that Elizabeth did give birth to a son. What do we learn about her from the events surrounding that miraculous birth?

📖 What first responses do you find in Luke 1:57–58?

_____

_____

_____

_____

Elizabeth's neighbors and relatives heard about the birth of her son. They came to see her and the newborn and, doubtless, to hear the story of how all this came to pass. What joy Elizabeth must have shown as she detailed the miraculous beginnings, the months of seclusion and meditation, the meaning of his birth, and her expectation in the coming Messiah. We do not know how much she shared, but enough was said for her neighbors and relatives from near and far to recognize that God *"had displayed His great mercy toward"* Elizabeth. They continually rejoiced with her.

What happened on the eighth day, the day when John would be circumcised? Look at Luke 1:59–60 and record your insights. What do you see about Elizabeth?

_____

_____

_____

_____

_____

_____

The Law instructed God's people to circumcise their newborn sons on the eighth day after birth (Leviticus 12:3). Zacharias and Elizabeth gladly obeyed the Law and came to circumcise John. This was also the time when they would announce the name of the child. The custom among the people was to name the child after one of the relatives, perhaps the father or grandfather, and the people assumed that this would be the case with this newborn son. They expected the name Zacharias to be the first choice, and that is what everyone expressed. Zacharias could not tell them the name since he had been stricken silent. As with so many other aspects of this child's birth, a surprise awaited everyone. Elizabeth emphatically stated, *"No indeed; but he shall be called John."* Here we see her faith and confidence in the word sent from God by the angel.

Word Study
THE FULLNESS OF TIME

Galatians 4:4 says, *"But when the fullness of the time came, God sent forth His Son, born of a woman, born under the Law."* That fullness of time for the birth of Jesus also meant the fullness of time for the birth of the forerunner, John. "Fullness" is a translation of *pleroma*, a Greek word that describes a vessel filled with oil or nets full of fish. The word for "time" is *chronos*, the root of the English word "chronology." It refers to <u>measured time</u> as opposed to another Greek word for time, *kairos*, which refers to a "season" or "era" of time and focuses more on an <u>opportune time</u>, when something is set to be accomplished. *Chronos* can encompass several times of *kairos*. Jesus and John came at the exact time (*chronos*) measured by the Father. Jesus affirmed more than once that within His *chronos*, His *kairos* "time" had not yet come (*kairos*—opportune time to accomplish certain things) (see Luke 1:20; John 7:6, 8). Jesus accomplished all He came to do—on time (John 17:4).

How did Zacharias respond to all that was occurring according to Luke 1:61–63?

_____

_____

_____

What happened to Zacharias after he wrote John's name on the tablet? Look at Luke 1:64.

_____

_____

_____

Did You Know?

GOD'S GIFTS TO BARREN WOMEN

God gave Isaac to Abraham and <u>Sarah</u> (Genesis 21:1–3), Reuben and other sons to Jacob and <u>Leah</u> (Genesis 29:31–32), Joseph to Jacob and <u>Rachel</u> (Genesis 30:22–24), Samuel to Elkanah and <u>Hannah</u> (1 Samuel 1—2), Samson to Manoah and <u>his wife</u> (Judges 13), and John to Zacharias and <u>Elizabeth</u> (Luke 1).

The neighbors and relatives were not persuaded by Elizabeth's bold statement, and they began to make signs to Zacharias about what this child's name should be. Zacharias then asked for a tablet and immediately wrote, **"His name is John."** He too was walking in faith, obeying the word God had commanded concerning the name of this child. *"At once"* God opened Zacharias' mouth, and he began to speak, just as the angel Gabriel had promised.

📖 When Zacharias' tongue was loosed and *"he began to speak in praise of God,"* a full song came forth. Luke 1:67–79 is the record of that song of praise. What is the wellspring of this song according to Luke 1:67?

What was Zacharias' focus in verse 68?

_____

_____

_____

_____

Zacharias *"was filled with the Holy Spirit,"* and, under the direction and inspiration of God's Spirit, began to bless and exalt *"the Lord God of Israel."* He focused on the redemption God was bringing, knowing that his son would announce the coming of the Messiah.

📖 Read the entire song (1:68–79) slowly and carefully, perhaps even out-loud. You may want to read it several times. (There are over 30 quotes or allusions to a passage in the Old Testament in this song.) Note your insights.

_____

_____

_____

_____

_____

_____

Look again at the second part of this song given in Luke 1:76–79. Picture the aged Zacharias looking at his infant son. Then, think of Elizabeth standing there, listening, looking, and pondering all that she was hearing and seeing. What elation she must have experienced! What might she have been thinking? Note your insights.

_____

_____

_____

_____

_____

Doctrine

THE PRAISES OF ZACHARIAS AND DAVID

Zacharias' song begins with the same words David used in blessing young Solomon as the new king. Solomon was the continuity of the Davidic line leading to the coming Messiah King, the Son of David (1 Kings 1:48). Zacharias spoke of the salvation that God had raised up *"in the house of David,"* referring to the coming Messiah (Luke 1:68–69).

This song is marked by the richness of the Old Testament promises, assurances Zacharias and Elizabeth had read and heard for over sixty years. The events of the last nine months had given both of them much upon which to meditate, much for which to thank God. Zacharias, no longer silent and now full of the Spirit of God, praised God for the salvation He provided through the Messiah, the seed of David. God was fulfilling His promises made to Abraham and bringing what He had revealed through the prophets. Zacharias rejoiced in God's mercy and His covenant faithfulness. God was about to work mightily through this son, John, and then accomplish salvation through His own Son, Jesus. Then, people could know and serve God *"without fear, in holiness and righteousness before Him all our days."* Zacharias' song rose with a heavenly melody as he thought of his son, the messenger of the Messiah. The salvation He would bring meant forgiveness of sin, mercy unmeasured, light in the darkness, life instead of death, and peace instead of strife. What a Savior!

Luke 1:65–66 gives us the record of what happened in the days and weeks, even months, after John's birth. What was the response of all the neighbors and those living in the area? Record your observations and insights.

_____

_____

_____

_____

Word Study

THE SON IS LIKE THE SUN AND THE STARS

The Scriptures speak of Jesus as the *"Sun of righteousness [rising] with healing in its wings"* (Malachi 4:2 NKJV), the *"Dayspring"* or *"Sunrise from on high"* (Luke 1:78), and the *"morning star"* (2 Peter 1:19; Revelation 22:16).

As a result of all God had done in and through the lives of Zacharias and Elizabeth, a holy fear came upon all the people around them—in the neighborhood, in the hill country, and beyond, among all who heard the story … and the songs. Before their watching eyes and listening ears they rehearsed these mighty deeds of God. This was no passing news item, no short-lived story. Verse 65 says, *"All these matters were being talked about,"* the verb tense signifying they *kept on* being talked about and thought about. As people heard the story, they recognized the touch of God on this child's life—*"the hand of the Lord was certainly with him."* They wondered what would become of him. What would God do?

Luke 1:80 tells us, *"the child continued to grow, and to become strong in spirit, and he lived in the deserts until the day of his public appearance to Israel."* Zacharias and Elizabeth raised John for a time. Their faith, their prayers, and the things God had taught them doubtless touched John. That, coupled with the touch of God on his life, helped him become strong in spirit. At some point John went into the deserts to live and to be taught of the Lord. There, the Lord gave him the message he would herald. At the age of thirty, he began to faithfully proclaim the coming of the Messiah, preparing hearts to receive Him. About six months later, Jesus came to John where he was baptizing at the Jordan River. The Dayspring, the Sunrise from on high, was dawning, and the songs Zacharias and Elizabeth had heard began to sound more clearly than ever.

JESUS CHRIST ON JOHN'S LEGACY

In Luke 7:28, Jesus said, *"I say to you, among those born of women, there is no one greater than John; yet he who is least in the kingdom of God is greater than he."* What an honor to John **and** to his mother, Elizabeth, for Christ to say this.

For Me to Follow God

Elizabeth **DAY FIVE**

God meant for us to walk in joy, to have a song in our hearts. We have heard the songs surrounding the lives of Zacharias and Elizabeth, songs of the salvation God provided through Jesus Christ. Those songs came from the Lord. Zacharias knew the Word of God—they had the light of the Old Testament including the many prophecies of the salvation God would bring. When God revealed His work in their lives, and they, by faith, mixed that with the Word in their hearts, a song came forth. The same is true for us. As God gives us light through His Word and we follow, we experience the song of His Spirit. When the light dawns and faith follows, the song comes. As we fill our hearts with God's Word and then obediently walk in His will, we experience the song of following God. How can we make sure we are following like He wants us to follow? Let's look at some Scriptures that point the way.

📖 Where is the first place we should go to make sure we are walking in the light? Read John 8:12 along with John 1:4 and record your observations.

_____

_____

_____

_____

_____

_____

When the light dawns and faith follows, the song comes.

Jesus declared, *"I am the light of the world."* If we want light, we must come to Jesus. He is the source of light; as a matter of fact, He **is** the light. He made it clear that if we are to walk in His light we must **follow Him** (present tense, keep following Him, listening, trusting, obeying). As we follow we can personally experience the **"light of life,"** and we *"shall not walk in the darkness."* The Greek word for "life" used in that verse is *zoe*, which refers to more than physical life. It is the kind of life Christ has to offer us: an everfruitful, fully satisfying resurrection life—eternal life. Jesus tells us that He is *"the life [zoe]"* (John 14:6). John 1:4 states, *"In Him was life [zoe], and the life was the light of men."*

Jesus promised that when one follows Him he *"shall not walk in the darkness."* *Skotia*, the Greek word for "darkness" does not just describe general darkness, but is a word that focuses on the personal consequences or fruit of darkness. As we follow Jesus day by day, we avoid the fruit of darkness and enjoy the fruit of light. That is the place of a song.

What can hinder us? What can cause us to stumble in our walk? Read 1 John 1:5–9 and record your insights.

_____

_____

_____

_____

_____

When we walk in fellowship with God who is the Light, we have all the light we need. However, we can choose to sin and step out of that fellowship of light. Sin is stepping into the darkness. When we walk in the darkness of selfishness, we cannot have fellowship with God or with anyone else. We have to come back to Him, back to a right fellowship with Him, back to walking in the Light. This does not mean that we lose our salvation or our relationship with Him. We lose the joy of that salvation. Once we come to Jesus and begin following Him as our Lord and Savior, we have an eternal relationship. However, we can lose the closeness of our fellowship. We do that by not dealing with the sin we have chosen. As soon as we sin, we need to confess it, forsake it, and replace it with what is right. Then we should thank the Lord for His forgiveness and cleansing. When we do that we are stepping back into the fellowship of light. There we experience the joy of His light, the fullness of His life, and the song of His heart.

What does Psalm 119:130 add about how we can walk in the light of the Lord?

_____

_____

_____

What helpful picture do you find in Psalm 119:105?

_____

_____

_____

_____

The Psalmist said *"the unfolding of Thy words gives light,"* picturing the symbolic opening or unrolling of a scroll so the words of Scripture can be seen, read, and clearly understood. The words of God are like lights to light the way, like a lamp for the feet shining on the path ahead. The picture in verse 105 is of an ancient eastern lamp held near the ground, giving light to the path just ahead, enough light to keep from stumbling and to guide the way step by step.

God assures us that *"the unfolding"* of His Word *"gives understanding to the simple."* As we read and hear and meditate on God's Word, He gives us understanding and wisdom so that we avoid the pitfalls of *"the simple."* There is a play on words in the Hebrew language. The word translated "simple" (*pthiy*) means "wide open" referring to someone who is open to anything that comes along, therefore easily open to folly or to a wayward path, even to walking about in the dark. When we open or unfold the words of God, we avoid being wide open to anything that comes along, any folly or foolish choices. Instead, we see clearly which way to go.

In the New Testament, we find added encouragement. Colossians 3:16 says when we let the Word of Christ dwell in us richly, we open the way for a song in our hearts and praise on our lips. The same results are seen in Ephesians 5:18–21. When we surrender to the control of God's Spirit, He gives us light for the way and puts a song in our hearts. That affects all our relationships, making them what God wants—we encourage and serve others and we walk with a song of praise and thanks to God. That is the fruit of light, the result of the salvation Jesus brings.

In Ephesians 1:18–23, Paul gives an additional thought about walking in the light. There he prays for believers to *"be enlightened,"* to have the light of understanding about the hope we have, the inheritance that awaits us, and *"the surpassing greatness of His power toward us who believe."* When we understand that the power that raised Jesus from the dead is the power of His life in us, then we can walk confident in whatever we face. For Elizabeth, He was greater than barrenness and old age and all the physical limitations that were hers. He is greater than any obstacle we might face, even death. Wherever He leads, we can follow, confident that He will give us enough light, enough strength, and a certain song.

APPLY What about you? Is there a song in your life? If not, what is holding back or stopping the song? Who is the person, or what is the event or situation or circumstance that has made you silent instead of singing, worried instead of peace-filled, fearful instead of confident? Stop and talk to the Lord about whatever you are facing. If there is a sin that you must deal with, deal with it. If you are facing a situation beyond your control, let the Lord deal with it **in His power.**

_____

_____

_____

_____

By His presence, Jesus wants to make Himself real in whatever you are facing, whatever is defeating you, whatever is silencing you. He wants to bring light to your path and a song to your heart **now**. As a matter of fact, He wants each day to start with a new song, fresh evidence of the fullness of His Spirit in your life for this day.

Remember this, yesterday's grace, peace, and power will not fit today's need. God is the God of fresh "manna" each morning, sufficient grace each moment, and enough wisdom for each mystery life brings. Like Elizabeth, you should believe Him and His Word. He will fulfill all His will and bring you through into the fullness of His salvation and the joy of His song.

Look in Psalm 119:9–11, 97–104 and record the effects of God's Word in a person's life. Compare that with Ephesians 5:1–21 and Colossians 3:12–17. What do you see about walking in the light, walking in the Spirit, and walking in God's Word?

Yesterday's grace, peace, and power will not fit today's need. God is the God of fresh "manna" each morning, providing sufficient grace for each moment and enough wisdom for each mystery life brings.

Did You Know?

SONGS OF SCRIPTURE

In addition to the songs of Gabriel, Mary, and Zacharias in Luke 1, we find many other songs in Scripture. These include the Song of Moses and Miriam (Exodus 15:1–18, 21), Moses (Deuteronomy 32:1–43), Deborah (Judges 5:1–31), Hannah (1 Samuel 2:1–10), David (2 Samuel 22:1–51), Jonah (Jonah 2:2–9), the Angels at Bethlehem (Luke 2:13–14), Simeon (Luke 2:29–32 and 34–35), in the New Song to the Lamb (Revelation 5:9–14), and the Song of Moses and Song of the Lamb (15:3–4). In addition, are the many psalms of David and others. First Kings 4:32 mentions that Solomon composed 1,005 songs. We were created to sing in fellowship with our Lord. God loves to hear his people singing His praises.

Why not spend a few moments with the Lord in prayer right now?

Lord, I praise You and exalt You as the Lord of Life, the Light of the world, and the One who brings light and a song to darkened and defeated hearts. Thank You that Your timing is always right, even when I want You to hurry up to catch up to my timing. Thank You that You do not bow to my time table, but call me to bow to You and Your timing. Thank You that when You say "No" to my request, You are really saying "Yes" to Your best in my life. May I learn to trust You as I wait on Your "best"—the best answer at the best time in the best way. Father, there are days when a song is slow in coming or missing altogether—perhaps because of sin; perhaps because I don't understand Your silence to my request; or maybe because I don't see the full picture of what You are doing. Through Your Word, give me light on the path so I can deal with any sin You see. Give me perspective to trust You at a new level of faith when I am in a time of waiting. May I encourage others to believe You and affirm them when they do, like Elizabeth affirmed Mary. Thank You for Your tender mercy, Your forgiveness, and Your readiness to guide us in the way of peace—into the place of a song. May I sing in my heart to You each day, confident in Your Word, trusting You for the way You are watching over me and for the way You are working out Your will. I love You. In Jesus' Name, Amen.

APPLY Elizabeth followed God. What have you seen in her life that has made an impact on your life? Write a prayer to the Lord or record a journal entry in the space below.

_____
_____
_____
_____
_____
_____
_____
_____
_____
_____
_____
_____
_____
_____
_____
_____
_____
_____

Notes

Palestine in the Time of Jesus

- ☐ Extent of Herod's kingdom
- ■ Herodian fortress city
- ○ Decapolis city (time of Herod)
- • Other city
- ▲ Mountain

ABILENE

Abila

ITUREA

Sidon

Abana R.

Damascus

SYRIA

▲ Mt. Hermon

Leontes R.

Caesarea-Philippi

Dharpar R.

PHOENICIA

Tyre

GAULANITIS

TRACHONITIS

Raphana

L. Hula

J. Jarmuk ▲ Hazor

GALILEE

Chorazin

Capernaum • Bethsaida

Gennesaret

Gergesa

TETRARCHY OF PHILIP

Ptolemais (Acco)

Sea of Galilee

BATANEA

Mt. Carmel ▲

Cana

Magdala

Tiberias • Hippos ○

Jarmuk R.

AURANITIS

Nazareth

▲ Mt. Tabor

Gadara ○ Abila

Mediterranean Sea

Nain

Bethany beyond Jordan

Kishon R.

Dor

Megiddo

Caesarea (Strato's Tower)

Scythopolis ○

Pella ○

Dion

Jordan R.

SAMARIA

Salim?

Gerasa ○

DECAPOLIS

Sebaste (Samaria)

▲ Mt. Ebal

Mt. Gerizim ▲ Sychar

Amathus ■

Me Jarkon

Jabbok R.

Joppa

Antipatris (Aphek)

Alexandrium

PEREA

Philadelphia (Amman)

(SEMI-INDEPENDENT MUNICIPALITY)

Jamnia

Emmaus

Cyprus ■ Jericho

Esbus (Heshbon) ■

Azotus (Ashdod)

▲ Mt. Olivet

Jerusalem Bethany

Medeba

Bethlehem

Hyrcania ■

Ashkelon

JUDEA

Herodium ■

Machaerus ■

Hebron

Gaza

Adora

Dead Sea

Arnon R.

N A B A T E A

Masada ■

IDUMEA

Arad

Beersheba

Malatha ■

Besor R.

Zered Br.

0   10   20   30 miles

0   10   20   30 kilometers

© 1999 MapQuest.com, Inc

The Woman at the Well

LIVING WATER FOR A WORSHIPING HEART

Jesus declared that *"the Son of Man has come to seek and to save that which was lost"* and assured His followers that He *"did not come to be served, but to serve, and to give His life a ransom for many"* (Luke 19:10; Matthew 20:28). He traveled about from village to village and town to town preaching the kingdom of God and calling men and women to repentance and faith (Mark 1:14–15, 38–39; Matthew 9:35). Jesus wanted people to come to Him to know the eternal life He could give (*"I came that they might have life, and might have it abundantly"*—John 10:10b). His heart reached out to people. Matthew 9:36 gives us this picture of the heart of Jesus: *"And seeing the multitudes, He felt compassion for them, because they were distressed and downcast like sheep without a shepherd."*

When we turn to the Gospel of John we see Jesus reaching out calling people to Himself and to the life He alone could give. John 3 records the encounter with the inquisitive, seeking, Jewish ruler, Nicodemus, as he sought to find some answers from this Rabbi. Nicodemus called Him *"a teacher come from God"* (John 3:2 NKJV). Jesus walked him through the truths about being born again or "born from above" by the Spirit of God. He

> ### Did You Know?
> ### SAMARIA
>
> **Samaria** encompassed the region north of Jerusalem (see map on left), an area that spanned approximately forty miles from north to south and thirty-five miles from east to west. It covered the territory allotted to the tribes of Manasseh and Ephraim (Joseph's sons). Samaria is also the name of the capital city of the northern tribes designated as Israel when Israel and Judah split in 931 B.C.

WHERE DOES SHE FIT?

2200 B.C.	1950	1700	1450	1200	950	600	100 B.C.	A.D. 1	A.D. 100

HAGAR
2100?–2040?

Daniel
619–534?

ELIZABETH
75 B.C.?–A.D. 10?

REBEKAH
2040?–1915?

Solomon
991–931

WOMEN of the
Gospels
10 B.C.?–A.D. 50?

LEAH
1948?–1885?

Judges Rule
1385–1051

David
1041–971

LOT'S WIFE
2100?–2066

RACHEL
1943?–1899

Joshua
1495–1385

ABIGAIL
1036?–976?

Nehemiah
480?–400?

Jesus Christ
4 B.C.?–A.D. 30?

THE
SUBMISSIVE
WIFE

BATHSHEBA
1016?–961?

Ephesians 5;
1 Peter 2—3

Isaac
2065–1885

Moses
1525–1405

JEZEBEL
889?–841

Abraham
2165–1990

Jacob
2005–1858

Samuel
1105–1022

WOMAN at Well
40 B.C.?–A.D. 50?

focused Nicodemus on the ways of God and how the Son of Man had come to bring eternal life. He spoke of Moses lifting the serpent in the wilderness and how the Son of Man would be lifted up in a similar way so that any who looked to Him in faith could know eternal life. This gift was from God Himself who *"gave His only begotten Son, that whoever believes in Him should not perish, but have eternal life"* (John 3:16). Jesus spoke to others of this gift of God, and this week we will see more clearly what He meant.

When we turn to the next chapter, John 4, we find Jesus having an entirely different kind of encounter. He was still reaching out in compassion, seeking to save the lost, but this time He was in Samaria. There He met a woman at Jacob's well outside the village of Sychar. We know her as the "woman at the well" or the "woman of Sychar." She was one of the women most in need of "living water" and most receptive to what Jesus said about that "water." We can learn much from Jesus and from this woman He encountered. The woman at the well can show us what it means to follow Jesus and know the gift of God's "living water" as we worship Him in spirit and in truth.

Woman at the Well

DAY ONE

Did You Know?
JACOB'S WELL

Jacob's Well was located outside the village of Sychar on the plot of ground Jacob purchased outside the city of Shechem. He bought it from Shechem's father, Hamor, for one hundred pieces of silver (see Genesis 33:19 NIV) and allotted it to his son Joseph. The bones of Joseph were buried there after the children of Israel came out of Egypt (Joshua 24:32). The well dug out of limestone is nine feet in diameter and is located at the base of Mount Gerizim (see map on p. 150). The name of the nearby village, **"Sychar,"** may be derived from the name of the ancient city of Shechem.

JESUS MEETS A WOMAN OF SAMARIA

J esus knew His mission. He was sent by the Father to fulfill the Father's will, which was to seek and save the lost and reveal the Father to them. But as Jesus carried out His Father's will, He faced opposition from the Jewish religious establishment. John 4:1 explains that when Jesus knew the Pharisees had heard about the many who were coming to Him and being baptized as His followers, He left Judea and headed north toward the Galilee region. He took the most direct route going from Judea through Samaria. After several hours, Jesus and His disciples came near to the village of Sychar, the location of the ancient city of Shechem (see map on p. 150). He stopped at a well there; the well Jacob had dug about seventeen hundred years earlier. It was "the sixth hour" (around noon according to Jewish time or six P.M. Roman time), and the disciples went into the village to buy food. Jesus, weary from the journey, sat by the well, where a woman of Samaria came to draw water. Much to her surprise, Jesus asked her for a drink of water. What is the setting for this encounter? What adventure did the Father have for His Son in Samaria?

📖 What do you find about the relationship between Jews and Samaritans from John 4:9?

_____

_____

_____

_____

_____

The relationship between Jews and Samaritans had a long history dating back to the eighth century B.C. We get some idea of the relationship when we look at the events in the book of Nehemiah. Look at one of those events and record your insights from Nehemiah 4:1–2 (around 445 B.C.).

_____

_____

_____

_____

_____

_____

_____

A quick look at history will help us understand what is going on at Jacob's Well. In 722 B.C., the Assyrians conquered and deported the Jews from northern Israel, the region known as Samaria. In their place the Assyrians colonized the land with Gentiles from many nations and many religious backgrounds (2 Kings 17:21–24, 29–41). These colonists intermarried with some of the Jews and their descendants became known as "Samaritans." The Samaritans opposed the Jewish exiles who returned from Babylonian captivity in the days of Zerubbabel, and again from Persian captivity in the days of Ezra and Nehemiah (Ezra 4:1–5, 7–23; Nehemiah 4). The Samaritans even built a rival temple on Mount Gerizim, and though it was destroyed in 128 B.C., they continued to worship on that mountain. Jews of Jesus' time looked upon Samaritans with racial and religious contempt; therefore, the hatred and rivalry between Jews and Samaritans ran deep. Most Jews avoided traveling through Samaria altogether, choosing instead to bypass this territory through Perea on the east side of the Jordan River (see map on p. 150). Jews and Samaritans usually did not talk with one another, nor was it the custom for men to say anything to passersby who happened to be women. Yet Jesus ignored both of these time-honored traditions. The woman was obviously surprised that Jesus would speak to her since Jesus was a Jewish male.

📖 Read John 4:10. What did Jesus tell her?

_____

_____

_____

_____

The conversation with the woman at Jacob's Well took a surprising turn, as Jesus directed the conversation away from the differences between Jews and Samaritans by speaking about a gift, *"the gift of God,"* and how He could give that gift. Jesus also spoke about *"living water."* What did this mean?

📖 What additional insights do you see about *"the gift of God"* in Ephesians 2:8–9?

_____

_____

_____

_____

Word Study
"THE GIFT OF GOD"

"The gift of God" spoken of in John 4:10 is translated from the Greek word, *"dōréa,"* and refers to a **free gift**, emphasizing the graciousness and generosity of the giver.

Jesus seemed to indicate that if this woman knew the gift of God and Who it was that spoke to her, her whole life would change. We find in Ephesians 2:8–9 that this gift is the gift of salvation by grace through faith. It can never come as a result of works or amount of works, so that no one receiving this gift could possibly boast before man or before God. If the woman at the well knew who Jesus was as the Giver of the gift of God, then she would ask Him and she could have this gift. He would give her *"living water,"* a picture of the salvation that only Jesus can give. The woman was puzzled about Jesus' statements concerning water, since Jesus had no instrument to draw water out of Jacob's well, and there appeared to be no other place to get water. What was He talking about?

📖 Jesus wanted the woman to know more about this offer of "living water." What did He tell her in John 4:13–14? How did she respond according to John 4:15?

_____

_____

_____

_____

_____

Jesus clearly explained that there are two kinds of water, one that quenches thirst temporarily and another that quenches "thirst" permanently. That second kind of water does not come from a well like Jacob's Well. It is a gift from Jesus Himself. It is *"living water"* that goes deep into a man or woman and in that place becomes a well of water springing up, always available, never running dry. This "living water" is eternal, and in drinking it one experiences eternal life. The woman readily agreed to get this water if she could. What would it take?

"Living water" refers to pure, running water as opposed to cistern water or some other standing water, which could be stagnant, even polluted. The people of Jesus' day recognized living water as water that came from freeflowing rains, from rivers, from springs, or from wells fed by a spring. It was refreshing, life-giving, abundant, and free—a true picture of the salvation Jesus brings.

Woman at the Well   **DAY TWO**

THE SAMARITAN WOMAN MEETS THE MESSIAH

When Jesus began talking to the woman of Sychar, He was focused on His mission to seek and to save the lost. He knew that the woman whom He met at the well was spiritually thirsty, and He was ready to guide her to the thirst-quenching *"living water"* only He could provide. How would this happen? What would the woman have to do to get this water? What would it really mean to her once she received this "water"? The woman was about to find out.

📖 Read John 4:16–18. What did Jesus ask, and then what did He reveal?

_____

_____

_____

_____

In light of the woman's desire for *"living water,"* why do you think Jesus brought up the issue of her marital status?

_____

_____

_____

Jesus asked the woman to call her husband, to which she responded, *"I have no husband."* Then Jesus revealed the truth about her life. She had had five husbands, and the man she was then living with was not her husband. He pinpointed her sin as a step toward giving her *"living water."* He pointed out her spiritual deadness so He could give her eternal life.

The woman stated her belief that Jesus must certainly be a prophet. In making that statement, she was admitting that He had spoken the truth about her. Anyone who could pinpoint her life and her sin in that way surely must be a prophet who knew God in a supernatural way.

📖 Look at John 4:19–20. What topic did the woman bring up? Why do you think she did this?

_____

_____

_____

_____

The woman began talking about the right **place** for worship. She wanted the focus moved off herself and her lifestyle onto another topic. Since Jesus had pointed to an issue of right versus wrong in her private affairs, she decided to shift the conversation to an issue beyond her situation—a right-versus wrong-debate between *"our fathers"* (the Samaritans) and where they worshiped and *"you people"* (the Jews) and where they worshiped. Jesus was much more interested in a **right heart** for worship rather than the **right place.**

📖 Jesus gave very clear directions about the right place for worship and the meaning of true worship. He also gave a personal prophecy about this woman. Record what you find in John 4:21–24?

_____

_____

_____

_____

The geographical place for worship was not an issue in Jesus' mind (Jerusalem or Mount Gerizim). The issue was and still is the place of the heart. God seeks those who worship Him *"in spirit and truth."* Jesus made a personal prophecy about this woman. He clearly stated that this woman would *"worship the Father"* but it would not matter whether she worshiped in Jerusalem or on Mount Gerizim (4:21). The focus of the heart and the condition of the heart is always God's concern. How did this issue of heart-felt worship relate to the woman to whom He was talking? What is the connection between what Jesus said about worshiping in spirit and truth and His earlier discussion about the woman's live-in boyfriend? How do her living arrangements and Christ's teaching on true worship tie in to the matter of receiving living water? We will seek answers to these questions shortly, but first let's look at a specific application point.

 APPLY How is your heart now? Is there some sin you are trying to cover up? (Like the woman at the well, do you want to change the subject when you are under conviction?) Deal with whatever the Holy Spirit has shown you. He will always lead you to the truth.

Therefore with joy you will draw water from the wells of salvation.

Isaiah 12:3 NKJV

🔍 *Did You Know?*
❓ **MOUNT GERIZIM**

Mount Gerizim is the mountain in Samaria from which the Israelites pronounced the blessing (Deuteronomy 11:29–30; 27:11–12). It stands opposite Mount Ebal, the mountain from which the curses were pronounced (Deuteronomy 11:29; 27:13; Joshua 8:30–35). Around the time of Alexander the Great, the Samaritans built a temple for the worship of God on Mount Gerizim. According to the historian Josephus, John Hyrcanus, the Maccabean, destroyed that temple in 128 B.C. Just as in Jesus' time, the current inhabitants of this region still regard Mount Gerizim to be holy. (See map on p. 150.)

Are you truly worshiping the True God?

The New Testament uses three Greek words for worship: *proskuneō, sebomai,* and *latreuō.* The word *proskuneō* literally means "to kiss the hand toward someone," carrying the idea of honoring or showing reverence with a kiss of homage. *Proskuneō* can also mean to bow, kneel, or prostrate oneself before another, emphasizing the **attitude** and **action of submission.** The word *sebomai* means "to worship and adore," emphasizing the **attitude of reverence** with the root idea being "to fall before." *Latreuō* means to wholeheartedly serve the will of the one being worshiped, not out of compulsion, but freely. The word *sebomai* emphasizes the **action of service.** John 4:24 uses *proskuneō.* Matthew 4:10; Luke 1:74; 2:37; and Romans 12:1 use *latreuō. Sebomai* is used in Mark 7:7 and Acts 16:14; 18:7, 13.

When we look at Jesus' words in John 4:10, 13–18 and 21–24, there are some very important connections. Jesus had introduced the woman to the fact that there was a *"gift of God"* to be given. Then He began showing her who He is as the Giver so that she could ask Him for that gift. When Jesus brought up the issue of the woman's lifestyle, He was revealing truth. He was seeking to get her to the truth about Himself and the truth about her life. He wanted the woman to experience the joy of the "living water" He offered, but He knew that sin had to be dealt with first. She had to be honest about her sin. To get *"living water"* from Jesus, one must first ask for it. The woman had asked for the "living water" (verse 15), but that asking must also be in line with a knowledge of who Jesus is and **how** He gives *"the gift of God"* (living water). How did this *"living water"* connect to worshiping in spirit and truth? Let's look at the woman's response to Jesus.

📖 What happened in the life of the woman at the well in John 4:25–30. What was the turning point for her?

_____

_____

_____

_____

_____

When the woman at the well first began to talk with Jesus, she did not know He was the Messiah. She did know that the Messiah would announce the truth about all things (especially the things about God and true worship). Jesus then revealed Himself as the Messiah, *"I who speak to you am He."* In the Greek language He literally said to her, "I AM" (*ego eimi*), the designation for the Lord in the Old Testament (Exodus 3:14–15). When Jesus revealed Himself to her, the connection was made in her heart. When He turned to her as Messiah, faith was born. She turned to Him, knowing somehow He could take care of her sin. She was willing to surrender to Him and His salvation. At that point, the woman lined up her life before Him as her Messiah and knew He could give her living water.

Woman at the Well DAY THREE

THE DISCIPLES LEARN A LESSON

When Jesus' disciples came from the city of Sychar with food, they saw the woman and Jesus talking with her. The disciples were quite surprised to find Jesus talking to an unknown woman. After all, what Jesus was doing was not something normally done by the men of that day, especially towards a Samaritan woman. They wondered why He did this and what it was He was seeking. Though they said nothing to Jesus, the questions were filling their minds—Why would He speak with a *woman* and more over, why would He speak with a *Samaritan* woman? Jesus had some truths they needed to understand about the Messiah and His mission. The woman, filled with the new knowledge of Jesus as Messiah, left her water pot and ran to the city to tell any who would listen about this Messiah (John 4:27–30). What would happen next?

📖 Though the disciples did not question Jesus about the woman, there were other questions occupying their minds. What was their focus according to John 4:31 and 33?

_____

_____

_____

_____

The disciples were puzzled about Jesus conversing with the woman of Samaria, yet they said nothing to Him. They immediately pleaded with Jesus to partake of the food they had purchased. *"Rabbi, eat,"* they kept on telling Him, but apparently He was not as interested in their food as they thought He should have been. More questions came to their minds, and this time they spoke them out loud, "Did someone else already bring Him something to eat? Why is He not eating? Eat, Rabbi!" (see verse 33). They did not recognize the significance of the conversation Jesus had just had with the woman or the significance of her leaving her water pot and running back to the village.

📖 Read John 4:32 and 34. What was Jesus' response to the disciples? What was His focus?

_____

_____

_____

_____

Jesus' *"food,"* that which filled Him and satisfied Him, was something the disciples did not yet understand. They did not know about it. His *"food"* was a spiritual food that satisfied beyond the physical dimension, deeper than the physical realm. His focus was on an eternally satisfying food—the will and work of His Father. That which satisfied Him like no earthly, physical food could was doing the will of His Father. That was what the Father **sent** Him to do. In doing His Father's **will** day by day, moment by moment (or meal by meal), Jesus would fully accomplish the Father's **work**. That was Jesus' focus—a focus that went far beyond the temporary bread and meat and water of everyday existence. He had just talked to the woman of Samaria about *"living water"* and eternal life; now He was talking to His disciples about "living food" and the eternal will of His Father. There was more the disciples needed to see at this very teachable moment.

📖 What word picture did Jesus use in John 4:35–38?

_____

_____

How does this word picture connect to what He previously said about His Father's will and His Father's work?

_____

_____

_____

> *"Jesus said to them, 'My food is to do the will of Him who sent Me, and to accomplish His work.'"*
>
> **John 4:34**

📖 When Jesus said, "lift up your eyes, and look on the fields . . . white for harvest," what would the disciples have seen (John 4:35, 39)?

_____

_____

_____

_____

Jesus began talking with His disciples about a harvest. Apparently, the field of Samaria had just been sown, and the first sprigs of green were barely visible. According to the calendar, harvest time was still another four months away, yet Jesus said that the fields were already *"white for harvest,"* ready for reaping.

Jesus was saying there was a spiritual *"harvest"* of "food" that could feed the disciples and Him right now. But what did He mean? How does this picture of the harvest relate to what had just happened with the woman at the well and the villagers she had gone to speak with at that very hour?

_____

_____

_____

_____

Salvation does not depend on one's location (Jerusalem, Mount Gerizim, or wherever) or on one's race (Jewish, Samaritan, or whatever) but on knowing Jesus Christ as the Living Water, as true Lord and Savior.

At about the same time Jesus was introducing the subject of the harvest, the woman of Samaria was approaching with many of the villagers of Sychar, people who knew something new and different had happened to this woman of their village. Though the disciples at first probably looked out at the fields of barely-visible sprouts, the true harvest that Jesus was referring to was the multitude of villagers—lost souls intrigued by the news of the Samaritan woman and thirsty for the "living water" that she had just received. Just as Jesus said, the fields were ripe for a soul harvest! Jesus had just spoken to the woman and revealed Himself as the Messiah, and she believed Him. She was one of the true worshipers the Father was seeking. As the True Prophet He was, Jesus had said that she would worship the Father and know His salvation, but it would not matter whether she was Jewish or Samaritan or whether she worshiped in Jerusalem or Mount Gerizim (4:21). The only thing that really mattered was whether she knew Christ as the source of *"living water."*

📖 When Jesus said, *"Already he who reaps is receiving wages, and is gathering fruit for life eternal,"* who is *"he who reaps"*? Who has already come to know life eternal (John 4:35–38)?

_____

_____

_____

_____

_____

It is evident that Jesus was the one who had already begun reaping a harvest.

The first fruit of the harvest in Samaria was this woman of Samaria, the woman at the well. Jesus began getting the disciples involved in the harvest. He wanted the disciples to rejoice with Him and come to know the satisfaction of this "food" He knew but which they did not yet understand. What would this mean for this village? How would they respond to the woman and to this "Messiah" she spoke about? How would the disciples see both the concepts of sowing and reaping? We will provide answers to all these questions in the reading for Day Four.

MEET THE NEW SAMARITAN WOMAN

What a day in Sychar! This woman, already well known in the city, came running into town and began telling everyone some amazing news. What she said and the way she said it got their attention. What happened next shows us something about the harvest Jesus talked about.

📖 Read John 4:25–30 and 39–42. What did the woman tell the villagers?

_____

_____

_____

_____

_____

What does her statement tell you about her?

_____

_____

_____

The woman ran to tell the villagers about this Jesus who *"told* [her] *all the things that* [she had] *done."* She was honest and transparent from the heart. That statement was a public admission that said in essence, "All of you know what kind of life I have lived. This man revealed the sin in my life, and He is right. You must come see Him. Surely He is the Christ." They came to see for themselves.

📖 Verse 38 is connected to verse 39 with the conjunction *"and."* What insights do you see in John 4:35–38 as they relate to verse 39?

_____

_____

_____

_____

The Father seeks those who will worship Him in spirit and truth.

The Father seeks those who will worship Him in spirit and truth. When Jesus revealed Himself as the Messiah, the woman realized the full picture that included her sin, her Savior, and her surrender to Him. When she saw Jesus for who He is, she became honest about her sin; she was going in the right direction. Jesus knew this honesty was essential if she were to worship in spirit and truth like the Father wanted.

 We too must deal with sin. We must deal with what is on the inside, for it is on the inside where the real person is. You see, God wants "real people" as His worshipers—people who surrender to Him from the heart and worship Him with everything in them. Have you honestly dealt with your sin and your surrender to Jesus? Do you know Jesus as your Lord and Savior? If you don't know Jesus as your savior, now would be a good time to read the final section of this study workbook, "How to Follow God" that begins on page 207.

📖 How did the Samaritan villagers respond to Jesus according to John 4:39–42?

_____

_____

_____

_____

When the Samaritan villagers heard the woman's testimony and saw her honesty and transparency, they knew something had changed about her. They knew this Jesus must be someone very unique. They came to see Him and Jesus revealed Himself as the Christ to them. They, too, believed in Him as their Savior, their Messiah. They, too, became worshipers of the Father and of the Lord Jesus in spirit and truth—knowing He could take care of their sin debt and change their believing, yielded hearts. The Father still seeks such as these to be His worshipers and His followers. We will see more about this in Day Five.

Have you dealt with your sin and your surrender to Jesus? Do you know Him as your Lord and Savior?

Woman at the Well 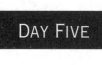 DAY FIVE

FOR ME TO FOLLOW GOD

"For God so loved the world that He gave His only begotten Son, that whoever believes in Him should not perish, but have eternal life."

John 3:16

The Father is still seeking those who will worship Him in spirit and truth, who will deal honestly about their sin and wholeheartedly surrender to Him. Jesus is still saving those who come to Him for that *"living water"* since He ever lives as the Giver of eternal life—to all who will ask in faith. Those who ask in faith find Him faithful to give the "gift of God," that eternal life, and begin them on a journey of following Him as their Savior and Lord. What does it mean to know this *"gift of God"* and to follow Him for the rest of our days?

📖 Jesus spoke to the woman at the well of the *"gift of God."* We can learn much about that "Gift" and the Giver of that Gift by looking up the verses below. As you search each Scripture passage, record what you learn about the *"gift of God."*

John 3:16–17

_____

_____

_____

Romans 3:24

_____

_____

_____

Romans 5:15–17

_____

_____

_____

Romans 6:23

_____

_____

_____

2 Corinthians 9:15

_____

_____

_____

Ephesians 2:8–10

_____

_____

_____

James 1:17

_____

_____

_____

> *"Thanks be to God for His indescribable gift!"*
>
> *2 Corinthians 9:15*

God gave His only begotten Son, the greatest gift given of all time and eternity. Through the gift of His Son, Jesus, God the Father can give us the gift of eternal life. When we receive the gift of eternal life, we are also *"being justified as a gift by His grace"* (Romans 3:24). Jesus paid the price of redemption to redeem us out of slavery to our sin, and He did so as a gift, an abounding, free gift out of abundant grace. By His giving we can receive the gift of righteousness and reign in life through Jesus. This is truly an *"indescribable gift"* (2 Corinthians 9:15) in its magnitude, in the love God demonstrates in giving it, and in the eternal effect on our lives. This combined gift of justification and eternal, abundant life can never be something we can boast about as though we did anything to merit it or earn it. We can only boast in the great love of *"our great God and Savior, Christ Jesus; who gave Himself for us that He might redeem us from every lawless deed and purify for Himself a people for His own possession, zealous for good deeds"* (Titus 2:13b–14). This gift comes from above, from the Father of lights who is ever true, never shifting in His love or His giving. How amazing He is!

We have looked at the *"gift of God."* We know that God is love and it is the nature of love to give. What further insights do the Scriptures show us about how love gives? Look up the verses below and record your insights and applications. As you read these verses, think of how God has shown **you** His love? Then look at how you have shown love to **God** and to **others**.

John 10:11, 17–18 with John 15:13–14

_____

_____

_____

_____

_____

John 13:35 with 1 John 3:11; 4:11

_____

_____

_____

_____

_____

_____

John 14:15

_____

_____

_____

_____

_____

_____

_____

Romans 5:5–10

_____

_____

_____

_____

_____

Romans 13:8

_____

_____

_____

_____

_____

" . . .our great God and Savior, Christ Jesus; who gave Himself for us, that He might redeem us from every lawless deed and purify for Himself a people for His own posses- sion, zealous for good deeds."

Titus 2:13–14

1 John 3:1

_____

_____

_____

_____

1 John 3:16–18

_____

_____

_____

_____

_____

Jesus chose to lay down His life out of love. No man forced Him to die on the cross. No army of Rome or any other nation could have done that. He showed His love to us as His friends. He died for us not when we were worthy or when we were deserving but when we were helpless, ungodly sinners in His sight, even enemies of His. He loved us so much; He has called us His children, the very children of God. If we love Him, we will obey His commandments, heeding all He says to us. We will also love one another as brothers and sisters in Christ. We will be open to give to needs and share what we have. We must ever be reminded that we always owe love to one another. Each of us is always in a position of being loved by our Father and of needing love from one another.

This love of God means so much. At its heart is a Father's heart. John 4:23 says, _"for such people the Father seeks to be His worshipers."_ Those who worship in spirit and truth will worship **the Father,** and He will be **their Father.** The woman at the well discovered this. Each person who comes to Jesus as Lord and Savior finds that God is his or her Father. What does this mean to each of us?

📖 What do you find about God being our Father in these verses?

John 14:21–23

_____

_____

_____

_____

Romans 8:14–17

_____

_____

_____

_____

_____

> ### At the heart of God's love is a Father's heart of love.

Did You Know?
❓ ADOPTION

Adoption in Roman law and in Scripture could not be revoked. An adopted child could not be disinherited or abandoned according to Roman law. How much more secure are we who have been adopted into the family of God by our heavenly Father!

2 Corinthians 6:16–18

_____

_____

_____

Galatians 4:4–7

_____

_____

_____

Ephesians 3:14–19

_____

_____

_____

_____

1 John 3:1–3

_____

_____

_____

Word Study
"JOINT-HEIRS"

We are _"Joint-Heirs"_ (KJV) or _"Fellow Heirs"_ (NASB) with Christ (Romans 8:17). The Greek word (_sugklēronómos_) refers to the possession we receive as a gift from our Father. We receive and participate in this inheritance or possession equally with our Lord Jesus. How awesome to be adopted as full sons and daughters of our heavenly Father!

We are loved by the Father, the Son, and the Spirit. God wants our love in return. The Son gladly discloses Himself to His loving followers and makes His abode with each one. This is a permanent (an eternal) relationship. As a father, God adopts us into His family and promises to lead us by His Spirit. We can cry out "Abba! (like the cry of "Daddy," or "Papa"), Father!" He assures us that we belong to Him as we walk with Him. We also have the promise of being joint–heirs with Jesus (see Romans 8:17 KJV). Knowing that we may face suffering with Jesus, we are also assured that we will be glorified with Him. Day by day as the sons and daughters of God the Father, we can know His presence and His leadership as our Father, just as the children of Israel knew God's presence and leading in their journey with Him. We also have the inner strength of His Spirit promised to us. We can even know the experience of His love at deeper and deeper levels as we continue our walk with Him. Then, because we are God's children, we have an awesome future to which to look forward, even the confident expectation of being changed fully into His likeness.

Someone once shared with me four characteristics about what makes a gift meaningful. Read each of these in light of what you have just read about the love of God and the _"gift of God."_ Spend a moment thanking the Lord for His _"indescribable gift."_

What makes a gift meaningful to a person?

- ✓ The one who gives the gift.
- ✓ The value and nature of the gift.
- ✓ How long the gift lasts.
- ✓ The ability to share the gift with others.

Think of how Jesus fulfills all of these. He is THE GIFT OF GOD. Take some time and talk to Him about these things.

_____

_____

_____

_____

_____

_____

_____

_____

_____

_____

APPLY How have you been sharing this "gift" with others? Are there some friends, family members, or acquaintances that need to hear from you about this gift. Ask the Lord for an opportunity to talk to them about their relationship to Jesus Christ, then begin looking for an open door to speak to them. Write the names of some people for whom you are praying and with whom you are seeking an opportunity to speak.

_____, _____,

_____, _____,

_____, _____,

_____, _____,

_____, _____,

_____, _____,

Spend some time with the Lord in prayer right now.

Lord, thank You for the *"gift of God,"* the *"living water"* of Your life. You are the perfect gift, of inestimable value, greater and more precious than any amount of silver and gold. Thank You that You are eternal and Your gift of life is eternal. Your love is unshakeable, unending, ever giving. Thank You that I can never be separated from Your love, that I am a child of Yours, adopted, secure, forever. I look forward to the inheritance You have promised, the home You are building, the grace You will be ever giving, but most of all—the fullness of Your loving, holy, and joyful presence. May I worship You as You deserve, surrendering daily to You and Your Word, always listening and seeking to obey You from a loving heart. May I love with Your kind of love, giving to others as You would have me give. Thank You for the presence of Your Spirit and the power You give to love You and others. I know I love You and others because of what You did in my heart—You first loved me. Thank You. I love You. Amen.

What difference has Jesus made in your life?

Thinking back on the life of the Samaritan woman and what a difference Jesus made in her life, take a moment to consider the difference Jesus has made in your life. In light of that, write a prayer to the Lord or make a journal entry.

_____

_____

_____

_____

_____

_____

_____

_____

_____

_____

Notes

Notes

lesson

Women of the Gospels

EXPERIENCING JESUS AND FAITHFULLY FOLLOWING HIM

What would it be like for Jesus to give you His undivided attention, to stop what He was doing just to hear your story? What would you think if Jesus wanted to meet with you alone to assure you of His love and care and victory over whatever you are facing? On the other hand, how would you respond if Jesus seemed reluctant to answer the need of your heart? Or, what would it mean to you if, when others criticized you, Jesus spoke up and defended you? Even more, what if you found out that He was absolutely delighted with the way you expressed your love, devotion, and worship to Him? In this week's lesson, we will see these very things occurring, and you will find encouragement for your heart, or perhaps conviction of sin over some area in your life, or even comfort for a point of pain. Hopefully, you will discover a fresh strength for following Him day by day.

The Gospels reveal several women who were faithful and loyal followers of Jesus, both in His earthly ministry and in the early church established after His death and resurrection. These women were from various backgrounds

WHO ARE THE WOMEN OF THE GOSPELS?

The women featured in this lesson came from various backgrounds and stations in life. They included common village women and women from higher socio-economic levels. The one common thread that marked them all was this: Jesus made an eternal impact on them, and they followed Him with a whole heart.

WHERE DOES SHE FIT?

2200 B.C.	1950	1700	1450	1200	950	600	100 B.C.	A.D. 1	A.D. 100

HAGAR
2100?–2040?

Daniel
619–534?

ELIZABETH
75 B.C.?–A.D. 10?

Solomon
991–931

REBEKAH
2040?–1915?

WOMEN of the Gospels
10 B.C.?–A.D. 50?

LEAH
1948?–1885?

Judges Rule
1385–1051

David
1041–971

LOT'S WIFE
2100?–2066

RACHEL
1943?–1899

Joshua
1495–1385

ABIGAIL
1036?–976?

Nehemiah
480?–400?

Jesus Christ
4 B.C.?–A.D. 30?

THE SUBMISSIVE WIFE

BATHSHEBA
1016?–961?

Isaac
2065–1885

Moses
1525–1405

Ephesians 5;
1 Peter 2—3

JEZEBEL
889?–841

Abraham
2165–1990

Jacob
2005–1858

Samuel
1105–1022

WOMAN at Well
10 B.C.?–A.D. 50?

and various stations in life. They included common village women and members of higher levels of society. The one thing that marked them all was this: Jesus made an eternal impact on them, and they followed Him with a whole heart. They can show us much about what it means to follow Him.

Some of the women we will study this week will be very recognizable. Others will be new to many. Some of these women are well known, others are not known at all by name, only their story is told. Regardless of how well each is known, each one followed Jesus in a way that impacted those around them and in a way that can impact each of us as we look at their walk.

Women of the Gospels

DAY ONE

Experiencing the Healing Touch of Jesus

While Jesus began ministering throughout the cities and villages of Galilee, many began to take notice of Him. The *"gracious words"* He spoke made an impact on many (Luke 4:22). The way He opened the Scriptures to their understanding struck a chord of spiritual hunger in village after village. One of the most noteworthy aspects of His ministry was His ministry of healing. The prophets spoke of a Messiah who would come with a touch of healing. Malachi said it this way, *"The sun of righteousness will rise with healing in its wings"* (Malachi 4:2), and the Rabbis taught that the Messiah would be able to heal all sorts of diseases and sicknesses. When Jesus came He did just that. How did that impact the people? When we read the gospel accounts, we find many who experienced the healing touch of Jesus, among whom were several women. These women became faithful followers of Jesus, and studying their lives can help us do the same.

 One of the first accounts of Jesus' healing touch occurred in the town of Capernaum, Jesus' second "home" during His ministry. Read Mark 1:29–31 along with Luke 4:38–39 and record what happened.

_____

_____

_____

_____

_____

_____

_____

_____

It was Saturday, and Jesus along with his disciples had been at the synagogue. They came into the home of Simon Peter. Andrew and Peter (who were brothers) and their cousins, James and John, were with them as well. Peter's mother-in-law was sick in bed *"suffering from a high fever,"* experiencing all the aches and pains that go with it. This illness was more than 'just a little touch of something.' *"They"*—probably Peter (and most likely his wife) and the disciples—spoke to Jesus about her. Jesus came to her bed, took her hand, rebuked the fever, and raised her up. The fever immediately left her.

What was the response of Peter's mother-in-law according to verse 31?

_____

_____

_____

_____

Peter's mother-in-law immediately got up and began serving the guests. She was completely well—full of energy and ready to joyously serve those in the home of Peter and her daughter. This was significant in light of what would happen later that day.

Mark 1:32–39 tells us a great crowd gathered at the house that evening, and many were healed and many set free from demons. The next day, Jesus left Capernaum and began going through the towns nearby as well as throughout the region of Galilee, preaching the kingdom of God and ministering in various ways.

Luke 8:1–3 records Jesus' ministry in the various towns and villages. What do you discover in 8:1 about His travel? What was His primary emphasis according to Luke 8:1?

_____

_____

_____

_____

Jesus traveled from city to city, from one village to another, speaking to all who would listen. His primary focus was proclaiming and preaching the kingdom of God, the rule of Jesus over the hearts and lives of His followers. Jesus told people the message of the kingdom, emphasizing the good news of His forgiveness of sin and of the power of His reign. This included the details about the righteous character of this kingdom, the power of His kingdom, and ultimately His eternal reign as King.

Who was with Him during these days? Read Luke 8:1–3 again and list those mentioned.

_____

_____

_____

_____

What marked the women who were following Jesus, according to Luke 8:2?

_____

_____

_____

_____

Did You Know?

THE SUPPORT OF RABBIS

The support of rabbis and their disciples was not unique to Jesus and the Twelve. It was a common practice for devotees and disciples of a particular rabbi to support him out of one's personal wealth. We find support for Jesus and those who ministered with Him (such as the 70 and the 12) not only in Luke 8:1–3 but also in Luke 10:4–8, and then in the life and ministry of the apostles and others in 1 Corinthians 9:4–11, Philippians 4:15–18; Galatians 6:6, and 1 Timothy 5:17–19.

Did You Know?
THE VILLAGE OF MAGDALA

The village of Magdala, located about three miles from Capernaum (see "Palestine in the Time of Jesus" map on p. 150), rested on the western shore of the Sea of Galilee. It was a busy town, actively involved in the fishing industry and also known for dye works and some textile businesses. It is possible that Mary Magdalene had earnings from one of these industries allowing her to give of her substance and have the freedom to travel with Jesus and His disciples. In any case, she gave of what she had and followed Jesus with a faithful heart.

Jesus' companions included His twelve disciples as well as several women who had been healed of various sicknesses and demon possession. The women named were Mary Magdalene, Susanna, and Joanna (the wife of Chuza) who was Herod's steward. The year was around A.D. 28, and Chuza was serving under Herod Antipas, ruler over the regions of Galilee (north Israel) and Perea (area east of the Jordan River). As a steward, Joanna's husband acted as an overseer, taking care of the financial and property matters for Herod as well as managing the education of the children in the royal household. Joanna would have been a lady in the upper echelon of society. She made a bold choice in following Jesus and serves as an example of how the hand of God reaches to many different places to touch many different lives. Each of these women experienced the healing touch of Jesus in some way and chose to follow Him, devoting special time to traveling with Him and the disciples.

What part did these women play in the ministry of Jesus and the Twelve?

_____

_____

_____

_____

As a result of the impact of Jesus on the lives of these women, they gladly contributed to the ministry expenses faced by Jesus and the Twelve. Luke 8:3 says they were "*contributing*." The Greek word translated "contributing" is *diakoneō*, pointing to one serving or providing whatever is needed to care for the practical needs of someone else. The root idea pictures someone waiting on a table, serving food. This contribution was not a one-time gift, but an act of continuous giving from what each woman personally possessed. It is evident that the motive of these women was gratitude for all Jesus had done for them. In addition, they followed because they were spiritually hungry to hear Him as He preached and taught. They wanted to serve in any way possible and learn as much as possible as He ministered to the people of the land.

We have seen the names of three of the women who experienced the healing of Jesus—Mary of the village of Magdala, otherwise known as Mary Magdalene, Joanna, and Susanna. Who were the "*many others*" who were part of those that traveled and contributed to the support of Jesus and the Twelve? We do not know for certain who these were, but we find several incidents in the Gospels of women who were not only healed physically by Jesus, but also changed spiritually—they became faithful followers of the Messiah.

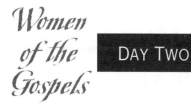

Women of the Gospels　DAY TWO

EXPERIENCING THE COMPASSION AND FORGIVENESS OF JESUS

Jesus healed in many ways. He touched the lives of many people with many and varied needs. As He went from place to place, He was sensitive to those around Him. Like His Father, He cared for the widow and the orphan, for the child and the aged, for the down-and-out sinner and the up-and-out Pharisee. We will see His compassion in action in Day

Two, a compassion that understands the needs of the heart and the hearts of the needy.

📖 As Jesus journeyed from Capernaum into the cities of the Galilee region, He came to the city of Nain. There we see Him touching the life of another woman and her son. What can we learn from this? Read Luke 7:11–15. Record what you discover about the widow and about Jesus.

_____

_____

_____

_____

_____

What did Jesus do according to Luke 7:14–15?

_____

_____

_____

📜 **Word Study**

THE YOUNG MAN RAISED FROM THE DEAD IN LUKE 7:14

Jesus, His disciples, and a large but eager crowd entered the city of Nain in the Galilee region. There they met another crowd, one that was mourning the death of a widow's son, probably in his 20s or 30s. When Jesus saw the funeral procession and the widow, *"He felt compassion for her"* and told her *"Do not weep."* Then Jesus boldly came to the coffin and touched it, stopping the procession. According to Old Testament law, this touch would defile a person (Leviticus 21:11; Numbers 19:11–16). However, this particular occasion was different. Like the outpouring of a fresh spring rain, washing away the stench of a stagnant pool, Jesus' pure and holy life could overcome death. Instead of defilement affecting Him, Jesus brought His holy power and purity to this funeral procession. Jesus spoke to the young man and commanded him to rise from the dead. Immediately he *"sat up and began to speak"* and Jesus gave this son back to his mother.

The Greek word, *neaniskos,* translated *"young man"* in Luke 7:14, refers to a man in the vigor of his life, usually no more than forty years of age. This man likely died in his late twenties or thirties. We do not know how long he lived after Christ raised him from the dead, but chances are good he lived many years after Christ raised and healed him.

📖 Luke 7:16–17 gives the results. Describe what happened.

_____

_____

_____

_____

Fear seized the crowd who saw this miracle take place, yet they began to glorify God. They kept saying, *"A great prophet has arisen among us!"*— noting Jesus as that great prophet. They saw in Him the evident presence and power of God. Their statement, *"God has visited His people!"* describes their awe that God was personally showing His great care. He was **there** with them, and they were amazed. The Greek word for "visited" (*episkeptomai*) means to look upon thoroughly, to comprehend the need fully, and to act graciously to meet the need. People began to talk and the report spread from the Galilee region throughout the land of Judea to the south and then to the regions around there.

Extra Mile
MULTIFACETED MINISTRY

Look at Luke 7:21–22 for a summary of the many things going on in Jesus' ministry. Note the different kinds of ministry and the numbers of people touched by Him.

📖 Soon after, Luke 7:36–50 presents another woman in the Gospels and her encounter with Jesus. Here is how it occurred. In the Galilee region, lived a Pharisee named Simon, who asked Jesus to dine with him. Jesus went to his house to eat. There we see the awesome care of Jesus for someone else in great need. What happened after Jesus arrived according to Luke 7:37–39?

While Jesus reclined at the table with Simon the Pharisee, a woman from that city entered the house bringing an alabaster vial filled with perfume. She knelt down, weeping, and began to wet Jesus' feet with her tears and to wipe them with her hair. This woman was *"a sinner,"* probably a prostitute, and she began to kiss Jesus' feet and anoint them with the aromatic oil. Her tears revealed a heart convicted over her sin and a heart that sought to honor Jesus.

What do you discover in Luke 7:39?

_____

_____

_____

_____

_____

He did not voice it out loud, but in his thoughts Simon the Pharisee began to question who Jesus was, thinking that if He were a true prophet He would know the character of this woman and would not let her touch Him. This Pharisee was doubtless thinking of the Old Testament law that would label her as unclean, being a prostitute. By her touch, she would make Jesus ceremonially unclean, and surely Jesus would not want that.

How did Jesus respond to Simon? What did He say about this woman? Read Luke 7:40–48 and record what you discover.

_____

_____

_____

_____

Put Yourself In Their Shoes
THE JAR OF ALABASTER

An alabaster vial filled with perfume was a very costly item and as a gift showed great love and devotion on the part of the woman in Galilee (Luke 7:36–50). Alabaster, a beautiful kind of marble, was often carved into vials or flasks to hold fragrant oils. The oils could be very expensive as well. In an incident similar to the one in Galilee, we read of Mary of Bethany breaking a flask and pouring perfumed oils on Jesus in a home in Bethany (Matthew 26:6–13; Mark 14:3–9; John 12:2–8). The disciples noted its value at over three hundred denarii, more than an average yearly wage (John 12:5). The vial of the woman in Galilee at the home of Simon the Pharisee was also very expensive and points to her great love for Jesus. He made evident His delight in receiving such love.

Jesus spoke up, knowing what Simon was thinking. He presented him with a story of two debtors, one with a debt of five hundred denarii, an amount equal to five hundred days' wages or almost two years of income for the average laborer of that time. The other debtor had a debt of fifty denarii, about two months' income for the average laborer. Neither debtor could pay what was owed, yet the moneylender *"graciously forgave"* both of them their debts. The question Jesus posed focused on the heart of each debtor. Which one would love the moneylender more? Which would show more gratitude? Both Simon and Jesus agreed that the one forgiven the greatest debt would show the greatest love. Then, Jesus turned from that story to real life. He focused on the woman and began to compare her outward display of love to Simon's hospitality (or lack thereof). The woman wet His feet with her own tears and wiped them with her hair, while Simon did not even offer the common courtesy of washing his guest's feet. There was no customary kiss of greeting from Simon, while the woman continued to kiss Jesus' feet, even as they talked. Again, Simon did not anoint Jesus' head with oil, but the woman anointed His feet with perfume, a much more valued gift.

What added revelation did Jesus speak in Luke 7:47–48?

_____

_____

_____

Jesus made it clear that He understood who this woman was; He knew she was "a sinner," but that did not stop Him from ministering to her. She had a great sin debt, and Jesus declared it forgiven. He saw her great heart of love as an indication of repentance and faith in Himself. It was obvious who loved Jesus more.

 How did the people respond to Jesus in Luke 7:49? What was Jesus' final word in Luke 7:50?

_____

_____

_____

Jesus' declaration of forgiveness of sins amazed the people at Simon's home. Jesus not only told the woman her sins were forgiven, but that her faith had saved her. She could now walk in peace having experienced His compassion and forgiveness. She was just one of many women in the Gospels touched by Jesus in a life-changing, eternity-changing way.

APPLY How about you? Have you been touched by Jesus? Has your life been changed? Have you experienced His forgiveness of **your** sins? How are you showing your gratitude to Him? If you have never come to Jesus in repentance and faith, now is the time to do that. If you know Jesus as your Lord and Savior, but are struggling over some area of sin or dealing with unforgiveness in some way, realize He has fully forgiven you and paid the debt for your sin by His death on the cross (Colossians 2:13–14). To understand these things more fully, you may want to read **"How to Follow God"** at the end of this book. Whatever the case, please know that you can experience what each of these women experienced. You can follow Him in the joy of forgiveness and the peace of a loving fellowship each day.

Later, in Luke 8, we find the record of a woman who experienced the power of the healing touch of Jesus. In Day Three we will look at her story.

Have you been touched by Jesus? Has your life been changed? Do you know His forgiveness of your sins?

EXPERIENCING THE POWER OF JESUS

Word about Jesus continued to spread as He healed and taught and preached. The people were amazed at His wondrous words. They marveled at His power to heal; even the demons were subject to Him. What kind of man was this? No rabbi ever taught like this. No man had the power He obviously had. On one of His ministry tours, Luke 8 informs us that when Jesus returned to Capernaum, a waiting crowd welcomed Him, wanting to see and hear Him once again. The Gospel records give the details

Did You Know?

ANCIENT MEDICINE

Ancient physicians like the ones mentioned in Mark 5 were limited in what they could do. However, much like today, physicians of that time prescribed various remedies for wounds or pain. One remedy for wounds was an oil mixture such as the one mentioned in the parable of the good Samaritan—a mixture of olive oil and wine (Luke 10:34). We read of pain-killing medicines such as the wine mixed with myrrh offered to Jesus on the cross (Mark 15:23). The Mosaic Law set forth health guidelines that included preventive and treatment procedures for rashes, skin diseases, leprosy, the proper handling of a dead body, the use of quarantine, as well as an uncompromising diet of "clean" foods.

of a significant encounter with a woman there. This encounter reveals a woman with genuine faith, faith enough to act enough, trusting Christ for a great need. As a result, she received what she needed . . . and so much more! Let's look at her story.

📖 Read Luke 8:40–43 along with Mark 5:21–26. In the midst of a crowd surrounding Jesus, and with an urgent request coming from Jairus, we are introduced to a woman. What do you find about this woman? What were the circumstances of her life? Look carefully at her life and think about the consequences of all that was going on in her life.

_____

_____

_____

_____

_____

_____

A woman in Capernaum heard that Jesus had come to town and, like many others from the city, was eager to see Him. This woman had suffered from a flow of blood, some sort of hemorrhage, possibly a tumor, for twelve years. What did this mean to the woman? Think of what the loss of blood did to her physically. She would have likely been weak, often tired, and prone to suffer other related illnesses because of this malady. Such a condition also must have affected her emotionally. Being physically drained would likely mean that she was easily emotionally drained. Add to all these complications the fact that she *"spent all that she had"* trying to get well. So she was financially drained as well. Financial constraints crippled her even further and could have made her a burden to her family members. But there is still one other way in which this woman was impacted by her illness. How do you think this woman's social and religious life was impacted (negatively or positively) by her sickness?

📖 Read Leviticus 15:25–27 and Numbers 5:1–4 and record what you find about anyone with a condition like that of this woman.

_____

_____

_____

God's law declared that where there was a flow of blood, there was uncleanness. That meant this woman was in a perpetual state of uncleanness. She could not enter the synagogue with the others—family, friends, and neighbors—on Saturdays. She would not be able to enter the Temple area in Jerusalem on any of the Feast days (or any other day) because there was never a point when she would be considered clean by the standards of Old Testament law; she was always considered unclean. Not only that, but at home, everywhere she sat was unclean. Anyone she touched became unclean and would have to go through the process of being ceremonially cleansed in order to go into the synagogue or Temple. Think of what this meant in her home with the members of her family. Think of those in the town. No one would want to get near her. All these difficulties added up to a desperate situation, a wearying, discouraging dilemma.

She had tried to find the remedy. During those twelve years, she visited several doctors, and none could help her. She depleted her funds, going from one physician to another. Not only were the physicians unable to help her, but her condition also grew steadily worse. Could Jesus help her?

📖 Read Mark 5:27–28. **What** did this woman do, and **why** did she do what she did?

_____

_____

_____

_____

_____

This woman heard about Jesus. Think about what she may have heard. He had healed people in village after village, city after city. Even in her own city of Capernaum, several had been healed in the months leading up to this day. Jesus had even healed some lepers—and leprosy was perhaps the most dreaded disease of that day, ultimately resulting in the sufferer being branded as "unclean." Perhaps she heard about these healings of the "unclean." Whatever she heard obviously gave her hope. A great crowd was pressing in all around Jesus. She came up in the crowd, knowing that those in the city who knew her would not want to be near her in her uncleanness. She was trying to get to Jesus. She said in her heart, *"If I just touch His garments, I shall get well."* So she came toward Jesus, pushing through the pressing crowd, and she reached out and touched His cloak, His outer garment, and immediately knew she was healed.

There is an additional element in this story that we can easily miss because we do not have all the details in this passage. When the woman reached out to touch the outer garment of Jesus, Luke 8:44 says she touched *"the fringe of His cloak."* This most likely refers to the corner of the garment and probably one of the tassels attached to the corner. What significance is this? There is a connection here that reveals her belief in Jesus as the Messiah and shows us that this touch was a touch of faith. What is the connection?

In Numbers 15:37–41, we read the Lord commanding His people to sew tassels on the corners of their garments as a constant reminder of His commandments **and** of their need to obey His law. This is mentioned in Deuteronomy 22:12 as well. The Hebrew word translated *"corners"* in Numbers and Deuteronomy (*kanaph*) is translated *"wings"* in Malachi 4:2, a verse that speaks about the coming of the Messiah. He, as *"the sun of righteousness,"* would come forth in righteousness and, in the purity and wholeness of His life, would have healing in His *"wings."* That was the understanding of the people in the days of Jesus. They were expecting a Messiah who would have healing power. From the testimonies she had heard, the woman with the issue of blood concluded that Jesus was the Messiah. Therefore, she sought to touch the fringes or the tassel of His outer cloak, believing that He had the power to heal her. Her action was no superstitious idea about Jesus' clothes. It was a touch point for her faith, faith in Jesus as the Messiah.

🖋 *Did You Know?*

❓ **WHAT A CROWD!**

When Jesus came ashore at Capernaum, *"a great multitude gathered about Him."* As He walked into town with Jairus, the crowd was *"pressing in on Him."* In Mark 5:24, 31, the Greek word *sunthlibo*, translated *"pressing in,"* pictures the people pressing in from all sides. In Luke 8:42, the Greek word *sumpnigo*, translated *"pressing against,"* could literally be translated "choking," both passages giving the picture of the crowd squeezing in on all sides. That is the crowd the woman had to get through to touch Jesus' garment.

Word Study

THE GARMENT AND THE FRINGE

The garment (outer garment) referred to in Mark 5:27 is the *himation*, a mantle or cape worn over the tunic (*chiton*). It was a rectangular piece of wool worn over the body or over the shoulders in the day and used as cover at night. For this reason it could not be taken as a pledge of payment by a creditor (Exodus 22:25–27). In obedience to Numbers 15:37–41 and Deuteronomy 22:12, the Jews attached a tassel to each corner of the cloak. It was one of these tassels (Greek—*kraspedon*), translated *"fringe"* (Matthew 9:20), that the woman in Mark 5:27 grasped. Examples of this outer cloak can be found in Matthew 5:40; 9:20–21; 14:36; 21:7–8; Mark 5:27, 28, 30; Luke 8:44; John 19:2; Acts 7:58; 12:8; 22:20, as well as 🔖 📖 the Greek translation of 1 Samuel 21:9 and Isaiah 3:6–7. The *"fringe"* or tassel (*kraspedon*) is also mentioned in Matthew 23:5; Mark 6:56; Luke 8:44; and Zechariah 8:23 (translated *"skirt"* or *"garment"* from the Hebrew word, *kanaph*).

📖 What happened to the woman according to Mark 5:29 and Luke 8:44?

_____

_____

_____

_____

_____

_____

📖 What was Jesus' response according to Mark 5:30–34 and Luke 8:45–48?

_____

_____

_____

_____

_____

Word Study

A DOUBLE BLESSING?

When Jesus spoke to the woman healed of the issue of blood, He used two different words for wholeness or healing. In Mark 5:34, He said first, *"Daughter, your faith has made you well* [or whole]*,"* using the Greek word *sozo,* often translated "saved" and many times referring to spiritual wholeness. (*Sozo* can also refer to physical healing.) In the second part of His blessing, He said, *"Go in peace, and be healed of your affliction,"* using the Greek word, *hugies,* for *"healed,"* rooted in *hugiaino,* the word from which we get our English word "hygiene," a word that relates to any conditions or practices that are conducive to one's overall health. It is very possible that Jesus gave this woman a double blessing in light of her faith in Him as the Messiah.

Did You Know?

"FRINGE" BENEFITS

Both Matthew and Mark record that many sick in several villages, cities, and even in the countryside sought to touch the "fringe" (*kraspedon*—the tassel) of Christ's outer cloak. *"As many as touched it were cured"* (Mark 6:56; see also Matthew 14:36).

As soon as the woman grasped Jesus cloak, Mark states emphatically, *"Immediately the flow of her blood was dried up."* Luke the physician tells us the flow of blood *"stopped"* at once. It was a miracle. She felt the difference in her body and knew she had just been healed. Just as quickly, Jesus turned and asked who had grasped His garments. The disciples did not know what to say, since a great crowd was pressing in on Him. Jesus knew that someone had touched Him in such a way that His very power (*dunamis*) had touched that person. The woman came prostrating herself before Jesus in fear and trembling, telling Jesus and the crowd all that had happened, *"the whole truth."* When He heard her testimony, Jesus joyfully spoke words of comfort to her, pointing to her faith in Him; Jesus implied both a spiritual healing as well as an evident physical healing. His statement could be translated, *"Daughter, your faith has made you well* [or has saved you]*; go in peace, and be healed of your affliction."*

But the fact that this woman was miraculously healed is not the end of her story but is really the beginning. For from that day on, everything would be different—spiritually, socially, physically, financially, emotionally, and eternally. She was able to enter into life in Capernaum in a new way. Perhaps she joined the *"many others"* mentioned in Luke 8:3 and followed Jesus in the various towns and villages. In any case, in one way or another, she certainly served as a witness of the power of Jesus and an example of true faith.

 This woman's faith was based on what she learned from the Word of God and what she heard about Jesus that matched that Word. The more you know Jesus and His Word, the more likely you are to walk in true faith, faith that asks and acts enough. How is **your** knowledge of His Word? How is your time in prayer? Let this woman's example encourage you in your faith. Call on Him, grasp His heart in prayer as you let His Word grasp your heart each day. Then, leave the results with Him.

EXPERIENCING THE RESURRECTION LIFE OF JESUS

In Days One through Three, we have seen several women touched by Jesus in significant ways, ways that revealed His compassion, His power, His love, and His forgiveness. Some of these could have been part of the *"many others"* who followed Jesus from town to town, hearing Him and helping support Him in ministry (Luke 8:3). We do not know every woman who did this, but we do know certain ones. Among the predominant women was Mary Magdalene, along with some other women from Galilee. What else do we know about them? The Gospel records are hardly silent about these women. Today, we will look at where and how they followed Jesus, and in looking at them we will learn some things about what it means to be a faithful follower—even in the darkest of days.

Jesus spoke to His disciples about the coming Cross. Luke 24:6–8 speaks of several women being with Jesus as He talked about the Cross and His resurrection. This conversation would have taken place when Christ was in Galilee and, later, on the journey to Jerusalem to fulfill that very mission of the Cross. These women heard much of what He said, what He taught, and what He prayed. We observe in these women that they were faithful disciples of the Lord Jesus, intricately involved in what He was doing and adequately equipped to assist in the ministry of God. What did they learn in the events surrounding the crucifixion and resurrection? What did God do in their lives?

📖 What do you discover about Mary Magdalene and some of the other women in John 19:25 and Mark 15:33–41, especially verses 40–41? Be sure to list all the people mentioned? Where and when do the circumstances of these verses occur?

_____

_____

_____

_____

_____

_____

Mark 15 reveals Jesus dying on a cross as bystanders watched and listened. There were Roman soldiers there, the centurion even commenting that this man was like no other prisoner of Rome: *"Truly this man was the Son of God!"* Looking on at the cross were several women, **Mary** the mother of Jesus, her sister **Salome**, the mother of James and John, **Mary Magdalene**, **Mary** the wife of Cleopas and mother of James and Joses, and **other women**. These women *"used to follow"* Jesus *"and minister to Him"* while He was in Galilee, traveling from town to town. The word *"follow"* pictures a continual following over an extended period of time. They had traveled to Jerusalem with Him, experiencing the myriad moments of ministry on the way as well as the momentous events of His final week in Jerusalem before His death. Now they stood watching their Messiah die.

Extra Mile

JESUS' CRUCIFIXION AND RESURRECTION

Jesus spoke of His crucifixion and resurrection during the final months before these events took place. Several of the women from Galilee heard Christ tell of these prophesied events when He was in Galilee and remembered Christ's words after His resurrection (Luke 24:6–8). Read the following passages of Scripture: Matthew 16:21–26; 17:22–23; 20:17–19; Mark 8:31–37; 9:30–32; 10:32–34; Luke 9:22–25; 9:43–45; 18:31–34. Three separate accounts are recorded in these pasages. The first account was at Caesarea Philippi, the second in Galilee, the third on the final journey to Jerusalem.

Did You Know?

? GOD USES EARTHQUAKES

God uses earthquakes to communicate a message, sometimes a wake-up call ("pay attention"), sometimes a judgment rendered. There was an earthquake at the crucifixion of Jesus as well as on Resurrection morning (Matthew 24:7; 27:51; 28:2). Earthquakes occurred at the giving of the Law at Mount Sinai (Exodus 19:18; Psalm 68:8), at the judgment of Korah and his family (Numbers 16:31), and at Mount Horeb, when God was speaking to Elijah (1 Kings 19:11). Isaiah warned Jerusalem of the punishment of the Lord that would come primarily through an earthquake (Isaiah 29:6), and Jeremiah spoke of the Lord dealing with the nations in the same way (Jeremiah 10:10; 49:21). Other prophets spoke of God's work through earthquakes (Joel 2:10; Nahum 1:5; Haggai 2:6), and in the final days, several earthquakes will be part of God's judgments on the earth (Revelation 6:12; 8:5; 11:13–19).

Did You Know?

? ONE ANGEL OR TWO?

Some of the accounts of the resurrection mention one angel, others mention two. Which account is accurate? Both. At times the writer focuses on the work or words of one angel and at other times the appearance and words of two angels (Matthew 28:2–7; Mark 16:5–7; Luke 24:4–7).

[For a look at the chronology of these days, see the Chart: **The Women Involved in the Events of the Crucifixion, Burial, and Resurrection of Jesus** at the end of this lesson.]

📖 Matthew and Luke also present the record of these faithful women at the cross (Matthew 27:55–56; Luke 23:48–49). They continued with Him through everything He faced. Where do we find them next? Read Matthew 27:55–61, especially verses 60–61. What were their plans according to Luke 23:53–56 and Mark 16:1–3?

_____

_____

_____

_____

_____

_____

After Jesus died, Joseph of Arimathea obtained permission to bury the body of Jesus. He carried Christ's body to his own tomb hewn out of rock, and there he placed the body. Mary Magdalene and the other Mary apparently had stayed at the cross and then went to the tomb with Joseph watching every detail of where he placed Jesus. These women then returned to the place they were staying and prepared spices and perfumes. Their plan was to come and anoint the body with those spices on Sunday morning after the Sabbath day of rest. That is what they sought to do, but when Sunday came, some things had changed.

📖 Early on Sunday morning (about sunrise), several women went to the tomb of Jesus to anoint His body with the spices and perfumes they had prepared. What did they find? What happened at the tomb? Read Matthew 28:1–4, Mark 16:1–8, and Luke 24:1–8 and record your findings.

_____

_____

_____

_____

_____

📖 Think about what these women must have been thinking. Read Luke 24:9–11 with John 20:1–2. Did they believe Jesus had risen from the dead?

_____

_____

_____

_____

When the women approached the garden, they were wondering how they were going to remove the stone, but when they got there it was already moved—the result of an earthquake and the work of angels. The guards who had been there were apparently gone or still unconscious (see Matthew 28:1–4)—having experienced the earthquake and the fearful appearance of one of the two angels. The women looked inside the tomb and saw an angel who told them Jesus had risen from the dead just as He said He would. They remembered Jesus saying this would occur, and they saw the place where He had been. One of the angels told the women to go and tell the disciples the good news and promised that Jesus would meet them in Galilee. They immediately raced to the eleven disciples *"and to all the rest"* who were with them and told them what they had seen and heard from the angels. Mary Magdalene was not sure what had happened. Even with the angel's announcement, she still thought the body had been removed somewhere. The disciples did not believe the report of the women, but Peter, John, and Mary Magdalene ran back to the tomb to see.

John 20:3–10 reports that Peter and John ran to the tomb, with John getting there first—though Peter entered the tomb before him. They saw the linen wrappings with the head linen set apart. They pondered about what all this meant and left the garden. Apparently Mary Magdalene stayed behind after they left. She stood there weeping, not knowing where the Lord's body had been taken. It seemed that things were only getting murkier. What would happen next?

📖 Read John 20:11–18 then Matthew 28:8–10 and summarize what you find.

_____

_____

_____

_____

Mary stood weeping and looked once again into the empty tomb. This time there were two angels where the body had lain. They questioned her about why she was weeping, and she confessed her perplexity over where the body of Jesus had been taken. She turned around and saw a Man standing there who spoke to her and also asked why she was weeping. Mary assumed it was the caretaker of the garden, and she asked Him if He knew where the body was, even offering to come and take the body away. The Man, who was none other than Jesus, spoke to her, *"Mary,"* and she recognized Him. *"Rabboni,"* she said, acknowledging Him as her Master and Teacher. She grabbed Him, and Jesus responded, telling her to stop clinging to Him, but to go and tell *"My brethren"* about His coming ascension back to the Father. Mary Magdalene's devotion was evident; she was one of the last to leave the cross and one of the first to see the tomb. She was now the first to meet the resurrected Lord. Mary rushed back to the disciples and told them she had actually seen the Lord. A group of women at the tomb then came and told the disciples the Lord had appeared to them on the way back from the tomb.

Luke 24:13–49 reveals that later that day, Jesus appeared to Simon Peter and to two disciples (not of the Twelve) on the road to Emmaus. The eleven surviving disciples, except Thomas (Judas was dead), gathered together that Sunday night and were discussing these things when Jesus Himself appeared in the room (without opening or entering the door!). Of course, the disciples were very frightened. Jesus calmed their fears and assured them that it really was He raised from the dead, just as He said would happen. He even pointed to His hands and feet and ate some broiled fish to show He was not a disembodied spirit. We also read there the commission He gave them: go and proclaim forgiveness of sins in His name. He had paid the sin debt for any and every kind of sin, and anyone could receive His for-

Word Study
"RABBONI"

The word *"Rabboni"* [Greek—*rhabboni*] in John 20:16 can also be translated "Master" or "My Great Master" and refers to a teacher or master of highest honor. It is transliterated from the Hebrew *rhabbi*, which means "great one" or chief. There were three levels of this title: **1)** *Rab* points to an honored one at the lowest level; **2)** *Rabbi* means "my master" and carries greater honor and dignity; and **3)** *Rabboni*, "my great master" is the title of highest honor. In Jewish history only seven people were officially given this title, each being of the school of Hillel. Nicodemus called Jesus *"Rabbi"* and acknowledged that He came *"from God as a teacher"* (John 3:2). Jesus fulfilled Moses' prophecy of the "Prophet" raised up by God (Deuteronomy 18:18–19). Blind Bartimaeus and Mary Magdalene addressed Jesus as Rabboni (Mark 10:51; John 20:16).

giveness. His resurrection victory over death was the eternal seal that assures a person that he or she can know forgiveness and the eternal life He alone can give.

📖 After the resurrection and ascension of Jesus, we see these women once again. Where are they and what are they doing? Read Acts 1:9–14, noting verse 14, and record your findings.

_____

_____

_____

_____

_____

Jesus met the Eleven on another occasion and promised them once again that the coming of the Holy Spirit would be soon. They would know the Spirit's power for witnessing about who Christ is and what He had done. Jesus then ascended to Heaven, and two angels proclaimed to the men that He would return in the same way as He left. The disciples returned to an upper room, where for the next ten days they met, prayed, and talked over the commands Jesus had given them. The women were there with them. Oneness of mind marked this group of about 120 believers (1:15) as they devoted themselves to prayer.

Acts 2 tells us that when the Holy Spirit came on the Day of Pentecost, each of these believers, both men and women, were filled with the Holy Spirit and testified of the mighty deeds of God. Certainly, they spoke of the mightiest deed—the life, death, and resurrection of the God-Man, their Lord Jesus Christ. Peter then proclaimed that, by faith in Jesus, one could receive forgiveness of sins and eternal life, all part of the very presence of the Holy Spirit in one's life. As a result, that day about three thousand men and women placed faith in Jesus Christ as their Lord and Savior, the beginning of a new life for each of them and the beginning of the Church and the new work of Jesus Christ through His Holy Spirit—a new work that involves you and me. How does our involvement with the Holy Spirit apply to everyday life? We shall see in Day Five.

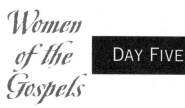

FOR ME TO FOLLOW GOD

How can we faithfully follow Jesus each day? When we look at Him and the way He interacted with people He met from day to day, we see an awesome Man, but more than a Man—He was and still remains the Son of God, who showed His great compassion, love, and forgiveness to thousands. He is the God-Man, who by His power created all that exists, and by that same power healed and restored many. Today, Jesus calls us to follow Him as Lord—the Lord who is worthy of our love and allegiance. How can we walk in a way that is both honoring and pleasing to Him, faithfully following Him like the men and women of the Gospels did?

To answer that question, first of all, we need to think of what it means to **follow**—a step at a time, listening, watching, obeying, desiring to please Him.

What pleased Jesus two thousand years ago? When we look at the lives of the various women (and men) in the Gospels, we see at least three or four common elements among those who followed Him, things that brought great delight to Jesus. One of these common threads was genuine **faith in and obedience to** Him. Christ was always full of joy when He saw real faith that agreed with and obeyed His Word. Another common thread was a **giving/loving** heart (a loving heart is a giving heart)—when Christ saw someone giving out of a heart of love and devotion, He had great delight. Another delight to Jesus and yet another common element found in those who truly followed Him was a **thankful** heart—a heart that acknowledged the goodness and grace of God. The questions each of us needs to ask ourselves are as follows:

- ☐ Am I a delightful, faithful follower?
- ☐ Am I walking in faith, trusting Jesus and His Word?
- ☐ Am I giving/loving in word and deed?
- ☐ Am I marked by a thankful heart?

Let's look at three more women who can help us answer those questions?

📖 The first woman is found in Matthew 15:21–28. Read that account (You may want to read the account in Mark 7:21–29 as well). What is your first impression of this woman's encounter with Jesus and the disciples?

_____

_____

_____

_____

_____

Jesus went to the region of Tyre and came into a house with His disciples. A Canaanite woman (Mark tells us she was of the Syro-Phoenician race), a Gentile, heard that Jesus was there, and she came begging Him to heal her daughter. Jesus appears at first almost to ignore her, and the disciples wanted Him to send her away—not exactly an inviting picture of a giving/loving heart. Jesus said His first calling was to the *"lost sheep of the house of Israel,"* implying that the Gentiles would come later. What was the response of the woman?

Look carefully at the interaction between Jesus and the woman in Matthew 15:24–28. What do you see about this woman? What do you see about Jesus?

_____

_____

_____

_____

This woman began to beg for help. Jesus said *"the children's bread"* (the blessings promised to the children of Israel) is primarily for the children (Israel) rather than for the house dogs (Gentiles). (He used a word for personal pet dogs [*kunarion*] owned by a family, not the stray street dogs of the day.) Jesus was not being harsh or derogatory to this woman. He merely pointed out the fact that the gospel first went to the Jews, then to the Gentiles, and that gen-

Think of what it means to follow— a step at a time, listening, watching, obeying, desiring to please Him.

🖋 **Did You Know?**

② **WHO ARE THE GENTILES?**

The term **Jews** refers to the descendants of Abraham through Isaac and then Jacob. Jacob had twelve sons, each the head of one of the tribes of Israel, with Joseph's tribe named through his sons Ephraim and Manasseh. The **Gentiles** are all the other nations and people groups of the world. The Greek word *ethnos* (root of the English word "ethnic") is usually translated "Gentiles," or "nations."

uine faith was required of both categories of people for salvation (see Romans 1:16–17). Jesus often tested the hearts of His hearers by looking for a faith response. This woman had called out to Him. *"Lord, Son of David,"* a title for the Messiah. Did she really believe that He was the Messiah? Her response shows that she did indeed, for her faith was genuine. As she so boldly stated, even "the little dogs" have opportunity to eat the Master's bread—even if from the floor. She showed a humble heart, willing to receive from Jesus what He alone could give in whatever way He wanted to give it. Note this: **she did not give up on the character and grace of Jesus.** She believed He could and would help her and heal her daughter. Jesus was delighted with the response of faith and healed her daughter that same moment.

APPLY What about you? Are you **trusting** Jesus in your situation? Are you walking in **faith**, trusting His timing? Remember, delays are not denials as this woman found out. Are you **obeying** what you know to obey? Are you seeking Him in His Word and calling on Him in prayer? Look to Him. As with the woman in Tyre, He will be faithful to respond to you.

There is a second woman that can help us evaluate where we are in our walk in following Jesus. Read Mark 12:41–44 (also found in Luke 21:1–4). Describe what you "see" about this widow and about Jesus.

_____

_____

_____

_____

Jesus and His disciples were in the Temple complex in Jerusalem, specifically the Court of the Women, where there were thirteen trumpet-shaped vessels for receiving offerings for the Temple. Jesus watched the rich put in their money, some giving large sums. Then He noticed a widow put in two small coins, two mites equal to less than an hour's wage for most workers of that day.

Immediately, Jesus got the attention of His disciples and told them an amazing truth: this woman essentially gave more than anyone else. She was the poorest of the "poor," the Greek word, *ptōche,* referring to one at the worst level of poverty—helpless, with little or no means of even securing food. All that she had, she gave—two mites. She gave knowing that she would have to trust God for work to be able to buy any food. Jesus, knowing her heart, commended her giving and pointed to it as comparatively more than what others present at the Temple gave on that day. She gave all that she had, while the others gave only a small portion of their abundance. Jesus did not say this to condemn the others, but to show how God looks at giving and to honor the action of this faithful widow.

APPLY How is your **giving** (Matthew 6:19–34; 1 Timothy 6:17–19)? Do you give to the Lord through your local church (1 Corinthians 16:1–2; 2 Corinthians 8:1–9; Romans 15:24–28)? Do you meet your responsibilities at home, in paying your bills, and in daily business matters (1 Timothy 5:8)? Are you obedient to the Scriptures, giving to meet the needs of others as you have opportunity (Galatians 2:10; Ephesians 4:28)? Remember, the amount is not the main thing; **the heart of giving** is most important—and, of course, a giving heart will give generously. You see, a true follower of Jesus is a giver.

📖 A thankful heart is certainly one of the signs of a follower of God. We see this in another woman in the New Testament. To get the full picture of this woman, read Luke 2:22–38. Look carefully at the life of Anna in verses 36–38. What do you find about her?

_____

_____

_____

_____

_____

Anna, an 84-year-old prophetess, became a widow after only seven years of marriage. She lived in the Temple area, which contained several places where priests could stay during their assigned service time. Apparently, Anna was given a place there after the death of her husband. She was known for her life of devotion to *"fastings and prayers."*

On a certain day, Joseph and Mary were at the Temple, offering their required sacrifices for purification and for presenting the baby Jesus before the Lord as the firstborn son (Exodus 13:2, 11–15). There, a man named Simeon, being led of the Spirit, came into the Temple and saw them. He took the infant Jesus in his arms and blessed the Lord for the salvation He had brought in this Child. He spoke a blessing to Joseph and Mary and prophesied the future of this son and the impact He would have. In one of God's divine appointments, Anna came into the Temple at that moment. Seeing the Child Jesus, His mother, and Joseph, and hearing the words of Simeon, Anna was overwhelmed with gratitude and praise and gave thanks to the Lord. God revealed to her that this Child was at the center of God's redemption of His people, and she spoke *"of Him"* to many.

 APPLY What about you? Do you **praise** the Lord and **give thanks** to Him (Ephesians 5:20; Colossians 3:16–17)? Do you give thanks for all that the Lord has given you and for all He has done for you (1 Thessalonians 5:18; 1 Timothy 4:3–5)? Like Anna, are you giving thanks for the redemption God has provided?

We have been introduced to many women in the Gospels, each unique in her own way, yet in some ways like each one of us. It would be good at this point to pause and reflect on where we are in our following. Read over the questions listed below. Check the one (or ones) that hit home in some way and talk to the Lord about these matters.

- ☐ Like the woman of Tyre (in Syro-Phoenicia) do you refuse to give up on the character and power of Jesus? Are you marked by true **faith**?
- ☐ Like the widow with two mites, are you **giving** with a generous heart?
- ☐ Like Anna, are you giving **thanks** for this Child born for you and your redemption?
- ☐ Like Peter's mother-in-law, are you **serving** in the strength Jesus gives? (see 1 Peter 4:10–11)
- ☐ Like the "sinner" woman, are you marked by **love, gratitude, and giving** toward Jesus? How are you showing love? How are you giving?

🚶 *Extra Mile*
HEALED ON THE SABBATH

Look at the crippled woman of Luke 13:10–17, who was healed on a Sabbath. Read the story and discover Jesus' care, even in the face of opposition to His healing her. Think of His care for **you** (1 Peter 5:7).

- ❑ Like Mary Magdalene, are you living in the awe of Jesus as your living Rabboni—**Master**, the Source of your wisdom and the Master of the way to walk in life? Are you telling others that Christ is a living Lord and Savior they can know personally?
- ❑ Like the woman with the issue of blood, are you walking in **faith** based on what you have heard and learned through the Word of God?
- ❑ Like the many women who followed Jesus, contributing to His ministry, are you **investing your life** (time, resources, energies, etc.) in the kingdom of God? Are you seeking **first** His kingdom?

What specific actions do you need to take? What is God showing you that you need to do as you resolve to be a faithful follower?

_____

_____

_____

_____

_____

_____

Lord, thank You that You change lives, that You are the same yesterday, today, and forever. Thank You for leaving a record of the faithful women who followed You, a record that encourages me to trust You with the circumstances, even the frustrations of my life. You are good. You are full of compassion and willing to forgive the worst and the lowest. I am glad that covers anyone willing to come to You for forgiveness and a new life. Thank You that You have the power to heal and forgive and change anyone. May I be a witness of Your love and forgiveness, of Your indestructible, eternal life, and of Your call to come, believe, and receive You as the only Lord and Savior. Thank You for giving me that eternal life and for the promises of all that lies ahead. In Jesus' Name, Amen.

Write your own prayer to the Lord or make a journal entry of what the Lord is saying to you about faithfully following Him.

_____

_____

_____

_____

_____

_____

_____

_____

For further information on other women in the Gospels, see *Following God: Life Principles from the Women of the Bible*, **Book One.** There you will find the story of Mary and Martha of Bethany and Mary, the mother of Jesus.

The Women Involved in the Events of the Crucifixion, Burial, and Resurrection of Jesus

Not all the women involved in the events of the crucifixion, burial, and resurrection were together for each event. Some were at one place, some at another. Some involved are not named. All those named can be listed as follows: Mary, the mother of Jesus; Salome, who was the wife of Zebedee, sister of Mary, and also the mother of James and John; Mary Magdalene; Mary, the wife of Cleopas (Alphaeus) and mother of James (the Less or the Younger) and Joses (Joseph); Joanna.

ORDER OF PLACES/EVENTS	PEOPLE	SCRIPTURE
At the Cross during the Crucifixion.	Jesus, Mary mother of Jesus, Salome, Mary Magdalene, Mary (James and Joses), Roman soldiers	Matthew 27:55–56; Mark 15:22–41; Luke 23:33–49; John 19:23–30
At the tomb when Jesus was buried.	Jesus, Mary Magdalene, Mary (Joses), plus Joseph of Arimathea and Nicodemus	Matthew 27:57–61; Mark 15:42–47; Luke 23:50–55; John 19:38–42
At their lodgings they prepared some spices before the Sabbath and then bought more at the marketplace after the Sabbath. They prepared those to anoint the body of Jesus.	Mary Magdalene, Mary (James and Joses), Salome	Mark 16:1; Luke 23:56; Luke 24:1b
Sunday Morning—Earthquake at the tomb, Angel rolled away the stone, Roman guards shook for fear.	Angel, Roman guards	Matthew 28:2–4
At the tomb to anoint the body of Jesus. The women found the stone rolled away from the entrance to the tomb. Jesus was not there.	Mary Magdalene, Mary (James the Less), Salome, Joanna. The guards were apparently gone.	Matthew 28:1; Mark 16:1–4; Luke 24:2–3, 10; John 20:1
Two angels stood by them in shining garments and proclaimed that Jesus had risen just as He had predicted. They remembered Jesus' words.	Mary Magdalene, Mary (James the Less), Salome, Joanna, two angels.	Matthew 28:5–7; Mark 16:5–7; Luke 24:4–8, 10
They ran to Simon Peter and John and the rest to inform them that Jesus was missing and to tell them the message of the angels.	Mary Magdalene, Mary (James the Less), Salome, Joanna.	Matthew 28:7–8; Mark 16:8; Luke 24:9–11; John 20:2
Some ran back to the tomb and looked in, seeing the linen wrappings where the body of Jesus had been.	Peter, John, Mary Magdalene	Luke 24:12; John 20:3–9
Peter and John left the tomb. Mary Magdalene stayed at the tomb weeping. She looked into the tomb and saw two angels.	Mary Magdalene, Two angels	John 20:10–12
The angels questioned Mary about her weeping. She was still thinking His body had been placed somewhere else.	Mary Magdalene, Two angels	John 20:13
Mary saw Jesus and thought it was the attendant in the garden. This was the First Resurrection Appearance of Jesus.	Jesus, Mary Magdalene	John 20:14; Mark 16:9
Jesus questioned Mary about her weeping. She offered to take the body from wherever it had been laid. Jesus spoke her name, "Mary" and she recognized Him declaring, "Rabboni—Master." This was the First Resurrection Appearance of Jesus.	Jesus, Mary Magdalene	John 20:15–16
Mary Magdalene grabbed Jesus, and He told her to stop clinging to Him. He commanded her to go to the disciples, "My brethren," and tell them of His resurrection.	Jesus, Mary Magdalene	John 20:17

ORDER OF PLACES/EVENTS	PEOPLE	SCRIPTURE
Mary ran back to the disciples and told them, "I have seen the Lord," and told them what He had said to her.	Mary Magdalene, the disciples	John 20:18
Jesus met the other women on the road from the tomb. They "took hold of His feet and worshiped Him." Jesus commanded them to not be afraid, but to go and tell "My brethren" that He would meet them in Galilee.	"The women" (Matthew 28:5)	Matthew 28:9–10
Jesus also appeared eight other times after His Resurrection.	The two on the road to Emmaus, to Peter, to the disciples minus Thomas, to the disciples with Thomas, to seven of the disciples at the charcoal fire on the shore of Galilee, to more than 500 in Galilee, to James, to the Eleven at His Ascension, to Paul on the Damascus Road. It is likely that some of the women of the Gospels (named and unnamed) were at some of these appearances as well.	Luke 24:13–53; Matthew 28:16–20; Mark 16:12–20; John 20:19–29; 21:1–25; Acts 1:1–11; 9:1–19; 1 Corinthians 15:4–8

Women Who Are Named in the New Testament

NAME	SCRIPTURE	NAME	SCRIPTURE
Anna	Luke 2:36–38	Mary, Mother of Jesus	Matthew 1; 2; 12:46–50; 13:55–56; Mark 3:20–21, 31–35; Luke 1; 2; 8:19–21 John 2:1–12,; 19:25–27; Acts 1:14
Apphia	Philemon 2	Mary Magdalene (of the village of Magdala)	Matthew 27:55–61; 28:1; Mark 15:40–47; 16:1–11; Luke 8:2–3; 24:1–11; John 19:25; 20:1–18
Bernice	Acts 25—26	Mary of Bethany	Luke 10:38–42; John 11:1–46; 12:1–8
Candace	Acts 8:27	Mary, Mother of James the Less/the Younger and Joses (or Joseph). She is also known as the wife of Cleopas (also known as Alphaeus)	Matthew 10:3; 27:56, 61; Mark 15:47; Luke 24:10; John 19:25
Chloe	1 Corinthians 1:10–11	Mary, Mother of John Mark	Acts 12:12
Claudia	2 Timothy 4:21	Mary in Rome	Romans 16:6
Damaris	Acts 17:34	Persis	Romans 16:12
Dorcas (Tabitha)	Acts 9:36–43	Phoebe	Romans 16:1–2
Drusilla	Acts 24:24–27	Priscilla (Prisca)	Acts 18:2–3, 18, 24–26; Romans 16:3–5; 1 Corinthians 16:19; 2 Timothy 4:19
Elizabeth	Luke 1:5–80	Rhoda	Acts 12:1–17
Eunice	Acts 16:1–3; 2 Timothy 1:5, 3:14–15	Salome, Daughter of Herodias	Matthew 14:6–11; Mark 6:22–28
Euodias	Philippians 4:2	Salome, Wife of Zebedee, and also the mother of James and John	Matthew 20:20–28; 27:56; Mark 10:35–45; 15:40–41; 16:1–8
Herodias	Matthew 14:3–12; Mark 6:14–29; Luke 3:19–20	Sapphira	Acts 5:1–11
Jezebel	Revelation 2:18–29	Susanna	Luke 8:1–3
Joanna	Luke 8:1–3; 23:55; 24:10	Syntyche	Philippians 4:2
Julia	Romans 16:15	Tabitha (Dorcas)	Acts 9:36–43
Lois	2 Timothy 1:5	Tryphena	Romans 16:12
Lydia	Acts 16:12–15, 40	Tryphosa	Romans 16:12
Martha	Luke 10:38–42; John 11:1–46; 12:1–3		

Unnamed Women in the New Testament

NAME	SCRIPTURE	NAME	SCRIPTURE
Daughter of Abraham (Afflicted in her back)	Luke 13:10–17	Sister of Nereus	Romans 16:15
Daughters of Jerusalem	Luke 23:28–31	Sister of Paul	Acts 23:16–22
Daughters of Philip	Acts 21:8–9	Slave-girl with the spirit of divination	Acts 16:16–24
Daughter of Jairus	Matthew 9:18–25; Mark 5:21–43; Luke 8:40–56	Syro-Phoenician Woman (Canaanite)	Matthew 15:21–28; Mark 7:24–30
Hebrew Widows	Acts 6:1–5	Widow of Nain	Luke 7:11–18
Hellenistic Widows	Acts 6:1–5	Widow with two mites	Mark 12:41–44; Luke 21:1–4
Peter's Mother-in-law	Matthew 8:14–17; Mark 1:29–34; Luke 4:38–39	Women of Prominence at Antioch of Pisidia	Acts 13:50
Peter's Wife	Matthew 8:14–17; Mark 1:29–34; Luke 4:38–39; 1 Corinthians 9:5	Woman of Blessing	Luke 11:27–28
Pilate's Wife	Matthew 27:19	Woman Caught in Adultery	John 8:1–11
Rufus' Mother	Romans 16:13	Woman with the Issue of Blood	Matthew 9:20–22; Mark 5:25–34; Luke 8:43–48
Servant Girls at the charcoal fire in the courtyard at Caiaphas' house	Matthew 26:69–72; Mark 14:66–70; Luke 22:55–57; John 18:16–17	Woman of Sin at Simon's House	Luke 7:36–50
Sisters of Jesus	Matthew 13:55–56; Mark 6:3	Woman at the Well	John 4:1–43

Notes

The Submissive Wife

BIBLICAL PRINCIPLES FOR A HEALTHY MARRIAGE

*S*ubmission is a very important word for all of us to understand. When Scripture is properly presented as the God-breathed Word of God, then such terms as the word "submission" are easier to receive. But when God's Word is not properly taught, it causes much confusion in the Body of Christ. The term "submission," because of man's improper interpretation, is very misunderstood. It is crucial that we look at submission very carefully, for improper interpretation of the subject has caused knee-jerk reactions and much misunderstanding and pain, especially among women.

Submission is God's design. In our culture today, the devil has driven a wedge between man and woman, and one of the ways he has accomplished this is through words like "submission." The word has been used and abused in so many ways; it is no wonder we are in such a state of confusion on the subject. Yet submission is God's way; it is His design. Only His design works.

Many years ago, a man was asked by some friends to fly in the cockpit of a 727 jet that is owned by an oil company in Alaska. They let him sit in the jump seat behind the pilot, and according to my friend, it was an awesome, breathtaking

> *Submission is God's design for men and women. Everyone has a role of submission some place in life.*

WHERE DOES SHE FIT?

2200 B.C.	1950	1700	1450	1200	950	600	100 B.C.	A.D. 1	A.D. 100

HAGAR
2100?–2040?

REBEKAH
2040?–1915?

LEAH
1948?–1885?

LOT'S WIFE
2100?–2066

RACHEL
1943?–1899

Isaac
2065–1885

Abraham
2165–1990

Jacob
2005–1858

Joshua
1495–1385

Moses
1525–1405

Judges Rule
1385–1051

Samuel
1105–1022

Solomon
991–931

David
1041–971

ABIGAIL
1036?–976?

BATHSHEBA
1016?–961?

JEZEBEL
889?–841

Daniel
619–534?

Nehemiah
480?–400?

ELIZABETH
75 B.C.?–A.D. 10?

WOMEN of the
Gospels
10 B.C.?–A.D. 50?

Jesus Christ
4 B.C.?–A.D. 30?

WOMAN at Well
10 B.C.?–A.D. 50?

THE
SUBMISSIVE
WIFE
Ephesians 5;
1 Peter 2—3

experience. They took off from Anchorage, Alaska, and flew to Prudhoe Bay. When they were landing at the oil company's landing strip on Prudhoe Bay, the guest noticed that even though the weather was totally clear, the pilot put the plane on "instrument landing." That intrigued the guest, so he asked the pilot about it. The pilot said, "You don't know much about the weather in this part of Alaska, do you?" He said that a weather front could come in so quickly that you could be on the approach in clear weather one second and suddenly you would enter the densest fog you had ever seen. For that reason, according to the pilot, they landed using only instruments. The pilot exclaimed, "We only trust what we know works. Our eyes are not sufficient but the instruments are." Wow! You see, that story illustrates the point I want to make about submission. We had better depend on what God says, because nothing—and I say it again—none of our deeds will be deemed worthy in God's eyes, unless they are rooted in what God says in His book, the Bible. Submission is God's design not man's.

There is good news built into the word "submission." The good news is that when a wife chooses to submit to her husband, she will be enabled by God to follow through—no matter how difficult the circumstances may be. When any believer chooses to submit to the God-given order in his or her life, that one is given enabling grace to do the will of God. God energizes our choice to say, "Yes" to Him. It is then that He fills us with His Spirit, enabling us to be and do what He demands of us. Remember, what God demands, He and He Himself alone enables. We are living in a day when man is trying to create God in his own image. The parts of Scripture that we don't like, we tend to ignore as if we were walking through a cafeteria line and exercising our options based on what brings us pleasure. We must remember that we are not here on this earth to please ourselves, but God. There is really only one way to please God—by having a willing, obedient heart to do what God says. Such a devoted heart only comes with the understanding that He didn't leave us as orphans! He lives in us to do through us what we cannot do in our own fleshly power. It is amazing how the ability to accomplish various deeds for God comes only when we are first willing to be obedient to God's leading.

The Submissive Wife DAY ONE

GOD ENABLES WHAT HE DEMANDS

In Ephesians 3, two chapters before we find the command that the wife "submit" to her husband, we discover that God's power enables us to do whatever He commands us. Paul prays for the Ephesian believers in 3:16–17, *"that He would grant you, according to the riches of His glory, to be strengthened with power through His Spirit in the inner man; so that Christ may dwell in your hearts through faith."* Now, the Greek word translated "dwell" in verse 17 is the word *kataoikéo*. The word *kataoikéo* comes from two root words: *kata,* here meaning "down," and *oikéo,* meaning "house" or "home." *Kataoikéo* means "to settle down at home," or "to be at home."

With the understanding of the word "dwell" fresh in your mind, write out what "Christ dwelling in your heart" means to you.

_____

_____

_____

Christ dwelling in our hearts doesn't mean to "indwell," since that takes place when we receive Christ. It means Christ can "be at home" or feel divinely accommodated in the rooms of our hearts. Now, what rooms are in the house of our heart?

📖 Look up Luke 9:43–47 and write out what you discover in verse 47.

_____

_____

_____

_____

Verse 47 says that Jesus knew *"what they* [the disciples] *were thinking in their heart."* This statement can be puzzling to some. Some of you might be asking right now, "What does the **heart** have to do with the mind or **thinking**?" Hebrews 4:12 sheds more light on the connection between the heart and our attitude:

> *For the word of God is living and active and sharper than any two-edged sword, and piercing as far as the division of soul and spirit, of both joints and marrow, and able to judge the thoughts and intentions of the heart.*

📖 What connections do you see in this verse?

_____

_____

_____

The Spirit gives life to our soul; the marrow gives life to our bones; and so the *"intentions of the heart"* give life to our thoughts and attitudes. We don't really have "thought problems;" we have "heart problems" as believers. It is safe to say that when it comes to sin in our lives, "the problem of the heart is the heart of the problem."

🛑 **APPLY** Are you submitting to Christ as ruler of the room of your thoughts?

_____

_____

_____

📖 Look at Matthew 18:35 and write out what you discover about another room of the heart.

_____

_____

_____

Not only does Christ want control over the room of our thoughts, but He also demands control over the room of our attitudes. Perhaps there is someone whom you have not allowed Christ to empower you to forgive in your heart? Forgiveness comes only when we realize that we can't forgive in our own power, but must bow humbly before Christ, willing to submit and do

When, in humility, we submit to Christ and His will, He pours out grace—His enabling power to accomplish His will. Remember, God resists the proud, "but gives grace to the humble" (1 Peter 5:5).

what He demands. Christ is the one who forgives through us. But, we cannot understand this principle, nor will we abide by it, unless we are totally submitted to Him and to His Word.

 Whom have you not allowed Christ to forgive in your heart?

_____

_____

_____

📖 Look at John 14:1 and write out what you discover about another room of the heart.

_____

_____

_____

_____

What is it that "accommodates" or makes Christ feel "at home" in the room of our thoughts, attitudes, and emotions?

Jesus here describes "the room of our **emotions.**" Are you allowing Christ to rule over your emotions? Victory never takes place through our conquering of sin, but through Christ conquering us and by our total yieldedness to Him. We can live victorious lives when Christ is King of our emotions. As we are strengthened *"in the inner man"* as verse 16 of Ephesians 3 says, then God gets all the glory.

Now, how do you allow Christ to rule in these different "rooms" of your heart? Let's look again at our theme verse, Ephesians 3:17. It states *"so that Christ may dwell in your hearts through faith."* What is it that "accommodates" or makes Christ "at home" in the room of our thoughts, attitudes, and emotions?

_____

_____

_____

It is "faith" that accommodates the divine presence of Christ in our hearts. Faith incorporates so many things, such as a yielded heart to Christ, a willingness to obey His word, an attitude of total trust in Him and Him alone, and so forth. When we trust Him and His Word to the point of obedience, then we are accommodating Him in the different rooms of our hearts. Again, when it comes to sin in our lives, "the problem of the heart is the heart of the problem."

How are you doing in accommodating Christ in your heart?

_____

_____

_____

Everything He demands is enabled by Him when we walk surrendered to Him! So, whatever His commands, whatever His design, He enables us to be and do all that we are asked.

How does this study of God's enabling power apply to your life, especially in the area of submission? What has God spoken to you?

_____

_____

_____

_____

SUBMISSION IS THE EVIDENCE OF THE SPIRIT

E phesians 5:22 states: *"Wives, submit yourselves unto your own husbands, as unto the Lord."* (KJV). In this verse, the Greek word translated "submit" is the word *hupotasso*. It comes from two root words: *hupo*, which means "under," and *tasso*, which means "to arrange" or "to place in order." A husband and a wife are equals in God's sight. But, God specifically tells a wife to willingly place herself, as an equal, up under her husband's leadership because this is God's design. This word, "submit," is a beautiful word. It should in no way be construed as demeaning to the wife. In the context of Ephesians 5, submission is simply a function that fits the design that God made.

📖 Look at Ephesians 5:18. What is the two-fold command here?

_____

_____

Instead of wine, we are to be filled with the Holy Spirit. The command to be filled with the Spirit is in the present-passive tense. It literally means to **be continually filled** with the Spirit. We must constantly be under the control of the Holy Spirit. From what you learned in our Day One discussion, what is the key to being filled with the Holy Spirit (or accommodating Christ in your heart)?

_____

_____

_____

As Christians, when we step out by faith and decide to be obedient to God's commands, the Holy Spirit, through God's enabling power allows Christ, who dwells in our lives, to feel welcome and to permeate our thoughts, attitudes, and emotions. Now, look at the contrast in Ephesians 5:18 of being filled with wine (drunkenness) versus being filled with the Spirit. What is the contrast in your own words?

_____

_____

Paul's description of being drunk with wine helps us to realize that such behavior is subjecting oneself to the control of a foreign entity. The behavior of drunkenness is a picture of one who is out of control. However, you do not need to be a drunk to struggle with issues of control. Drug abuse, sexual addiction, pornography, unrequited anger, and many other transgressions

Word Study
DISSIPATION

Ephesians 5:18 says that getting drunk with wine is *"dissipation,"* a translation of the Greek word *asotia*, which is rooted in *asotos*, the word for prodigal living used of the wayward son in Luke 15:13. *Asotia* speaks of wasteful extravagance and squandering, a picture of one out of control because he or she is under the control of wine or any number of things the world has to offer. A person controlled by the Spirit lives a life ordered by God's will, not self-will, and is identified by self-control because that person is under God's control.

Doctrine
WHAT A WALK WITH GOD LOOKS LIKE

A person drunk under the control of wine walks differently, talks differently, thinks differently, has a different perspective on life—all leading to the dissipation and destruction of that person's life. One under the control of the Holy Spirit also walks, talks, and thinks differently, and has a different perspective, a Christ-centered perspective, on life—all in a right, life-filled relationship with God and in healthy relationships with others.

can eventually control the person who struggles with them. You might paraphrase Ephesians 5:18 to say "Do not be drunk or filled with any worldly influence, but be filled or controlled by the Spirit within you." Yes, the Spirit controls from within. Isn't it amazing, that as Christians, we already have what we are looking for (the Holy Spirit within us), yet most of the time, we do not even realize it? What an awesome reminder that God **lives in believers** in the person of His Spirit, who is the Spirit of Christ! The Spirit came to control us and to live Christ's life through us.

📖 Now, look at Ephesians 5:19–21 and write out the evidences of one who is being filled with the Spirit.

_____

_____

_____

What familiar word in our study is used again in verse 21 (KJV, NKJV, NIV)?

_____

You probably noticed the word "submit" or "submitting" in verse 21. (NOTE: The New American Standard Bible [NASB] uses the phrase, *"be subject to"* in place of the word *"submit."*)

Now lets look at verse 21. Do you realize that the Greek word for "submit" or "subject to" in Ephesians 5:22, *hupotasso,* bears the same meaning that is understood in verse 21? When God's Spirit is working in the life of a believer, the attitude of submission is an act of His enabling, and it is true of both man and woman, anyone who is following Jesus.

📖 Read Ephesians 5:22–24. What is the primary focus of the wife in verse 22?

_____

_____

_____

In verse 22, there is a heart-felt attitude pictured that inspires a wife to do what she is commanded by God to do. First, wives are commanded "to submit to [their] own husbands." Such behavior is strictly between a husband and a wife. Then Paul gives the key as to how this is to be done when he says "as to the Lord." That is the primary focus of a submissive wife. Verses 23 and 24 explain further that when a wife submits to her husband, she aligns herself up under him as the spiritual leader of the home, just as the Church is aligned up under Christ. The word "as" in verse 22 is used to compare and link two elements of submission. In other words, wives should submit to their husbands with the same attitude in which all Christians should submit to Christ. A Christian wife's submission to her husband is actually submission to Christ as she aligns herself under her husband's leadership.

🛑 APPLY Write out in your own words what Ephesians 5:22–24 means to you.

_____

_____

_____

Now, read verse 24 again. What are the limits of this submission?

_____

_____

Notice how the word *"submit"* in verse 24 is followed by the phrase *"in every thing."* Does this really mean there are no limits or exceptions as to how much a wife must submit to her husband? Now, to balance this principle, we must look at Colossians 3:18. Ephesians and Colossians are commentaries on each other to some degree. Colossians 3:18 states, *"Wives, be subject [hupotasso; submit] to your husbands, **as is fitting** in the Lord."* The word *"fitting"* is crucial here. It can also mean "proper." You see, the implied assumption in Colossians and in Ephesians (especially with the phrase *"wives should submit to their husbands in everything,"* [NIV]) is that husbands of Christian wives are Christ-loving men who are exemplary in their spiritual leadership. You may be asking right now, "But what if my husband is not a Christian?" This is an excellent question, for we know that not all wives have Christ-honoring husbands. So the phrase, *"as is fitting"* provides some degree of limitation as to when a wife should submit to her husband. In other words, when a wife is asked to do anything by her husband that is not "proper," or "fitting" in her walk with Christ, then she must defer to her True Master, Jesus Christ and respectfully decline her husband's request.

By no means am I suggesting that Christian wives with unsaved husbands are totally exempt from the submission principle. 1 Peter 3:1–2 commands women to submit to their husbands, even if those husbands are *"disobedient to the word"* of God. Peter goes a step further in this passage and states that a woman's loving and respectful behavior towards an unbelieving husband will go a long way towards winning him over to Christ. We will expound more on this commandment in 1 Peter in Day Four. But I want to reiterate that **only when a husband gives instructions that would seriously compromise his wife's devotion to the Lord, is she permitted to decline his request—and then she should do so with loving respect.** Wives must understand their submissive role and recognize that their role is part of God's design. However, wives are fully protected when asked to do anything that is not in the realm of what God would approve.

APPLY Now, with this in mind, answer these questions in your own words.

Why should a wife submit to her husband when he does not love her as Christ loves the Church?

_____

_____

_____

_____

What should a wife do when her husband asks her to do what she knows God will not allow?

_____

_____

_____

_____

Word Study

"AS IS FITTING"

Colossians 3:18 says, *"Wives, be subject to your husbands, **as is fitting** in the Lord."* The word "fitting" is a translation of the Greek word, *aneko*, which means "to come up to," or "to reach to," carrying the idea of something being due to one, or, in this case, due to the Lord. It refers to something that is proper, necessary, and appropriate in light of our relationship with the Lord. Submission is fitting because it is founded on who the Lord is and what He has designed the home to be.

Your answers to the above questions should have run along these lines: a wife is to submit to her husband unconditionally unless her husband requests that she do something that is diametrically opposed to God's will. That means she is to submit to her husband regardless of whether or not he loves her, or Christ, or the Church.

WHERE IS THE BALANCE?

Balance is a wonderful word in our Christian lives. We must find balance in our relationships at home. In our Day Three discussion, we will discover how to have a balanced view of submission, particularly the submission required of a wife to her husband.

📖 Read Ephesians 5:23. What does this say about the order that God has set up for husbands and wives?

_____

_____

_____

Now, look at this verse closely: *"For the husband is the head of the wife, as Christ also is the head of the church, He Himself being the Savior of the body."*

Who has God set up to be the "head" of the wife?

_____

It is very clear that God has set the husband in the position of headship or leadership over the wife. We can be assured that God has a divine purpose in this design, and that in His Word He has made clear what He desires regarding the husband's role in the family.

 How can we apply this? Think about the functions the head fulfills for the body. List a few of those.

_____

_____

_____

The head looks for the right direction to go, listens for the right advice in making choices, pays attention to any signals from the body that warn of danger or pain or that promise delight and joy. Just so, a husband as head is responsible to lead, to listen, to pay attention to what is going on in the life of his wife (and children). The head helps protect and provide for the body. That is God's design.

How can a body properly follow the head in a way that is fitting and healthy?

_____

_____

_____

Regarding the human body, the "head" looks for the right direction to go, listens for the right advice in making choices, pays attention to any signals from the body that warn of danger or pain or that promise delight and joy. A husband who is "head" of his household should operate in much the same fashion.

A wife following her husband as the head can help him become aware of things he might otherwise miss. She can help him respond to needs in the "body." One of the primary thoughts back in Genesis 2 pictures the wife as *"a helper suitable,"* someone to help Adam, to complete and complement him. That means a relationship of clear communication from husband and wife for each to know how to lead and how to follow. *The Amplified Bible* adds a perceptive note in Ephesians 5:22, *"Wives be subject—be submissive and adapt yourselves—to your own husbands as* [a service] *to the Lord."* That word "adapt" paints a picture of cooperating and adjusting, being willing to yield to his leadership and follow in the various areas of the home.

In all of this we must remember the full context. The wife's (and the husband's) primary focus is the Lord Jesus and following Him under the control of the Holy Spirit. The wife first follows the Lord as Head of the Church and then, in obedience to Him, follows her husband as head of the home. Of course, this following is easier the more the husband loves the wife, mirroring Christ and His love for the Church. However, regardless of what one partner does or does not do—if the husband fails to love like Christ or the wife fails to submit—the other is still responsible to obey the Lord and trust Him with the results.

What comparison does Paul give in his description of the husband's role in Ephesians 5:23?

_____

_____

_____

In Ephesians 5:23, Paul compares the husband's role of leadership to Christ's role as head of the Church. We should be careful in how we interpret this comparison. Paul is not saying that a husband's leadership of the home is in any way equal to Christ's leadership of the Church. Verse 23 concludes by identifying Christ as *"the Savior of the body* [church]." You see, Christ died for his Bride, the Church, and became the provider of eternal life—something a husband can never do. So, even though there is a comparison between husbands and Jesus Christ, there is also an inequality or contrast! In this Scripture passage, we also see that the husband is to love his wife. How is he to do that?

📖 According to Ephesians 5:28–29, how does the head treat the body?

_____

_____

_____

The head, the mind, is always looking out for the needs of the body. No man hates his own flesh (his body). He takes care of it. He "nourishes and cherishes it." He feeds his body and takes care to provide for the physical needs and comforts of daily life. The same should be true of a husband's leadership, care, and provision for his wife. His daily love for her, under the control of the Holy Spirit, makes for a healthy marriage and a harmonious home.

There may be a degree of frustration among some of you who still don't understand this concept of submission. "Where is the balance?" many wives ask. "Are we just a doormat for our husbands to walk all over as he pleases?"

Doctrine
📖 DAILY SUBMISSION

"Wives be subject—be submissive and adapt yourselves—to your own husbands as [a service] *to the Lord."* (Ephesians 5:22; Amplified Bible.) *"Let every person be in subjection* [hupotasso] *to the governing authorities. For there is no authority except from God, and those which exist are established by God"* (Romans 13:1). *"Submit* [hupotasso] *yourselves for the Lord's sake to every human institution. . . ."* (1 Peter 2:13a). Just as a wife is commanded to submit to her own husband, so God directs all of us to submit, "to arrange ourselves under," as Jesus did to His mother and Joseph (Luke 2:51), as a citizen to government (Romans 13:1), as the church to Christ (Ephesians 5:24), as a servant to a master (Titus 2:9), and as a believer to God Himself (James 4:7).

No. Paul makes it clear that while headship is reserved for the husband, both the husband and the wife should have a servant's heart toward one another (remember Ephesians 5:21). If both husband and wife are walking in the fullness of the Spirit as described in Ephesians 5:18-21, neither will be treated like a doormat. There is another aspect of this we need to see here because of some of the confusion in our culture, including Christian segments. To try and help you out in your understanding of submission and what it is not, let's look at another word for submit or obey that is never used in any command of God to a wife.

There are two basic Greek words that are translated in the New Testament as "obey" or "submit." The first Greek word is one we have already studied. It is the word *hupotasso.* This word is used in ways that imply that husbands and wives are **two equals,** even though the wife is commanded to align herself up under the husband's leadership of the family.

The second Greek word for "obey" or "submit" is *hupakouo.* It is a word that comes from two root words: *hupo,* which means "under" in the sense of authority; and the word *akouo,* which means to "hear with understanding." It conveys the idea of hearing under an authority and obeying without any questions. It suggests there should be no debate, no resistance, but only total obedience to commands from those you understand to be in authority over you.

Hupakouo is the word used in Matthew of the wind and the waves obeying Christ. (Matthew 8:27: *And the men marveled, saying, "What kind of a man is this, that even the winds and the sea* **obey** *Him?"*)

Hupakouo is used in command form in Ephesians 6:1: *"Children,* **obey** *your parents in the Lord, for this is right."* Note that the context describes the parent/child relationship. Ephesians 6:1 is not describing blind obedience. The attitude and actions of this type of obedience have boundaries in particular contexts. Here the verse says for a child to obey his parents *"in the Lord."* Just as wives are to submit to their husbands *"as to the Lord"* (Ephesians 5:22), children are to submit to their parents *"in the Lord."* In other words, this obedience is to be without question or resistance as long as the command is in line with God and His Word.

The word *hupakouo* is also used in Colossians 3:22, which says, *"Slaves, in all things* **obey** *those who are your masters on earth, not with external service, as those who merely please men, but with sincerity of heart, fearing the Lord."* It is estimated that in Paul's day, approximately eighty percent of the workforce in the Roman Empire consisted of slaves. Obviously, most countries today do not permit slavery anymore, but the principles taught in this verse can easily apply to an employer/employee relationship. The context of this verse suggests that slaves or, using today's vernacular, Christian employees should be conditioned with a servant-like heart that fears God and is marked with integrity. A slave or servant (or employee) is to do what his master (or supervisor) instructs with the understanding that he is not just pleasing his master, but he is also pleasing God by his actions.

The example in Colossians of the slave is used to describe the attitude with which we are to obey Christ. Hebrews 5:9, in speaking of Christ says, *"And having been made perfect, He became to all those who* **obey** *Him the source of eternal salvation."* But, the example is also used of our Lord Jesus and His choice to place Himself, **though equal to the Father,** under the Father's authority when He came to earth as the God/man. Philippians 2:8 says, *"And* *being found in appearance as a man, He humbled Himself by becoming* **obedient** *to the point of death, even death on a cross.*"

Remember that *hupakouo* means "to hear under an authority with full understanding and to obey without any question." With that definition in mind, is the word *hupakouo* ever used in the context of marriage? The answer is no when it comes to any command in Scripture. The only time it is used in reference to marriage is in 1 Peter 3:6: *"Thus Sarah* **obeyed** *Abraham, calling him lord, and you have become her children if you do what is right without being frightened by any fear."* The word for *"obeyed"* in this verse is the word *hupakouo*. The way *hupakouo* is used in this verse suggests that Sarah **chose to obey on her own**. She was not commanded to do this. This points to her attitude towards Abraham, an attitude that desired to do right as unto the Lord. But, other than 1 Peter 3:6, there is no other context in which *hupakouo* can be found when it relates to marriage.

So, is there any balance when it comes to wives submitting to their husbands? Yes! Wives are in no way to become doormats for their husbands, nor is it proper for a husband to "walk all over" his wife. As a husband and wife walk together, the husband is responsible to lead and the wife is responsible to follow, to adapt—not in a military style obedience, but in a mutual submission to the Lord Jesus as head of the church and in a mutual recognition of God's design in the home. A wife is not expected to do everything her husband says without question. However, she must understand her role in putting herself up under the husband's leadership over the family.

Write out all that God has said to you in today's study.

_____

_____

_____

Paul said of the oneness of Christ and the Church and of a husband and wife, *"this mystery is great."* (Ephesians 5:32). The Greek word for "mystery" in this verse (*musterion*) suggests something hidden that must be opened up by God or something that must be revealed by His Spirit in order for us to fully see, understand, and experience. That is certainly true of the relationship between Christ and the Church and between a husband and a wife. To begin seeing the mystery of God's design for marriage, the Spirit must open our understanding. Paul concludes his statement with *"Nevertheless, let each individual among you also love his own wife even as himself; and let the wife see to it that she respect her husband"* (5:33). To begin experiencing the fullness of Christlike love and Christlike submission requires the revealing, empowering work of the Spirit. (see also Matthew 13:11; Romans 11:25; 1 Corinthians 15:51; Ephesians 1:9; 3:3–6, 9; 6:19; 1 Timothy 3:16; Colossians 1:26–27).

CHRIST AS OUR EXAMPLE

I n First Peter 2, we find some wonderful words that describe our Lord Jesus Christ and how He lived. Peter begins by addressing the servants of the times. As we have seen, some estimate that eighty percent of the workforce of that time was slaves. So Peter says to those believers in that category:

> *Servants, be submissive to your masters with all respect, not only to those who are good and gentle, but also to those who are unreasonable. For this finds favor, if for the sake of conscience toward God a man bears up under sorrows when suffering unjustly. For what credit is there if, when you sin and are harshly treated, you endure it with patience? But if when you do what is right and suffer for it you patiently endure it, this finds favor with God.* (1 Peter 2:18–20)

📖 In the comparison in 1 Peter 2:18–20, what finds favor with God? (Note "favor" is mentioned more than once.)

_____

_____

When one is treated harshly for doing what is right and suffers patiently, bearing up under the harsh treatment in a godly manner, this finds favor with God—not the harsh treatment, mind you, but the right response to being treated unjustly.

Now look at the next verse (21): *"For you have been called for this purpose, since Christ also suffered for you, leaving you an example for you to follow in His steps."* Suffering is always a part of our surrendered walk in Christ. Christ's suffering elevates our own suffering, and our right response to suffering is so important. He left an example for us to follow. When people treat us wrongly for living rightly, we can look at His example to know how to respond rather than react, and we can trust Him to work through us with His power as we respond.

📖 Read 1 Peter 2:22–24 and write in your own words in the space provided below, what example Christ left for us as to how we should endure wrong treatment for doing what is right.

_____

_____

_____

_____

The word *"reviled"* comes from the Greek word *"loidoreo,"* meaning "to abuse with words." When Christ was abused as to His character, nature, and intentions, He did not revile back. The word for *suffering* is the Greek word *"pascho,"* which means intense physical and emotional pain. In Christ's case, great suffering was inflicted upon Him by those abusing Him with words and physical violence. Yet, Christ did not utter a single threat. The Greek word translated *threats* is the word *"apeileo,"* which refers to a verbal warning one might issue if he is preparing to retaliate. But instead of responding to verbal abuse with more verbal abuse and instead of threatening the ones causing Him pain, Christ *"kept entrusting Himself to Him who judges righteously."* Jesus handed Himself and His circumstances over to His Father.

 According to what we have learned this week, does Christ live in us? How are we enabled to be what He desires us to be? (Review Day One.)

_____

_____

_____

_____

As we surrender to the Lord and as we yield our personal pain and wounded spirits to Him, then God by His Holy Spirit energizes that choice and empowers us with His presence and His perspective.

Now, can the truth of God enabling us be applied to marriage?

📖 Look at 1 Peter 3:1–4 below.

"In the same way, you wives, be submissive to your own husbands so that even if any of them are disobedient to the word, they may be won without a

---

As we surrender to the Lord and as we yield our personal pain and wounded spirits to Him, then God by His Holy Spirit energizes that choice and empowers us with His presence and His perspective.

word by the behavior of their wives, as they observe your chaste and respectful behavior. And let not your adornment be merely external—braiding the hair, and wearing gold jewelry, or putting on dresses; but let it be the hidden person of the heart, with the imperishable quality of a gentle and quiet spirit, which is precious in the sight of God.

What insights do you see here?

_____

_____

These verses are evidence that the wife, enabled by Christ living in her, is able to reach a husband that is treating her wrongly out of a disobedient lifestyle. In the previous chapter, Peter describes the very truth of Christ and His total dependence upon His Father. Then he begins chapter 3 by saying, *"In the same way, you wives."* One Greek word here is translated *"In the same way."* It is the word *homoios*, meaning "likewise" or "in like manner." Just as Christ totally yielded Himself to His Father, we totally yield ourselves to Christ. As the Father was to Christ, Christ is to us. The Greek word for *submissive* in 3:1 is the word *hupotasso*. Peter tells the wives to trust Christ in their marriages and to respond to Him in total trust.

How can a wife, enabled by Christ living in her, reach a husband who is disobedient to the word, or even treating her wrongly out of a disobedient lifestyle? The answer is also found in verse 1—*"The behavior of their wives."* The Greek word translated "behavior" is the word *anastrophē*. It suggests "a changed behavior." This seems to imply that where there had been bitterness or anger, perhaps nagging or even retaliation on the part of the wife to the husband's disobedient lifestyle, there is now a "changed behavior." With Christ being "at home" in her life and with the enabling power of the Holy Spirit evident in her behavior, there will be greater opportunities to influence her husband. The Spirit of Christ continues molding and shaping her into the vessel through which He can reach out to her husband.

Write out in your own words what the behavior of a submissive wife looks like.

_____

_____

_____

_____

We must cover one more aspect of how a wife can soften an unrepentant husband. We have already learned that husbands can be won *"by the behavior of their wives"* (1 Peter 3:1).

📖 How does Peter describe that behavior in 1 Peter 3:2?

_____

_____

_____

_____

_____

_____

> ## Just as Christ totally yielded Himself to His Father, we totally yield ourselves to Christ.

Peter tells us that husbands *"may be won . . . as they observe your chaste and respectful behavior."* The Greek word for *"chaste"* used in this verse is the word *hagnós*. It is behavior marked by purity or innocence. The word *"chaste"* is coupled with the word *"respectful."* The Greek word for *"respectful"* in this verse is the word *phóbos,* meaning "fear." In the context of the passage, it applies to the fear of God.

Verse 3 says, *"And let not your adornment be merely external—braiding the hair, and wearing gold jewelry, or putting on dresses."* The Greek word translated *"adornment"* is actually the word *kosmos* and refers to the external way in which a wife adorns herself. It is interesting to me that the word *kosmos* normally means "world system." The world measures "beauty" in how one looks on the outside and how one is dressed.

 What does Peter say about the wife's "adornment" in 1 Peter 3:4?

_____

_____

_____

Peter instructs wives to let their adornment come from *"the hidden person of the heart, with the imperishable quality of a gentle and quiet spirit, which is precious in the sight of God."* Peter is not saying that outward adornment is bad. He is only asserting that inward beauty is far more important. Imagine a struggling wife who so respects God, that she has surrendered herself to Him and to His will. As a result, God uses the radiance of her inward surrender to impact and even overwhelm the disobedient husband!

APPLY What has this lesson taught you so far? Wives, has God shown you any area of your relationship with your husband that God would not approve of? Husbands, are you showing leadership and care in your home that is like Christ's leadership and care of His Church?

_____

_____

_____

Husbands or wives, what improvements need to be made in your home to make it more like the model families that Paul and Peter describe. Teenagers, what improvements are necessary in your lives in the area of submitting to parental authority?

_____

_____

_____

The Submissive Wife **DAY FIVE**

FOR ME TO FOLLOW CHRIST

One of the problems that every believer, whether male or female, encounters when it comes to living the Christian life is his or her own logical perceptions of his or her situation. We tend to think that God doesn't know what He is doing. We resort to humanistic reasoning and try to decide what we would do if we were God. This, of course, is a downhill ride with no place to stop.

In this application-based section of the lesson, let's take inventory of how we are doing when it comes to trusting God in what He says.

 Are you living the Christian life? If Christ dwells within you, do you allow Christ to empower you to be what you know you cannot be on your own?

_____

_____

Have you come to the place that you now realize the futility of your own efforts to solve any given situation?

_____

_____

_____

Secondly, have you realized that Christ is your victory and that through surrender to Him and to His Word you enter that victorious way of life?

_____

_____

Thirdly, do you possess a submissive spirit as evidence of God working in your life? Or is your attitude one of controlling others and working out your own solution instead of allowing God to guide you through His Word?

_____

_____

_____

Fourthly, do you realize that you have a God-given right to stand up when obedience to His Word is being challenged? Do you know that you are not a doormat? Are you being asked to do things that the Word of God does not allow? Do you know that you can and must stand up and, in a loving way, politely refuse? Do you realize that God is your ultimate authority?

_____

_____

_____

_____

Fifthly, do you realize that Christ lives in you and can do through you what you could never do on your own?

_____

_____

_____

Remember, if Christ was submissive to His Father in the midst of very ungodly circumstances, and if He lives in you, can He not enable you to do

Remember, if Christ was submissive to His Father in the midst of very ungodly circumstances, and if He lives in you, can He not enable you to do the same?

the same? It is our prayer that this time spent looking at submission has helped a Christian wife realize that she cannot be the wife God tells her to be unless He Himself lives His life through her. For men, it is our prayer that you have studied this lesson with an understanding that the Scriptures regarding godly submission for a wife do not give you license to be abusive or to lead your wives into sin. Far from it, her godly submission is a call to you to be ever more careful in your leadership of the home, remembering that godly submission applies to every Christian at some point. Everyone stands in a relationship with various God-placed authorities that calls for submission to them. Remember, what God commands, He enables, and when we obey He ultimately rewards and blesses. Let submission be your path to His blessings.

Spend some time with the Lord in prayer right now:

Father, I pray that You will enlighten all of us who may be studying this lesson with the wonderful truth of **Christ in us**—the hope of glory! I pray that You will help abused wives to focus on You, and I ask that You give them wisdom and strength to deal with the difficult circumstances around them. Lord, not everyone studying this lesson is married, but one day many of them will be. I pray that they will remember the godly principles of marriage and family studied in this lesson. May all of us, both men and women, understand that principles of obedience and submission are applicable far beyond the boundaries of our homes. Lord, we also thank You for encouraging us with Your Word to be submissive to our parents, our employers, the leaders of our churches, and others You have placed in authority over us. As we yield all the places in our hearts to Your Son, Jesus Christ, and make Him a welcome inhabitant in all of our lives, we depend on Your Holy Spirit to enable us to do what is humanly impossible in each of those areas. May You receive all the glory and praise, for only You are worthy to be praised! Amen.

Write your own prayer thoughts in the space provided below.

_____

_____

_____

_____

_____

_____

_____

_____

_____

_____

_____

_____

_____

_____

May all of us, both men and women, understand that principles of obedience and submission are applicable far beyond the boundaries of our homes.

How to Follow God

Starting the Journey

Did you know that you have been on God's heart and mind for a long, long time? Even before time existed you were on His mind. He has always wanted you to know Him in a personal, purposeful relationship. He has a purpose for your life and it is founded upon His great love for you. You can be assured it is a good purpose and it lasts forever. Our time on this earth is only the beginning. God has a grand design that goes back into eternity past and reaches into eternity future. What is that design?

The Scriptures are clear about God's design for man—God created man to live and walk in oneness with Himself. Oneness with God means being in a relationship that is totally unselfish, totally satisfying, totally secure, righteous and pure in every way. That's what we were created for. If we walked in that kind of relationship with God we would glorify Him and bring pleasure to Him. Life would be right! Man was meant to live that way—pleasing to God and glorifying Him (giving a true estimate of who God is). Adam sinned and shattered his oneness with God. Ever since, man has come short of the glory of God: man does not and cannot please God or give a true estimate of God. Life is not right until a person is right with God. That is very clear as we look at the many people who walked across the pages of Scripture, both Old and New Testaments.

JESUS CHRIST came as the solution for this dilemma. Jesus Christ is the glory of God—the true estimate of who God is in every way. He pleased His Father in everything He did and said, and He came to restore oneness with God. He came to give man His power and grace to walk in oneness with God, to follow Him day by day enjoying the relationship for which he was created. In the process, man could begin to present a true picture of Who God is and experience knowing Him personally. You may be asking, "How do these facts impact my life today? How does this become real to me now? How can I begin the journey of following God in this way?" To come to know God personally means you must choose to receive Jesus Christ as your personal Savior and Lord.

- First of all, you must admit that you have sinned, that you are not walking in oneness with God, not pleasing Him or glorifying Him in your life (Romans 3:23; 6:23; 8:5–8).

- It means repenting of that sin—changing your mind, turning to God and turning away from sin—and by faith receiving His forgiveness based on His death on the Cross for you (Romans 3:21–26; 1 Peter 3:18).

- It means opening your life to receive Him as your living, resurrected Lord and Savior (John 1:12). He has promised to come and indwell you by His Spirit and live in you as the Savior and Master of your life (John 14:16–21; Romans 14:7–9).

- He wants to live His life through you—conforming you to His image, bearing His fruit through you and giving you power to reign in life (John 15:1,4–8; Romans 5:17; 7:4; 8:29, 37).

You can come to Him now. In your own words, simply tell Him you want to know Him personally and you willingly repent of your sin and receive His forgiveness and His life. Tell Him you want to follow Him forever (Romans 10:9–10, 13). Welcome to the Family of God and to the greatest journey of all!!!

WALKING ON THE JOURNEY

How do we follow Him day by day? Remember, Christ has given those who believe in Him everything pertaining to life and godliness, so that we no longer have to be slaves to our "flesh" and its corruption (2 Peter 1:3–4). Day by day He wants to empower us to live a life of love and joy, pleasing to Him and rewarding to us. That's why Ephesians 5:18 tells us to *be filled with the Spirit*—keep on being controlled by the Spirit who lives in you. He knows exactly what we need each day and we can trust Him to lead us (Proverbs 3:5–6). So how can we cooperate with Him in this journey together?

To walk with Him *day by day* means ...

- reading and listening to His Word day by day (Luke 10:39, 42; Colossians 3:16; Psalm 19:7–14; 119:9).

- spending time talking to Him in prayer (Philippians 4:6–7).

- realizing that God is God and you are not, and the role that means He has in your life.

This allows Him to work through your life as you fellowship, worship, pray and learn with other believers (Acts 2:42), and serve in the good works He has prepared for us to do—telling others who Jesus is and what His Word says, teaching and encouraging others, giving to help meet needs, helping others, etc. (Ephesians 2:10).

God's goal for each of us is that we be conformed to the image of His Son, Jesus Christ (Romans 8:29). But none of us will reach that goal of perfection until we are with Him in Heaven, for then "we shall be like Him, because we shall see Him just as He is" (1 John 3:2). For now, He wants us to follow

Him faithfully, learning more each day. Every turn in the road, every trial and every blessing, is designed to bring us to a new depth of surrender to the Lord and His ways. He not only wants us to do His will, He desires that we surrender to His will His way. That takes trust—trust in His character, His plan and His goals (Proverbs 3:5–6).

As you continue this journey, and perhaps you've been following Him for a while, you must continue to listen carefully and follow closely. We never graduate from that. That sensitivity to God takes moment by moment surrender, dying to the impulses of our flesh to go our own way, saying no to the temptations of Satan to doubt God and His Word, and refusing the lures of the world to be unfaithful to the Lord who gave His life for us.

God desires that each of us comes to maturity as sons and daughters: to that point where we are fully satisfied in Him and His ways, fully secure in His sovereign love, and walking in the full measure of His purity and holiness. If we are to clearly present the image of Christ for all to see, it will take daily surrender and daily seeking to follow Him wherever He leads, however He gets there (Luke 9:23–25). It's a faithful walk of trust through time into eternity. And it is worth everything. Trust Him. Listen carefully. Follow closely.

Other Books in the *Following God*™ Bible Character Study Series

Life Principles from the Old Testament

Characters include Adam, Noah, Job, Abraham, Lot, Jacob, Joseph, Moses, Caleb, Joshua, Gideon, and Samson
ISBN 0-89957-300-2   208 pages

Life Principles from the Kings of the Old Testament

Characters include Saul, David, Solomon, Jereboam I, Asa, Ahab, Jehoshaphat, Hezekiah, Josiah, Zerubbabel & Ezra, Nehemiah, and "The True King in Israel."
ISBN 0-89957-301-0   256 pages

Life Principles from the Prophets of the Old Testament

Characters include Samuel, Elijah, Elisha, Jonah, Hosea, Isaiah, Micah, Jeremiah, Habakkuk, Daniel, Haggai, and "Christ the Prophet."
ISBN 0-89957-303-7   224 pages

Life Principles from the New Testament Men of Faith

Characters include John the Baptist, Peter, John, Thomas, James, Barnabas, Paul, Paul's Companions, Timothy, and "The Son of Man."
ISBN 0-89957-304-5   208 pages

Life Principles from the Women of the Bible (Book One)

Characters include Eve, Sarah, Miriam, Rahab, Deborah, Ruth, Hannah, Esther, The Virtuous Woman, Mary and Martha, Mary the Mother of Jesus, The Bride of Christ.
ISBN 0-89957-302-9   224 pages

Other Following God™ books are also available, including Leaders Guides!
Call for more information (800) 266-4977 or (423) 894-6060.
Log on to **amgpublishers.com** for more information about these books.